Still Fighting

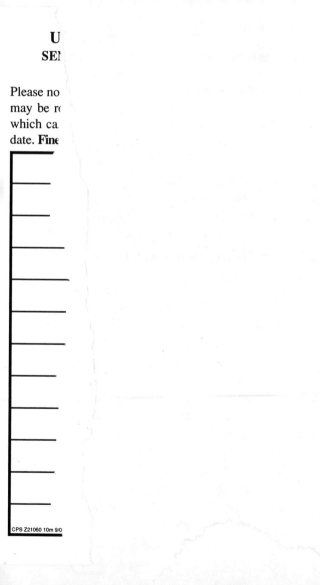

Pitt Latin American Studies

Billie R. DeWalt, *General Editor*

Reid Andrews, Catherine Conaghan, and

Jorge I. Domínguez, *Associate Editors*

Katherine Isbester

Still Fighting

The Nicaraguan Women's
Movement, 1977–2000

University of Pittsburgh Press

Published by the University of Pittsburgh Press, Pittsburgh, Pa., 15261

Manufactured in the United States of America

Printed on acid-free paper

10 9 8 7 6 5 4 3 2 1

LIBRARY OF CONGRESS CATALOGING-IN-PUBLICATION DATA

Isbester, Katherine.

Still fighting : the Nicaraguan women's movement, 1977–2000 /
Katherine Isbester.

p.   cm. — (Pitt Latin American series)

Includes bibliographical references and index.

ISBN 0-8229-4155-4 (cloth) — ISBN 0-8229-5757-4 (pbk)

1. Feminism—Nicaragua—History. 2. Women in politics—
Nicaragua. 3. Nicaragua—Politics and government—1979–
1990. 4. Nicaragua—Politics and government—1990–   I. Title:
Nicaraguan woman's movement, 1977–2000. II. Title. III. Series.

HQ1236.5.N5 I83 2001

305.42´097285—dc21

2001002661

For my mother, with love and gratitude

Contents

Abbreviations

AMNLAE	Association of Nicaraguan Women "Luisa Amanda Espinoza"
AMPRONAC	Association of Nicaraguan Women Confronting the National Problem
ATC	Association of Rural Workers
CDC	Center for Constitutional Rights "Carlos Nuñez" (1990–)
CIERA	Center for Agrarian Reform
CISAS	Information and Assessment Services Center
CNF	National Feminist Committee
CONAPRO H-M	Nicaraguan Confederation of Professionals— Heroes and Martyrs
COSEP	Higher Council of Private Enterprise
CST	Sandinista Workers' Committee
EPS	Sandinista Popular Army
FOA	Broad Opposition Front
FSLN	Sandinista Front for National Liberation
IMF	International Monetary Fund
INIM	Nicaraguan Institute for Research on Women Nicaraguan Institute for Women (after 1993)
INSBBI	Nicaraguan Institute for Social Security and Well-being
Madres H-M	Mothers of the Revolution—Heroes and Martyrs
MAS	Ministry of Social Action
MIDINRA	Ministry of Development and Agrarian Reform

MINSA   Ministry of Health

MPU   Popular Unity Movement

NGO   Nongovernmental Organization

UNAG   National Union of Farmers and Ranchers

UNO   National United Opposition

Preface

NICARAGUAN WOMEN HAVE STRUGGLED and continue to struggle for their freedom. The history of the women's movement in Nicaragua is a fascinating tale of resistance, tactics, and women's faith in themselves while they and their nation went through profound social, political, and economic changes. Nicaragua changed governments twice in eleven years, first in 1979 from the Somoza dictatorship to Sandinista revolutionary socialism and next in 1990 from Sandinismo to Catholic neoliberalism. Each government had its own ideology about the role of women in society, and each implemented its ideology through public policies. For each government, the women's movement had to redefine itself rapidly, producing new leaders, new forms of organizations, and new understandings.

Yet there has also been a high degree of continuity. Although grassroots participation waxed and waned, short-term goals were reworked, and the internal organization of the movement changed, the ideal of gender equality and freedom remained the focus. Some of the leaders of the women's movement under the Somoza dictatorship became the Sandinista leaders during the 1980s, participated in the creation of semi-Sandinista women's groups in the late 1980s, and assisted the emergence of the autonomous women's movement in the 1990s. One can compare statements and strategies as a woman shifted her position from guerrilla fighter to government bureaucrat to NGO consultant. Indeed, one can chart the growth of experience and repertoire of skills of the participants of the social movement.

In addition to the continuity of political players, there was also a continuity of political organizations. It was not unusual for the same women's organization to be active over a decade, allowing comparison of its strategies, identities, and impact on the rest of the women's movement. The extent of continuity and change in the Nicaraguan women's movement, concentrated in a short time period, contributes to the uniqueness of this analysis.

Existing approaches to the study of women's movements are of limited value due to both the special circumstances of the Nicaraguan situation and the scope of this study from the women's movement's inception in 1977 to the fall of the Chamorro government in 1996. Some analyses are useful for examination of discrete time frames: for example, the role of the activists just after the revolution or their response to Chamorro's structural adjustment. In order to analyze the Nicaraguan women's movement over its entire historical length and breadth of activity, I have drawn on European, North American, and Latin American thinking to develop social movement theory. To be successful in its organizing and goal attainment, a social movement must have three mutually reinforcing components: an autonomous identity, a use of resources appropriate to that identity, and a focused conflict. The presence of all three elements accounts for the movement's success, while the absence of any one undermines its viability. This theoretical approach also explains the relationships between the women's movement and the three Nicaraguan governments, which ranged from combative to cooperative.

The data upon which this argument is based were collected during field research conducted in Nicaragua between December 1993 and August 1994 and subsequently between December 1994 and the end of January 1995. When I arrived in the country the women's movement was already strong and well organized, and during my time there it grew in numbers, scope, internal cohesiveness, and political influence. It also lost its most powerful network, with bitter ramifications for the individuals and groups involved. Thus, I witnessed not merely the building and the maintenance of the movement but also the dissolution of one of its main players.

I conducted my research through in-depth interviews with actors in the social movement, sometimes following up with as many as two more interviews with key actors. I also interviewed some of the people who work with NGOs that operate within the women's movement. In an effort to gain a broad understanding of the forces against which the women's movement was operating, I interviewed members of the National Assembly, male leaders of other social movements, and women outside the women's movement. In all, I conducted over one hundred interviews, although not all of them will be quoted in this book. With the exception of a conversation with a Costeña woman, all interviews were conducted in Spanish. Unless otherwise stated in the bibliography, I have translated all Spanish language literature and interviews myself.

In addition, I conducted extensive archival research in the libraries in Managua. Because many of the people active today in the women's movement became involved in the 1980s and even the 1970s, it is useful to compare their present understandings with statements that they made in the past. People's memories became blurred over time, and newspapers and documents were useful for clarifying details.

To my surprise, I found that the most critical part of the field research was attending the movement's group and network meetings, organizing meetings, symposiums, and conferences. In these public spaces, I witnessed individuals forming groups, groups organizing into networks, networks organizing political action, and political action creating both identity understandings and unpredictable results in the public sphere. I watched tensions grow and witnessed how they were (or were not) resolved, how issues were chosen, language changed, leadership functioned, strategies were formulated, and identity was created. I witnessed the daily workings of a social movement and grew to appreciate its organic intricacy.

This analysis does not incorporate the women's movement of Nicaragua's Atlantic Coast region except when it intersects with the Pacific Coast women's movement. After doing a series of interviews in both Blue Fields and Puerto Cabezas, I realized that the women's movement there has fundamentally different goals, resources, and identity understandings from the movement on the Pacific Coast. The depth of difference between the two movements arises from differences in ethnicity, language, religion, economic development, political representation, and history. In order to do justice to the women of the Atlantic Coast, a second volume on just the Costeña women's movement will have to be published.

I was fortunate that I had the time and the financial support to stay and pursue my research in Nicaragua for as long as I did. I am thankful for the support provided by the International Development Research

Centre's Young Canadian Researchers Award, the University of Toronto Open Fellowship, and the Sir Val Duncan Award. I am also grateful for the University of Toronto Small Research Grant, which enabled me to hire a research assistant, Cathy Feingold, to update my manuscript for publication. Although the many people who had to suffer with me over the research and the writing this book are too numerous to mention, I would like to thank some people in particular. I am grateful to my mother-in-law, Mevrouw Jan-Tineke Gorter-'t Hooft, for offering me the space and support needed to finish the manuscript. I would also like to thank my doctoral committee members for their insights, support, and work. For their critical reading of rough drafts of the manuscript and thoughtful conversations, I would like to thank Dr. Lisa Mills, Cathy Feingold, and Kees 't Hooft. For permitting me to quote from her excellent and sadly unpublished ethnography of four Nicaraguan women, and for generously sharing her accommodation, friends, and wisdom with me, I would like to thank Dr. Vicki McVey. Finally, I would like to thank my family for their support. With some legitimacy, my mother can refer to this dissertation as "our thesis," for surely I could not have accomplished so much so fast without her steadfast belief in me and her hard work in contributing to this book.

Still Fighting

CHAPTER 1

Amparo's Story

THE STORY OF AMPARO RUBIO'S LIFE REFLECTS the lives of many women during the turbulent times of revolutionary upheaval, profound changes in government, and rapid redefinition of women's role in society.[1] By 1974, when Amparo became a guerrilla fighter for the Sandinista Front of National Liberation (FSLN), women were already well integrated into the guerrilla army. In fact, women were so thoroughly involved with the insurgency that they comprised 30 percent of the FSLN, with some rising to the rank of commander. Amparo was sufficiently skilled as both a leader and a fighter that she was one of those female commanders. After the revolution in 1979, she was a captain for the Sandinista defense. Once the revolutionary government had been voted out in 1990 and a right-wing government gained power, she led the women of her town to rise up for their rights.

Amparo had always been a fighter. And she had always been poor. She was born in 1957 to a working-class family in the north of Nicaragua, and as a child she had to help support her family by selling food on the streets. She sold bread in the morning before school, sweets during the lunch break, and after school fruits, eggs, sugar cane, or anything else she could find. Although so poor that she had no shoes, she was one of the best students in her school. She explains, "I knew how to put my attention on anything I wanted to do" (42). To protect her basket of goodies, her hard-earned coins, and her younger siblings from other kids, Amparo filled her basket with stones and carried a slingshot.

She sold to the rich people of the town and frequently got chased away from their houses for trying to watch their televisions. After seeing

1

the inside of one rich man's house, she remembered thinking, "Someday when I'm big, I'm going to work and I'm going to build a house for my mama, and I'm going to buy a television, and I'm going to buy a chair" (42). Those were grand dreams. At the time, her entire family lived in a one-room shack, which Amparo once tried to mortgage to pay for her infant sister's burial and her mother's operation. No one would take the deed of ownership, and Amparo had to beg for the money instead.

By the time Amparo had reached her teenage years, she was adept at survival and was mature beyond her years. "I don't think I was ever a child," she said. "The society we lived in made us into adults" (17). At thirteen, she left school and became a nurse's aide in addition to selling fruit in the streets.

It is important to appreciate that although Amparo and her family were poor they were not indigent. They had jobs, some education, and a home of their own. In Nicaragua, one of the poorest nations of Latin America, there was a sharp division between the wealthy and everyone else. Those with money had lots of it and led very pleasant lives: they had servants and all the luxuries they could want. Those who were not wealthy had very little at all and led precarious existences. People struggling to change this societal order had to first persuade the poor that this situation was morally wrong and could be altered. For Amparo, this revelation came through the Church.

At fourteen, almost by accident, she ended up at a weekend retreat run by a Christian-based community of the Catholic Church. At the time, the Catholic Church was riven by its shift to the poor. Called Liberation Theology, this new doctrine emphasized that the power structure in society denied people their fundamental rights and freedoms. It also suggested that people who fought against this sinful structure would be performing God's work and enlightening themselves in the process. Thus, at this weekend retreat, Amparo did not just attend mass and hear sermons about love and faith, but she also was told about her right to live, her right to clean water, and her right to earn a decent living (literally, her right to land for planting). She also learned about solidarity and how it was created, and, with time, she learned how to form groups, write memos to share ideas, and communicate those ideas to the illiterate peasants. In other words, Amparo learned how to organize people around the abstract idea of civil liberties. She learned how to fight back. "I was born in the Christian-based community . . . I loved it, I just loved it!" (83, 86).

The Christian-based communities had close contact with the FSLN. Although the FSLN as an organization was secular, a number of highly placed Sandinistas were deeply religious. The ranks of the FSLN included priests, monks, and Christian lay workers. Members from Amparo's Christian-based community put her in contact with a worker from the FSLN, also a woman. This woman, Monica Baltodano, gave Amparo reading material and talked to her at length about the FSLN. Amparo compared the goals of the FSLN with her own and the Christian-based community's and decided to join the FSLN. As a street seller, she could easily operate as a courier, follow the comings and going of the military personnel, and relate detailed information to the FSLN. She was sixteen.

Like so many other militants from both the FSLN and the Christian-based communities, Amparo was arrested. She later explained, "What happened was that after the first person was captured, the other *compañeros* were caught too, because someone in the prison . . . well, it's rare that he doesn't talk because of the torture" (85). Ironically, only a short time earlier, her father had lamented that Amparo was not a boy and thus could not fight back against the dictatorship. Even then, Amparo did not tell her family about her involvement with the FSLN. After her arrest, however, her secret was out and both her mother and her father fully supported her. Because Amparo was still a minor, she was eventually released.

Amparo went to Honduras for more training and then divided her time between fighting and training in the mountains and staying in safe houses. During this time, her first child was born. Amparo sent her baby to her mother to be raised. Amparo knew her child was being raised well but believed that she still suffered from not having her real mother. "Even just the right that a baby has to nurse . . . of this the Guardia [the military] and the dictatorship we had at that time, deprived her" (91). Amparo left her baby at three months and did not see her again until after the revolution. The knowledge of her existence was "the engine that moved" Amparo's life. "I had to return because of my daughter. I had to see her again. So I took care of myself for her sake. I did exercises so I would be in perfect physical condition. . . . I had to return alive so I could see my daughter. I always carried this thought with me" (96).

Amparo could not raise her own child because of the demanding life she led as a guerrilla fighter. She was trained in guerrilla combat, urban warfare, weapons, and tactics. All the trainees also had to be adept at mountain survival to be able to live in the remote northern mountains of Nicaragua. The discipline needed to belong to a guerrilla force surprised even Amparo, already a highly disciplined worker. With limited food, occasional shelter, and an ever-present fear of attack, the reality of basic survival was harsh. Comparing her later experiences as a captain in a professional army with those of being a guerrilla fighter, Amparo said, "Discipline is basic in the *guerrilla*. We are not talking about a military base. In the *guerrilla*, one has to be more rigid, have more order, greater strength, and more precise discipline. And I don't mean discipline in the way that you salute your officers, but in everything from food to baths" (106). She also had to be psychologically prepared for battle, although Amparo added that there is never sufficient training to offset the fear. "Anyone who says that he's not afraid in combat is lying" (96).

Amparo was not in the first wave of female combatants. Other women had blazed the trail for her. The first woman combatant joined in the mid 1960s, but it was not until the late 1960s and early 1970s that women joined in large numbers. These female pioneers would become famous in Nicaragua for shattering the image of the meek and ineffectual female. They had to fight not just the dictatorship but also the men within the FSLN for their rightful due. These women, like the Nicaraguan women's movement, would continue to fight for truth, equality, and freedom into the next millennium, even when that fight pitted them against the hierarchy of their own political party.

One of the more prominent guerrilla fighters turned politician is Dora María Téllez. As a twenty-two-year-old ex–medical student turned guerrilla fighter, she gained national prominence when she participated in the 1978 military assault of the National Palace, Somoza's seat of government. She became famous again when she led the takeover of the town of León during the final Insurrection. After the revolution, Téllez became the minister of health during the Sandinista government of the 1980s, doing such an impressive job that she was praised by the political adversary who inherited her job with the change in government in 1990. After an unsuccessful campaign in 1991, in 1994 she became the first woman to be elected to the elite governing committee of the FSLN, the

National Directorate. Disappointed with the lack of democratic governance within the FSLN, she broke with it, helping to found in 1994 the most prominent of the Sandinista factions, the Movement for Sandinista Renovation (MRS), and then the third way alliance, the Democratic Movement, in the year 2000. Throughout her years in the public eye, Téllez has been notable for her intelligent political analysis, her personal style of calmness, kindness, and dignity, and her implacable courage in the fight for democracy.

Although fame may have bypassed her, Amparo benefited from the breakthroughs the female pioneers like Dora María Téllez had made. She did not, for example, experience much sexism within the ranks of the FSLN. When Edén Pastora, the famous Commander Zero who led dashing assaults on Somoza's strongholds, had her tied to a post and then thrown into a pit even though she had been assigned as his second in command, Amparo phoned Carlos Nuñez (later married to Milú Vargas, feminist lawyer), who got her released. Pastora never pretended that the issue between him and Amparo was anything other than her sex. So at the tender age of twenty-one, after three years of guerrilla fighting and training, Amparo was made second in command of a troop of her own.

In 1977, the FSLN decided that women who didn't want to be guerrilla fighters could nonetheless resist the dictatorship of Somoza. Sandinista women created the first women's organization in Nicaragua, the Association of Nicaraguan Women Confronting the National Problem (AMPRONAC). AMPRONAC organized women, demonstrated against the regime, and made alliances with other protest groups. For their activism, Somoza's army persecuted them. Despite state oppression, patriarchy, and their own inexperience, by 1979 AMPRONAC was one of the best organized and most influential protest groups in the country.

Amparo saw the dawn of 1978 from inside a prison, captured during a battle. She was released for reasons that remain unclear.[2]

The strength of the FSLN had slowly been growing. As it made alliances with disenchanted members of the middle class, the women's movement, working-class organizations, peasant groups, and youth organizations, it gained legitimacy, money, and skills. By 1978, the FSLN was fighting pitched battles with Somoza's army, the popular or mass organizations were fighting Somoza in their own ways, and Nicaragua was engulfed by widespread uprisings. Commerce ground down, schools and universities closed, and cities were leveled by bombing and fighting. Even foreign affairs were conducted by both the FSLN and the state.

Amparo's troop was not as accepting of a female commander as her superiors had been. She said that winning over the men, getting them to accept her command, was her first battle. "It was very hard" (121). Amparo won their respect as both a leader and a fighter as her troop bettered its position strategically and she performed with greater courage than her men. About her experiences with men and women under fire, Amparo concluded, "I'll tell you something, the women in the *guerrilla*, we were hotter than the men. Many times I noticed that in combat. . . . It makes you understand why women achieved command positions" (121).

By July 1979, strategic cities had fallen to the FSLN and Somoza was using everything that he had to defend Managua. He hoped to win in a battle of attrition. The loss of life was horrific. Amparo, still second in command, was in the thick of the battle over the most hotly contested piece of territory. The decisive day was July 17, 1979, two days before the FSLN marched into Managua triumphant. But the Triumph had its price. Amparo remembered,

I give thanks to God, and to my *compañeros* in the battle, that I got out alive, because it was terrible. It was a terrible bombardment. I don't even like to remember it. The Guardia [the military] was shooting like crazy . . . it was crazy. In that moment, the Guardia was having to use all resources, cost what it may. . . . It was a massacre that can't even be named because really you didn't even know who to shoot at! You didn't know where they were shooting you from, so you were running around like crazy, trying to defend yourself. . . . The *compañeros* who were lying wounded in the little hospital in La Liberia, they joined us. They joined us on the front lines to repel that insane attack of the Guardia, a Guardia that was already defeated, no? (132–33)

Amparo was twenty-two and had been fighting for five years when she marched into Managua with the FSLN. "I can't even describe to you the joy I felt. It was like returning to life" (136).

Victory offered a new range of experiences for her. It was her first time ever in Managua, the only major city Nicaragua has. She had never seen traffic lights before. Or streetlights. Or big clocks. Not to mention the National Palace or the Cathedral. "What I felt, the joy. . . . I don't know if I cried, I don't know if I laughed, but I remember that, under that misty rain in Managua, I was happy" (137).

After the revolution, Amparo returned to her village to see her family. Her daughter, whom she had not seen for five years, rejected her. Her daughter said that Amparo was not her mother but a member of the Guardia and that the Guardia were bad people. It was "the most painful thing" (143). Many families were like Amparo's, suffering greatly due to the revolutionary uprising and only with difficulty repairing the damage done.

Soon after achieving power, the FSLN began implementing many of its social justice policies, which greatly benefited women. The new programs included literacy and health campaigns to improve the standard of education and public health; better rights for women, children, and workers; and land distribution for the peasants. Women became involved in the Sandinista government's reforms in order to advance their careers and to improve their legal status. Women participated in these reforms through Sandinista unions and neighborhood organizations, although the Sandinista women's organization, the Association of Nicaraguan Women "Luisa Amanda Espinoza" (AMNLAE), explicitly and consistently addressed women's needs.

Amparo returned to school, completing high school and even entering university. "It's true that because of participating in the Frente Sandinista I still don't have any money but the best wealth is what I learned. I learned to have confidence in myself, I learned how to pick up a pencil like I learned how to pick up a rifle. . . . I learned that you never stop learning" (141).

Soon after the revolution, Amparo moved from the army to the Ministry of the Interior, where she worked on formulating a code of civil liberties (the Statute of Rights and Guarantees). She really enjoyed her work there.

By the 1980s, the United States had a new president, Ronald Reagan, who authorized the funding of a new counterrevolutionary (contra) army based in Honduras that was composed of the remaining members of the Guardia, foreign mercenaries, disenchanted Nicaraguans, and kidnapped peasants. Through this army, the United States waged war by proxy. Nicaragua was once again engaged in civil warfare. The fighting was the worst and lasted the longest in the northern region beside the Honduran border.

Once again, Amparo's military skills were in need. She was sent to

Ocotal, the capital of the northern region, where she and the squadron she commanded were put in charge of defending the border towns from attacks. She also had to organize the communities to defend themselves, to build shelters, to learn about first aid, and to produce their own food in the event of a road blockade. Because so many young men had died in the uprising or were away fighting the civil war, these towns were heavily populated by women. So Amparo linked herself to the women's movement, focusing on raising women's morale and improving their abilities to defend themselves.

In the course of teaching the women armed combat, Amparo learned new ideas from them. The Ministry of the Interior had a more conservative understanding of gender roles than the women's movement had, and Amparo was chafing at these restrictions.

In 1969, the FSLN had published a manifesto detailing its support for women's rights in the event of a revolution. These promised rights ran the gamut from political to social to economic. It is safe to say that these promises were highly idealized, and women had to struggle for the enactment of these promises. Initially, much of the impetus for the struggle came from AMNLAE. Its high degree of organization, its new ideas, and its ability to force the FSLN to comply with its promises made the women's movement an influential political force. In the years just after the revolution, the women's movement made quite an impact on women and men throughout Nicaragua. Amparo was one of the women it affected.

In 1984, at the height of the civil war, the FSLN won Nicaragua's first free and democratic election with a substantial majority. But the war was taking its toll both economically and emotionally. Food shortages were common, and all stuffs were rationed. As the death toll from the war continued to rise without either side seeming to win anything, impatience with the new government began to grow.

The government was unable to continue to pay for implementing its social justice program and refused to enact many of its promises. Women's issues was one such area in which women were encouraged to wait for their just deserts. AMNLAE was not autonomous from the FSLN; in fact, the FSLN dictated AMNLAE's stance. Thus, AMNLAE, which had hitherto been a vocal and effective champion for women's rights, also advocated patience. As a result, by 1986, AMNLAE's early successes in achieving legal and social changes had slowed and its legitimacy to speak for women had been undermined. AMNLAE was unable to present issues such as reproductive health for public debate because the hierarchy of the FSLN did not consider such concerns politically expedient. When women in AMNLAE did become publicly critical of the FSLN's treatment of women in 1987, the FSLN threatened to shut down the organization. Thereafter, AMNLAE supported the FSLN, ignoring grass-roots women's demands in 1989 and again in 1991.

In 1988, George Bush became president of the United States. He did not have the compulsion to overthrow the Sandinista government that Reagan had. However, he was trapped by Reagan's legacy and therefore had to deal with the reality of Nicaragua's revolutionary government. In the 1990 general election, Bush endorsed the candidacy of Violeta Chamorro, the widow of a newspaper editor slain for criticizing the Somoza dictatorship, who headed a party formed from a coalition of other parties. Chamorro, who had the advantage of belonging to the upper class, had participated briefly with the Sandinistas when they first came to power and then joined the opposition. Furthermore, her own family had been split by the revolution into those who supported the FSLN and those who did not. For many Nicaraguans, she symbolized the plight of a typical Nicaraguan family. She promised to be the mother of all Nicaraguans and to bring peace and prosperity to Nicaragua. Bush promised that if she was elected, the military conflict would cease and the United States would fund the redevelopment of the nation. The Sandinistas could make no such promises. Chamorro's coalition won.

Although the war did indeed end with her election, armed ex-soldiers continued to roam the countryside. Poverty actually increased. Basic health care was eroded and once again children died from easily preventable diseases. Because Chamorro had extremely conservative views on gender roles, many of the rights that women had already won were reversed. The women's movement, severely weakened by its long association with the FSLN, underwent a painful self-criticism and reorganization that took several years. By 1993, the women's movement had begun to reestablish itself as a political force. As a compilation of women's groups, including AMNLAE, the women's movement grew rapidly in number, projects, and influence.

For many, life got worse in the 1990s. Amparo lost her job at the Ministry of the Interior. Northern Nicaragua, which had suffered so much under both the revolutionary uprising and then the postrevolutionary war, was simply forgotten. Amparo, seeing the rollbacks in essential services and civil rights, for which she had fought so hard, decided that something had to be done. She organized a group of women from all walks of life to protest the government's actions. The women included ex-soldiers, housewives, secretaries, high school students, and professionals, including lawyers. She called the group Frente Nora Astorga after a Sandinista lawyer, diplomat, and occasional combatant. It had approximately five hundred members. Housing, job training, education, and health care were key issues for the women in the northern regions. But neither the local mayor nor the national government would even respond to the letters that the Frente Nora Astorga wrote to them.

Finally, Amparo did what she did best—fought back. In April 1992, the Frente Nora Astorga militarily took over the town of Ocotal, the capital of the northern region. Those with military training had taught other women the basics. Those who spoke well handled the public communication and integrated all the sectors. The Frente Nora Astorga took over the town hall, the radio station, the post office (which was also the center for all communication in and out of the town), and other principal public buildings, as well as key roads in and out of town. They also took workers in those buildings hostage. The success of the campaign was helped by the reluctance of the police force to attack the women. Nonetheless, it was a well-planned military maneuver by one of Nicaragua's best and most experienced military leaders. Supplanting the women by force would have resulted in the loss of many lives on both sides.

After a week of negotiation, the Frente Nora Astorga and the national government signed an agreement. The Frente Nora Astorga received 165 building lots and construction materials to build the same number of houses, and twenty-five sewing machines. The government also promised to study the possibility of credit through local banks and to reforest 350 hectares. Because the Frente Nora Astorga received what they asked for, they voluntarily and peacefully relinquished control of the buildings. Said Amparo, without a trace of irony, "Now we're a women's organization, and what we want is to solicit help through the juridical process" (194).

The military action that the Frente Nora Astorga used for satisfaction of its demands was not the only such occurrence in Nicaragua. After fifteen years of civil war, people knew how to fight and fight well. Indeed, they lacked the skills to do much else. The Chamorro government offered soldiers on both sides of the conflict inducements of land, credit, and training to quit the armed forces. When the promised inducements never materialized, those soldiers rearmed to fight for their goods. Other ex-soldiers who could have farmed for a living discovered that it was easier to pillage, and they rearmed also. Other ex-soldiers rearmed, decrying the negotiations between Chamorro's coalition government and the FSLN. Soldiers were not the only ones who were irritated with the government. Elected members of the far right attempted a coup d'état, trade unions paralyzed the country on more than one occasion, and political parties were seemingly incapable of internal unity. Chamorro's coalition dissipated like chaff in the wind, and the FSLN split into rival factions that fought each other. Financially impoverished due to its economic policy and politically stalemated by long negotiations over public policy, Nicaragua teetered on the brink of utter chaos and anarchy.[3]

Amparo may have been able to help the women in her town to fight back, but she herself was unable to claim any of the benefits that came from the uprising. To keep the process as free as possible from the taint of corruption, Amparo refused all offers that would have lightened her financial burden. And so she saw out the Chamorro government while living back with her father, making food and selling it on the streets.

It would make a neat and tidy ending to suggest that Amparo and the women of Nicaragua had gone full circle from poverty to power and back again. Reality, however, is rarely so convenient. Amparo is still fighting for women's rights, still fighting to improve the lot of her community through all possible means: legal, political, economic, and, when all else fails, military. But now, unlike in the early 1970s, she knows what those rights are and has skills at her disposal to achieve them.

But even that is too neat and tidy to explain the transformation of Amparo from an impoverished and disenfranchised girl to an effective guerrilla fighter and political organizer. Similarly, the Nicaraguan women's movement requires an analysis that adequately explains its evolution from nonexistence in 1977 to an effective political organization under the Somoza dictatorship, the revolutionary government of the FSLN, and the right-wing conservatism of Chamorro. Social movement theory offers that analytical tool. The rest of the chapter will examine the strengths and weaknesses of social movement theory and outline how it applies to the Nicaraguan women's movement from 1977 to 1996.

Social movement theory developed in response to the rise of collective political actions that did not fit existing categories of party politics, interest groups, and social class activity. Movements around issues relating to women, ecological damage, religious concerns, old or young people, racial groups, and the disappearances of political activists called forth new kinds of explanatory theory. Two schools of analysis, resource mobilization theory and identity theory, staked out contrasting approaches. Today, many social movement theorists recognize that there are advantages to both schools of thought, and they combine elements from each to explain the growth and development of a social movement (Cohen 1985; Scott 1990; Escobar and Alvarez 1992; Dalton and Keuchler 1990; Morris and Mueller 1992; Foweraker 1995).

Despite the hybridization of social movement theory, some weaknesses of the original theories remain. These weaknesses are the objective definition of resources, the poor conceptualization of the role of public spaces, the narrow understanding of the role of grievance, and the definition of the impact of a successful social movement. These weaknesses will be highlighted during an overview of social movement theory.

Resource mobilization theory powerfully explains what materials (or resources) are needed for a successful social movement organization. The theory analyzes how a social movement organization or a protest group is able to maintain itself and grow through utilizing resources such as microprocesses of communication, leadership, preexisting domestic and international support groups, access to money, experience in organizing, degree of internal cohesion, variability and routinization of the flow of resources, and so on. It also includes the effect of changing political structures on social movements. For example, a change in the organization of the economy, of supreme court judges, or of government can offer a social movement an opportunity to make a sudden leap forward in pressing its claims.

Resource mobilization theory considers resources generally quantifiable and external to the group. (A notable exception is leadership, a variable impossible to measure.) Analysis of the emergence and growth of the Nicaraguan women's movement showed that a resource is not a quantifiable good, but rather the *perception* of what is a good. Thus, a resource is a resource only when defined as such by a social movement. Political oppression, lack of funding, and inexperienced leadership, all elements typically considered detrimental to social movement growth and maintenance, can be considered under certain circumstances as assets. Thus, resources are not goods external to the participants of a social movement, but rather goods defined as such by the participants.

Furthermore, a critically important resource is the structure of the social movement organization and the social movement itself. An appropriately organized internal structure complements and advertises the social movement's ethos and can thus be used to attract participants. The internal structure must facilitate the development of the other key components of a successful social movement: the creation of identity and goal attainment. A poorly structured social movement impedes identity creation, repels participation, and hinders goal attainment.

This approach to the mobilization of resources introduces the element of the subjective into the analysis. This proved problematic for resource mobilization theory because it assumed that human activity is based on utilitarian rationalism and cost-benefit analysis. As the paradigm continued to evolve, this ontology was heavily criticized and addressed through augmenting rationality or using psychology (Olsen 1965; Foweraker 1995, 24; McAdam, McCarthy, and Zald 1988, 709–10; Oberschall 1993, 24; Tarrow 1992, 5; Klandermans 1992, 86; Snow et al. 1986; McAdam, McCarthy, and Zald 1996, 24). Neither a rational analysis of solidarity nor a psychological presentation of political activism adequately explains the profundity of the belief system of activists and the risks that they take. In addition, these explanations cannot illuminate the interactions between the social movement and the larger political process and the individual and the social movement. "This deficiency is shared by the field as a whole" (McAdam, McCarthy, and Zald 1988, 698).

Eventually the resource mobilization paradigm arrived at a concept remarkably similar to identity (Marx Ferree 1992, 31; Friedman and McAdam 1992, 164). Identity theory has the great merit of focusing on the internal process of constructing meanings in a social movement. It begins with the assumption that human beings are meaning-shaping: that they create identities and that each identity group develops an ethos that can organize action, give an impetus to participation, and articulate an alternative to the status quo. The ethos is created through individuals resisting the dominant norms of society and interacting to form a like-minded group. The group's awareness, born of resistance and reflection, activates political engagement in an attempt to enact its alternative understanding.

The primacy of identity is of particular interest for the Nicaraguan case, as the women's movement there has fought over identity. Social movement theorists claim that identity-based social movements prefer to organize themselves through small collectives uniting into ad hoc networks (Melucci 1989, 60; Chalmers et al. 1997, 574–78; Tilly 1984, 305; Oberschall 1993; Clemens 1996). This resolves the tension between the need for the primacy of the identity and the need for cooperation and compromise to achieve specific political goals; in the collectives, the identity remains paramount, whereas in the network, the goal is explicitly political. The political action of a network of collectives is evident in the public realm through the use of public spaces: spaces in which the networks and the collectives meet, discuss, organize, and agitate. Public spaces connect the microspaces of the collectives with the political actions organized by the networks. In such a way, a decentralized social movement can confront a centralized state.

The women's movement's emphasis on identity formation with a complementary structure grants it a powerful base from which to grow because it can attract women of all classes and political affiliations. This issue has been a quagmire for more than one women's movement, and this is especially so in a nation just emerging from a prolonged civil war. However, an identity-based social movement tends to focus its identity on the body rather than on more abstract issues such as civil rights. Because identity formation grows on shared experiences and understandings, the basis has to be a widely held and utterly common experience. For women in Nicaragua, it is the physical experience of being female, although of course different groups will have experienced it differently. The experience of the body as the site of patriarchy produced an alternative also based on the body, which for the autonomous women's movement became an ethic of care. From this point, the ethic could evolve into any number of different political actions. Nonetheless, the emphasis on the body tended to shape the kinds of organizing it engaged in, limiting the effectiveness of the more traditional variety of political lobbying although facilitating nonpartisan legislative cooperation, international cooperation, and mass support for specific legal changes.

Both identity and resource mobilization theories inadequately conceptualize the relationship between civil society and the state. As a result, the arena in which they meet, public space, is also poorly theorized. Resource mobilization theory fails to recognize the importance of public spaces. Access to and use of public spaces could be considered valuable resources if they help to build the movement. Unfortunately, public spaces have not to date been identified as a resource. As a result, resource mobilization theory fails to analyze how resources are mobilized through political action in public spaces. This lacuna in resource mobilization theory can be traced to the dichotomized conception of state and civil society relations.

Because resource mobilization theory posits social movements wholly in civil society (Cohen and Arato 1992, ix, 509), it concludes that social and political changes occur solely through confrontations between the state and civil society wherein civil society and the state occupy distinct arenas and pursue mutually exclusive concerns.[4] It is much more realistic to postulate that civil society can have degrees of autonomy from the state. In fact, civil society and the state can be mutually embedded, for example, in a corporatist state (Wood 1995; Nielson 1995). Social movements and their utilization of public spaces can also have degrees of autonomy from the state. The extent to which the state and civil society are interwoven affects the techniques of political action. In a corporatist state, a social movement's public spaces can be created, funded, and directed by the state to achieve ends beneficial to both the social movement and the government. In a civil society with a high degree of autonomy from the state, public spaces are used to lobby the state and civil society or to strengthen the social movement's identity, or both.

In comparison, identity theory offers the possibility of understanding the unifying elements that bring actors together in public spaces, but it lacks a full conception of public space and the political work that is carried out in it. This is the lacuna of identity theory. The theoretical weakness is due to the absence of a concrete conception of the process of constructing political actions and meanings.

A fuller conception of public spaces can fill the theoretical void by giving focus to the political work that occurs in public spaces: choosing the social movement's goals and actions; persuading the state, other groups in civil society, and the movement's own members to accept new ideas; and challenging value-laden symbols. In each of the time periods of the Nicaraguan women's movement, these three kinds of political work were found in public spaces. Although the resources mobilized may have been different for each public space, and though the organization of the public spaces and the women's movement may have altered over the fifteen-year span, the actual work that the public spaces performed remained constant.

Another effect of the inadequate conceptualization of state–civil society relations is a poor understanding of grievance. Social movements become political because they resist and protest an aspect of state public policy or a societal norm. However, there is little appreciation of the difference between the three kinds of grievance inherent in all political structures: a generalized discontent with one's lot in life; a more focused conflict with a culturally constructed artifact, for example, the class system; or a specific complaint, such as a law that supports the class system (McAdam 1982, 33; McCarthy and Zald 1977, 1215; Melucci 1980, 210).

Two theorists from the resource mobilization school, Charles Tilly (1978) and Sidney Tarrow (1994, 1996), suggest that the rise of the modern state facilitated the rise of social movements by offering the social movements a focused source of conflict. "It was the rise of modern states and an international capitalist economy that provided the targets and the resources that helped movements to flourish and that laid the bases for today's social movements" (Tarrow 1994, 191). While Tarrow and Tilly might indeed be correct in regarding the development of social movements in the Western world, it is more difficult to apply their conclusion to Latin America, where state corporatism has been prevalent. Thus, a state might well provide the "target," but the involvement of a social movement with the operation of the government undermined the movement's ability to criticize it. Thus, a corporatist state is not an easy target, and social movements in this situation have to find targets other than the state. In the second half of the FSLN's rule in Nicaragua, AMNLAE sought to find a target, with limited success. It eventually lit upon scattering women's centers through the more remote regions of Nicaragua.

Frequently, social movements target societal norms and mores in the hope that by changing societal values they will consequently change the state's public policies as well. Societal values can be encapsulated in a symbol. Thus, the conflict between a social movement and society can be a specific complaint about a symbol. The battle between society and the women's movement over the control of the symbol of womanhood was evident in each and every phase of its activism.

Regardless of the nature of the target, for a social movement to be effective it must have an explicit complaint. For this reason, a specific complaint could be referred to as the social movement's goal. This goal becomes the focal point around which the social movement mobilizes short-term participation. A focused complaint also serves to create long-term commitment to the social movement: the movement can use the grievance to promulgate a more generalized statement of discontent and to suggest an alternative to the status quo. When the complaint is used to communicate the social movement's broader understanding, the specific grievance shapes the information disseminated. This, in turn, affects the kind of identity created. Furthermore, the specific grievance chosen will influence the resources mobilized. In such a way, a specific grievance interacts with the two other components of a social movement, shaping its growth.

The assumption of both resource mobilization and identity theories is that, with a clear target or a focused goal, an identity, and well-mobilized resources including a complementary internal structure, a social movement will be able to persuade and influence the state's public policies or societal values, or both.[5] This assumption unfortunately can be fallacious. The powerful Nicaraguan women's movement was unable to persuade the Chamorro government to alter its public policies relating to women. Indeed, the stronger the women's movement became, the more the government appeared to harden its stance against it. The more the government hardened its stance, the better target it made for the social movement. As conflict between the two political actors escalated, more people became involved in polarizing differences. This dynamic made public policy intransigent, resulting in the further impoverishment of women and, indeed, probably some deaths as well. This reality should temper the optimism found in much of the literature about the potential of social movements to ameliorate oppressive situations.

Nonetheless, the Nicaraguan women's movement did achieve some success, changing laws and persuading the state to at least cooperate with it internationally. It also had successes of the kind more difficult to see. The impact of social movements can be measured in the innovations that they stimulate: new models of organization, new patterns of behavior, and new understandings of cultural symbols. Unfortunately, the impact of altering a symbol does not allow one to make a direct correlation to changed public policy. Subverting the dominant cultural code and mobilizing resources against it are both part of the same field of changing power relations. Thus, they have a positive impact on each other. By successfully organizing participation through developing identity and a decentralized structure, the Nicaraguan women's movement has inspired other movements, for example, the homosexual rights movement, to organize. The women's movement has also successfully reappropriated the symbol of motherhood, perhaps for the first time. Although it is impossible to draw a direct correlation, these innovations should produce a ripple through Nicaraguan society, influencing it in years to come.

This theoretical framework, which suggests that the primary components of a successful social movement are an autonomous identity, a complementary use of resources, and a focused goal, is not a departure from other approaches to the study of social movements. Rather, my theoretical framework enhances and augments others' work. In recasting social movement theory, its weaknesses are overcome, rendering it more cohesive and flexible.

These three components of identity, resources, and goals, operating in a mutually reinforcing fashion, were critical to the success of the women's movement. The absence or presence of these three elements explains the women's movement from its inception to 1996: its relationship with the governing regimes, its changes, and its successes and failures.

AMPRONAC, the first women's organization in Nicaragua, was formed under dire circumstances and with few resources at its disposal. Yet it became one of the most influential protest groups operating against Somoza. Its success was possible only because it had the components necessary to create and maintain a social movement: an articulate identity, superb mobilization of resources, and a unifying goal of overthrowing the dictator.

After the revolution, AMPRONAC became AMNLAE. AMNLAE's initial success in achieving women's needs was eroded by the FSLN's reduced commitment. Without autonomy from the FSLN, AMNLAE lost its direction and floundered politically. As an organization, AMNLAE had contradictions built into its identity, goals, and strategies. These contradictions undermined AMNLAE's capacity to act efficaciously as a social movement. First, the identity that AMNLAE promulgated was the Sandinista identity of freedom and equality. Yet as the decade progressed, the FSLN increasingly resisted women's demands for freedom and equality. Second, AMNLAE's goals were always vague, shifting as the political need arose. Finally, the strategic organization of AMNLAE, which was hierarchical, corporatist, and nondemocratic, was alienating to most women. As a result, women's participation in AMNLAE decreased and its legitimacy declined.

Replacing AMNLAE, women's secretariats in Sandinista unions emerged as the most cogent voice for gender-based change in the late 1980s. Focusing on their specific union concerns and organizing around their particular union identity, the women's secretariats were able to broaden the space for effective criticism of the FSLN and to engage in effective action to alter the status quo. While the women's secretariats were not fully developed social movements due to their vulnerability to control by the FSLN, these secretariats were essential for reforming aspects of the existing system and for initiating the process of building women's identity autonomous from the FSLN.

After the FSLN fell from power in the 1990 general election, the women's movement had the opportunity to redefine itself separately from the FSLN and from the state. The reformation of the women's movement was inadvertently assisted by the newly elected government of Violeta Chamorro. This government was explicitly hostile to women's equality within the private and the public spheres. The Chamorro government changed laws to reduce women's public participation and initiated a harsh structural adjustment policy that reduced women's access to social services and employment opportunities. These legal, social, and economic changes offered the women's movement specific complaints around which it could mobilize.

The women's movement, recently autonomous from the FSLN, forged a new identity on gender concerns. It based its goals on health and human rights and reorganized itself horizontally through collectives, neighborhood groups, NGOs, and health and law clinics. Eventually, even the revamped AMNLAE and Sandinista women's secretariats joined. All these groups created their own identity. They then merged into horizontal networks to better achieve their specific goals. The use of public space became an important tool for the political arm of the women's movement, attracting new participants, challenging the government, and disseminating information from women's perspectives. This form of internal organization of a movement from group to network to public space required the mobilization of such resources as media, leadership, and funding. The presence of an autonomous, self-defined identity, appropriate use of resources, and a focused goal accounted for the successful organizing of the women's movement in the 1990s.

The rest of this book will demonstrate the validity of the theory by tracing the history of the Nicaraguan women's movement as it struggled over identity, resources, and goals, and the social, political, and economic environment in which it operated.

PART 1

The Sandinista Women's Movement, 1977–1990

CHAPTER 2

Overthrowing the Dictator, 1977–1979

IT WOULD BE DIFFICULT TO DESCRIBE Nicaragua's history as peaceful. In the twentieth century alone there was a coup d'etat, two American invasions, two guerrilla insurgencies, a corrupt dictatorship, a revolution, and a civil war. With its endemic violence and dictatorships, Nicaragua seemed to epitomize the stereotype of a Latin American nation. For most of the century, the stereotype of Latina women also seemed to be true in Nicaragua. Until the 1960s, the roles available to Nicaraguan women were typical for a poor Latin American nation: upper-class women were trophy wives with servants to do the household tasks, while poor women both worked outside the home and raised their children—frequently with heartrending suffering. Women's economic and social contributions went unrecognized, regardless of their class. This situation changed when women joined the FSLN as guerrilla fighters and organized their first women's movement.

Throughout the nineteenth and twentieth centuries, two parties, the Liberals and the Conservatives, jostled for political, and hence economic, power in Nicaragua. By the turn of the century, the ideological difference between the two dissolved and parties became largely personal as both developed into clan-based loyalties (Booth 1996, 423). After reformist and nationalist Liberal president José Santos Zelaya began negotiating with Germany and Japan to build a canal across Nicaragua, thus providing competition for the Panama Canal, the United States militarily supported a Conservative coup in 1909. The Conservatives made such a hash of governing that there was a rebellion of both Liberals and disenchanted Conservatives, prompting a second American invasion in 1912 to shore up the regime. With a short hiatus in the mid 1920s, the American marines occupied Nicaragua until 1933.

In 1925, the American government created and trained the National Guard, a combined army and police force, to defend the Nicaraguan presidency from rebellious elites and insurgent groups. In 1926, the Liberals, unintimidated by either the newly formed National Guard or the U.S. Marines, rose up again. Peace was reached in 1927 through the formation of a Liberal-Conservative governing alliance in which the United States changed its support from the Conservatives to the feistier Liberals.

In 1927, a Liberal nationalist and mystic, Augusto Sandino, refused to sign a declaration supporting the new American-backed president, supporting instead a constitutional presidency. With an army of two hundred men, Sandino retreated to the mountains and began a guerrilla war against the U.S. Marines and the National Guard. This warfare rapidly increased the size and capability of the National Guard until eventually the marines were able to withdraw in 1932.

After the Americans left, the general in charge of the National Guard, Anastasio Somoza Garcia, was invited by the new Liberal president to negotiate peace, the pretext being that Nicaragua was now free and sovereign and thus continued fighting was unnecessary. After one such meeting, Somoza had Sandino and all his lieutenants shot. Somoza then deposed, in 1936, the Liberal president and installed himself in power. Somoza Garcia ruled either overtly or through his puppets until 1956, when he was assassinated and his son, Luis Somoza Debayle, assumed power. In 1967, Somoza Garcia's second son, Anastasio Somoza Debayle, became president.

Whereas the final Somoza ruler had a reputation for unbridled venality, the first Somoza in particular was clever, so much so that he managed to given himself a patina of populism (Dunkerley 1988, 105). Somoza Garcia had to gain the acquiescence of the elite, as his status was due to his advantageous marriage with them, as well as his American support. Somoza was able to maintain himself in power by making alliances with both the Liberals and the Conservatives, by sharing money through patronage appointments and access to public funds, and by coopting the labor movement before repressing it. Despite the sharing, Somoza became the largest landowner in Nicaragua.

When it came to perpetuating his presidency, it certainly helped that Somoza had consolidated his power base in the National Guard. Somoza, who again achieved his rank of general by charming his American contacts, had to earn the loyalty of the National Guard. Somoza gained its loyalty by politicizing it around the presidency and by allowing the military to direct gambling, prostitution, and racketeering in Nicaragua. To instill fear, the military gained a reputation for extraordinary cruelty and violence, often arbitrary, including occasionally torturing a member of the oligarchy. Somoza summarized his political technique as, "Bucks for my friends, bullets for my enemies" (quoted in Booth 1985, 61).

Leonor Argüello de Hüper came of age during this period of Nicaragua's history. She was born in Managua to a wealthy oligarchic family in 1922. She met Sandino once as a child, and of course knew Somoza and his family. She described the lives of young wives and mothers like herself: "Since we were not supposed to think, we were not granted the privilege of knowing anything. A woman was supposed to stay at home . . . and be the kept woman of her husband (because they were never companions or friends, lovers maybe, but that was it). Women were objects. . . . [Women] didn't even know about how their husbands earned money, much less about politics. And as along as the husband was not a drunkard (oh, he could be a womanizer, most Latino men are), the women would put up with it. Marriage was forever" (quoted in McVey 1995, 36). For wanting to study law after the birth of her children, Leonor Argüello called herself "an oddity in my surroundings, a very strange person" (ibid.).

In contrast, Estabana Manjarreth Montoya, who was also born in 1922 but to a poor peasant family, grew up in a one-room house made of sticks and mud. She and her nine brothers and sisters and her father (her mother died in childbirth when Estabana was two) were all illiterate. The 1920 official Nicaraguan census called the job that she and 75 percent of other Nicaraguan women did "Domestic Office." It included preparing and making food, hauling water, gathering firewood, washing clothes in the river, and child-care. It did not include women's contribution to agricultural production or to the family income by making and selling food or services—which Estabana's mother and later her sister did.[1] As a young wife and mother, Estabana moved with her family around the northern area of Nicaragua in search of arable land. Throughout, Estabana baked and sold sweets on the street while her children did seasonal work on the plantations in miserable conditions (McVey 1995, chap. 1).

Despite the poverty of families like Estabana's, there was only limited unrest in Nicaragua in the first few decades after Somoza took power. This social and political peace was due in part to the repression of the National Guard, but was mostly due to a rapidly growing economy. When Somoza took power in 1936, Nicaragua was a coffee exporter with an economic infrastructure built around its production and export. Although new blocks of land continued to be put under coffee cultivation, the boom in the price of cotton after World War II created a sudden increase in the lands devoted to cotton. The diversification of the economy was furthered by a doubling of the lands devoted to sugar and cattle. In 1960, Nicaragua joined the Central American Common Market (CACM), which broadened its market and promoted industrialization. Between 1960 and 1970, manufacturing grew a cumulative 11 percent and continued to grow throughout the 1970s by a further 5 percent. As a percentage of its share of the gross domestic product, manufacturing rose from 13 percent in 1960 to 20 percent in 1978. From 1936, when Somoza took power, to 1950, the average growth rate of the gross domestic product was 4.6 percent, rising to 5.6 percent during the 1950s and 7.5 percent for the 1960s. This growth rate easily outstripped the population growth rate (Dunkerley 1988, 171, 202).

The modernization of agriculture and the industrialization of Nicaragua produced a small but growing middle class concentrated in the urban areas. Illiteracy, which was at 72 percent in 1920, dropped to 58 percent in 1950, with male and female illiteracy in the urban areas 32 percent and 35 percent, respectively.[2] Women's enrollment in universities rose from 10 percent of the student population in 1962 to 33 percent in 1978. The increasing public articulation of women, especially educated women, was reflected in women's franchisement in 1955.

Women's contribution to the economy was also becoming more visible. With education, the number of women entering the formal economy increased. This proportion grew to 22 percent in 1970 and to 29 percent in 1977 (Chinchilla 1983, 6), although it is estimated that almost one third of Nicaraguan households were headed by a woman, 85 percent of which worked outside the home (Collinson et al. 1990, 28). This fact suggests that the census grossly underestimated the number of working women. Agricultural work, in which many peasant women were involved, was still not counted. However, the number of women performing agricultural work declined as peasant families became dispossessed and migrated to the urban centers in search of work (Mason 1992, 76). There, many of these women sold homemade goods or became domestic servants. These economic activities belonged to the informal sector and were also not counted. Three quarters of all women in the labor force in Nicaragua in the 1970s belonged to the service sector, in which wages and job security were the lowest (Mason 1992, 77–78). The nature of the service industry did not allow for traditional methods of organizing workers through unions.

In 1961, three young men, Carlos Fonseca, Silvio Mayorga, and Tomás Borge, created the National Liberation Front (the immediate predecessor of the Sandinista Front of National Liberation [FSLN]). Inspired by the Cuban revolution of 1959 and Nicaragua's own national hero, Sandino, the trio created a new ideology of nationalist socialism achieved through armed peasant insurrection. This stance caused the young revolutionaries to split from the Nicaraguan Socialist Party, which advocated nonviolence and the organization of the urban proletariat.

The first actions that the FSLN undertook were routs. In 1967, the FSLN was almost completely obliterated at the battle of Pancasán. Included in those killed was Silvio Mayorga. The FSLN then took a long break from military confrontation. At that point, there was only one female guerrilla fighter with the FSLN, Gladys Baez. She escaped death at Pancasán only because she was recuperating in Managua from the tortures of the National Guard (Randall 1981, 177). There were, however, a number of female Sandinistas in the cities organizing students, safe houses, and supplies. Although the FSLN had lost every battle, the National Guard increased its repression, especially of the peasants in the northern area. This was a strategic error, because the battle for political rights and freedom was based in the urban centers, especially in the universities. And women were very much part of that battle.

Although the gross domestic product was increasing, the wealth was concentrated in fewer hands and the standard of living of the poorest people actually declined. Nonetheless, working- and middle-class wages rose until 1970 (or 1973, depending on the statistical model used), when growth from the CACM slowed and wages were unable to keep pace with OPEC-induced inflation. The increasing expectations and demands made by labor unions and professionals were met with repression. Somoza used the devastating earthquake in Managua in 1972 to acquire more power over the economy by controlling the flow of aid money and the postearthquake construction boom. The earthquake also had demolished the primary market for small and medium-sized businesses in Managua. The business class began to shift its allegiance away from Somoza (Booth and Walker 1993, 36, 62; Booth 1996, 425; Dijkstra 1996, 2).

By 1971, politically active students at both high school and university levels were being arrested. Parents, usually mothers, were being pulled into the political fray in the effort to protect their children (McVey 1995, 74). Women also had started to become politically visible through membership in neighborhood groups. These groups, organized after the Managua earthquake, sought collective solutions to problems, such as the lack of potable water, that individuals could not solve for themselves. Christian-based communities, in which women participated extensively, were also centers of antiregime mobilization.

On December 27, 1974, a Sandinista commando unit of thirteen guerrilla fighters, three of whom were women, took hostage the guests of a diplomatic party held by the American ambassador, Turner Shelton. In exchange for the hostages' freedom, fourteen Sandinista prisoners were freed. They and the Sandinista commandos were allowed to board a plane for Cuba and the Sandinista manifesto was published in the Nicaraguan daily papers. More important, it was a highly visible and successful action with female guerrilla fighters.

This commando action became the turning point for the FSLN in more than one way. Somoza became even more oppressive, and a number of Sandinista leaders were either killed or forced into exile. Carlos Fonseca, a founder and the guiding intellectual of the FSLN, was killed in 1976. The oppression, loss of leadership, and a ground swell of support for revolutionary insurrection caused arguments over strategies within the FSLN. With the death of Fonseca, discipline and unity were lost and the organization fragmented. One splinter felt that the Sandinistas must focus on organizing the urban proletariat, which was protesting the declining standard of living. Another splinter held that the Sandinistas must focus on mobilizing the peasants in the mountains, as Castro had done. By 1976, the Somoza dictatorship was seriously weakened, losing both domestic and international support, and the FSLN was fragmented, militarily defeated in the countryside, and decimated in the cities. The FSLN looked as if it might be left behind as the populace rose in spontaneous battle and organized itself into anti-Somoza groups (Nolan 1984, 68).

In 1977, Humberto Ortega, an FSLN militant, future general of the Sandinista army, and brother of future president Daniel Ortega, realized the possibility of failure (Marcus 1982, 59) and developed the ideology of the Third Tendency, or *Tercerismo*. The Sandinistas who agreed with Humberto Ortega were called the Terceristas. *Tercerismo* was a strategy for attaining revolutionary socialism through the organization of the masses into alliances under the direction of a vanguard party (Marcus 1982, 58).

The subject of the revolution, according to the Terceristas, would not be class per se but rather the masses in general. Sergio Ramírez defined the popular subject as "a conception of people as a class" (Dunkerley 1988, 242). The popular subject could reflect the liberating aspects of resistance and revolution, and thus could include women organizing as women. For that matter, it could include anyone organizing as anything. The logic was that capitalism exploited all people through its functioning and its ideology. Therefore, according to the ideology of *Tercerismo*, all were in need of liberation (Nolan 1984, 63–70; Nuñez 1988, 159). This approach to understanding oppression and liberation was accepted by many of the groups, such as the neighborhood committees, which were already resisting the dictator outside the FSLN. It also dovetailed with liberation theology and its Christian-based communities, which lent spiritual and logistical support for the FSLN, legitimizing its actions and ideology. The ideology of personal salvation through group alignment became the unifying ethos of the FSLN once it gained power in 1979. Redubbed "Sandinismo," it integrated all people into a governing ideology of social justice achieved through group liberation (Coraggio 1986, 12).

In 1977, the Sandinistas used this ideology to organize women as women, forming the Association of Nicaraguan Women Confronting the National Problem (AMPRONAC). AMPRONAC's peculiar name reflected the nonspecific nature of its resistance. There was no mention of either revolution or Sandinismo in its name or activities. It was not merely that its revolutionary origins were hidden; all partisan politics were eschewed. As a result, AMPRONAC was free to organize and define itself as it saw fit. Elizabeth Maier (1980, 51) elaborates: "AMPRONAC maintained a certain autonomy from the FSLN and at the same time maintained an organic relationship with it." The FSLN gave AMPRONAC the support it needed yet the space to define its own identity. This produced a wider scope for AMPRONAC's activism and an increasingly overt partisanship in favor of the FSLN. The emergence of such a successful women's group in so little time and under such adverse conditions was the result of a horizontal and democratic organization with an emphasis on self-discovery and self-definition rather than on furthering Sandinista goals, as well as the effective use of resources and a focused goal of overthrowing the dictator.

AMPRONAC was intended to be a human rights organization (Seitz 1992, 170; Lobao 1990, 194; Collinson et al. 1990, 139; Murguialday 1990, 40; *Central American Women Speak* 1983, xx). Nascent mothers' human rights groups were already spontaneously emerging. However, these early protests were not well organized or systematic (Murguialday 1990, 37–38). Nonetheless, these "mothers' clubs" made a difference to AMPRONAC's capacity to organize because they served as microcells of mobilization (McAdam, McCarthy, and Zald 1988). AMPRONAC contacted, integrated, and organized them. Building themselves on the mothers' clubs gave AMPRONAC ready access to already active women and allowed it to develop an image of a spontaneous organization of concerned mothers who were above the political fray.[3] AMPRONAC describes its emergence this way: "Within this socio-economic and political context [oppression], including the constant violation of our human rights, it is not hard to understand why as activists, mothers, wives, and sisters we felt the need to make our needs and demands heard in the midst of so much pain and injustice. Thus, for the first time in our history as Nicaraguan women, we began to organize" (*Central American Women Speak* 1983, 10).

However, this presentation of history is not entirely accurate because it omits the role of the FSLN in forging AMPRONAC. The role of the FSLN as AMPRONAC's creator must be recognized because it explains two phenomena: the extent to which the women's movement was controlled by the Party, even when that control was hidden and reduced, and the ease with which AMPRONAC abandoned its autonomy after the revolution.

Forming a women's movement based on human rights was an adroit move by the Sandinistas and clearly not accidental. In the 1960s, the FSLN twice tried to create a women's organization. Both attempts were dismal failures because of the emphasis on socialism rather than on women's concerns. "Its class character had dominated and frequently annulled any expression of feminine sectorial requests" (Murguialday 1988, 55).

The FSLN was conscious of the role that women played in undermining the socialist government of Salvador Allende in Chile (1970–1973) and in supporting the government of Fidel Castro in Cuba (Chinchilla 1983, 2; Schultz 1980b). It is reasonable to assume that they were also aware of the influential Madres de la Plaza de Mayo in Argentina, which helped to bring down the dictator there. It is not surprising that AMPRONAC superficially resembled the Madres de la Plaza de Mayo.

In April 1977, Sandinista commander Jaime Wheelock contacted Lea Guido and Gloria Carrión, two Sandinistas whose affiliation to the Party was well hidden (Murguialday 1990, 40).[4] He asked if they would form a mass-based women's group organized around women's problems (Randall 1981, 2). Although human rights was to be the new group's foundation, Guido fought hard to broaden women's consciousness, political action, and social base before and after the revolution (ibid, 4). Thus, the founding members of AMPRONAC broadened its appeal and its role, contributing to its success.

The task of organizing a mass movement out of depoliticized and repressed women in the midst of a revolutionary insurrection would be a Herculean task by any calculation.[5] According to Tilly (1978) and Anthony Oberschall (1993, 24–25), rapidly emerging social movements are based on well-developed associational groups that coalesce into federations. AMPRONAC was an exception to this rule. Although it initially used the mothers' clubs, these groups were too small, disorganized, and new themselves to produce effective political action. Instead, AMPRONAC had to learn how to develop itself; it had to learn how to mobilize its own resources.

Resources are both external to an organization and internal in how the social movement organizers decide how these resources should be utilized (McCarthy 1996, 149; Clemens 1996, 207; Melucci 1985, 801; Foweraker 1995, 51). Thus, resources are not merely quantities of goods available to the organization, but also the perception of those goods. This was especially the case with AMPRONAC. Some of the goods that the leaders of AMPRONAC perceived as beneficial to the organization could have been perceived otherwise, such as the lack of a known leader and the violent and desperate times in which the women lived. The four resources that AMPRONAC had available to it and that it used with skill were, first, documents outlining the FSLN's and AMPRONAC's platforms; second, the turbulence of the time, which brought new issues to light; third, support from upper and middle classes; and, fourth, its horizontal structure.

The horizontal organizational structure of AMPRONAC stemmed from Guido and Carrión's leadership. Surprisingly, Guido claimed little to no experience with union organizing and mass organizations. "At least [I knew] how a group like that was supposed to function," she said (Randall 1981, 2). Carrión, the American-educated sister of Sandinista commander Luis Carrión, had been active in the FSLN for some time. Presumably she too knew how a mass organization should function, if only theoretically.

Guido's and Carrión's relative inexperience appears to contradict the usual emphasis on leadership found in the resource mobilization school. Understanding the importance of experienced, recognized, and aware leadership "requires not so much a particular theoretical orientation as common sense" (McAdam, McCarthy, and Zald 1988, 716). Guido and Carrión solved the problem of their limited experience by organizing AMPRONAC horizontally. In effect, they did not lead. They immediately called a meeting of seven well-educated women who, if not outright Sandinista supporters, were critical of the Somoza regime. The seven included Leonor Hüper, longtime Sandinista supporter, member of one of the elite families, and future consul general to Los Angeles during the Sandinista years; Milú Vargas, daughter of the leader of the Conservative Party and future drafter of the Nicaraguan constitution; Nora Astorga, future ambassador to the UN; and Gladys Baez, the first woman guerrilla fighter for the FSLN (McVey 1995, 101; Daniel 1998, 55; Randall 1981, 179). It would be generous to consider Guido and Carrión as first among equals. Together, these nine women led AMPRONAC, provided it skills such as magazine printing, applied their education to the formation of its political and economic agenda, and funded it (Murguialday 1990, 40; Ruchwarger 1987, 48).

The horizontal organization that Guido and Carrión initiated continued throughout the span of AMPRONAC's existence, extending into alliances with like-minded resistance groups, creating democratically elected leaders and platforms, and convoking public assemblies to discuss key issues. How these organizational strategies emerged during AMPRONAC's struggle to organize itself and overthrow Somoza will be discussed in more detail.

Another resource that AMPRONAC perceived it had and that it wisely utilized was the turbulence of the times. The fomentation of revolutions traditionally calls all things into question, from the economy to personal relations. Dora María Téllez said, "Revolutions transform everything, make everything tremble" (quoted in Flynn 1980, 30). Revolutions allow us to imagine. The depth of transformation meant that women who would not otherwise have contemplated breaking the traditional gender model became engaged in socially alternative activities. AMPRONAC supported women who were nervous about being involved or who became active against the wishes of their husbands, thereby bonding women to AMPRONAC (Flynn 1980, 30; Schultz 1980a, 36; Ramirez-Horton 1982, 150). This aid not only increased women's participation in and depth of commitment to the movement, it also opened the door to the possibility of creating a new identity by generating support for a change in gender construction.

Finally, AMPRONAC used either the FSLN's or its own program of action to attract support, depending on the group to whom it was speaking. Poor women were looking for a new economic model and wealthier women were looking for a new gender model. The FSLN provided the former and AMPRONAC provided the latter. In this way, platforms were used as a resource for mobilizing participation. Initially, however, the vast majority of AMPRONAC's supporters came from the upper classes, which was evident in their statement of intent, written and voted on at their first assembly.

In August 1977, a mere four months after Jaime Wheelock first contacted Guido and Carrión, sixty women participated in AMPRONAC's first assembly. They elected an executive committee with Lea Guido as secretary general. They adopted three objectives: to fight for the participation of the Nicaraguan women in the study and for the solution of national problems; to defend the rights of Nicaraguan women in any and all sectors of their life, be it economic, social, or political; and to fight against all human rights violations (*Central American Women Speak* 1983, 10).

As can be seen, only the third point actually dealt with human rights. This is likely because Somoza threatened few of these families. Instead, there is more of an intent to broaden women's political participation and rights and then extend that demand to every sphere. Already, women were collapsing the public and the private spheres to form an identity based on gender. However, that gender identity included economic change only peripherally.

AMPRONAC used public spaces to forge its identity instead of building it through smaller women's groups and networks. This use of public spaces to forge a nascent identity is typical of emerging social movements and would occur again in the development of the Nicaraguan women's movement. It is also instructive that AMPRONAC had to publicly articulate its identity before it could perform any political actions.

Despite the inexperience of all, the connection was made between the autonomy of the women's organization and women's ability to define their own needs. The women of AMPRONAC were aware that women's needs would be met only if "we women organize ourselves separately, because it is us who can best defend women's rights. That is why we are fighting for women's increased political, economic, and social participation in our country" (Maier 1980, 156). AMPRONAC's identity may have been embryonic, but already the organization was insisting on autonomy.

One month after its first assembly, in September 1977, AMPRONAC organized its first public act: it denounced human rights abuses in the countryside by bringing one thousand peasants into Managua to tell their stories. The denunciation gained national and international attention. In its wake, AMPRONAC received "calls and letters from concerned women in other cities who wanted to organize themselves and follow suit. AMPRONAC chapters were founded in Chinadega, León, Matagalpa, and Carazo" (*Central American Women Speak* 1983, 10). The organization was becoming a movement, although at that point it couldn't be called a "mass movement," given that the total number of women involved dropped to twenty-five by the end of 1977 (Randall 1981, 5).

Participation of middle- and upper-class women skyrocketed after the January 1978 assassination of Pedro Joaquín Chamorro, the editor of the opposition newspaper, *La Prensa,* member of the upper class, and husband of the future president, Violeta Barrios de Chamorro. The assumption was that Somoza had ordered Chamorro's assassination, although later research would cast doubt on that. Within hours there were fifty thousand mourners and demonstrators at the Chamorro home, with spontaneous unrest and business strikes occurring throughout Nicaragua (Booth 1985, 159–60).

AMPRONAC presented the assassination as proof that no one was safe from the dictator. According to one participant who joined after the assassination, "In the beginning, it was elegant to be in AMPRONAC, it was fashionable. Mostly there were women of the highest class. The first meeting resembled a fashion show. You could smell French perfume" (quoted in Murguialday 1990, 42).

With its upper-class support and money, AMPRONAC occupied the United Nations building for twelve days in January 1978 as part of a national general strike to protest the assassination of Chamorro. On their last day, they organized a conference attended by six hundred women to demand news of their disappeared children.

Up to this point, AMPRONAC members had been protected by their high social status. However, after the general strike, Somoza's National Guard turned against even these women, and they suffered imprisonment and torture (Seitz 1992, 171; Randall 1981, 6–7).

Regardless of personal danger, AMPRONAC members maintained a high profile. Petition drives, hunger strikes, and demonstrations were organized at a time when very few were publicly protesting anything (Flynn 1980, 29). AMPRONAC used International Women's Day, March 8, to present its demands. On Mother's Day, a day of commercialized mother worship, AMPRONAC's slogan was "The best gift would be a free country." It was the first time that these days had been used for political purposes (Randall 1981, 14, 16).[6] When Somoza raised the price of staple goods in August 1978, AMPRONAC got women into the streets beating empty pots (ibid., 16). The women knew how to take popular cultural images of women and transform them into political statements. The battle for political control over the symbols of women happened in the public sphere because the content of a symbol is publicly held knowledge. Control of the content of symbols of women is an ongoing fight in Nicaragua.

As the scope of the political protest widened, it brought into question the long-term aims of the women. AMPRONAC began to operate in two currents: the more radicalized faction, which demanded broad democratic rights and the end to economic misery, and the more mainstream faction, which wanted to focus attention on human rights abuses only. The two currents were roughly based on those from the popular class and upper class, respectively. This development prompted a kind of identity and strategy struggle that determined the future course of AMPRONAC (ibid., 7, 15).

The FSLN, distrustful of the loyalty of upper-class women, was pushing for more involvement from the poorer barrios, where the women were suffering from greater abuses of all kinds. The FSLN assumed that more poor women would support the revolutionary cause than would middle-class or wealthy women. It assumed that it would be easier to mobilize poor women around the concept of a politically active woman.

The FSLN was correct in its strategy to place more confidence in the popular class. AMPRONAC garnered more support in the poorer neighborhoods than in the richer ones by integrating socioeconomic rights with political rights. Overall, working-class women responded and became more militant than did middle- and upper-class women (Flynn 1980, 29). As Michelle Saint-Germain (1993a, 126–27) notes, "Women's problems were seen as part of the economic, political, and cultural exploitation of people in general which would be solved when that exploitation was ended." To survive the economic changes and downturn, women had to be ingenious and determined (Chinchilla 1983, 6). Yet their livelihood remained fragile. According to Lea Guido, women's economic vulnerability was the "key factor in the unprecedented political participation of the women of the popular sectors" (Flynn 1980, 30). The FSLN offered women an alternative economic model, which allowed AMPRONAC to mobilize in poor neighborhoods.

The economic model presented by the FSLN heavily stressed the working class and the peasants, who they hoped would unite to overthrow their oppressors in classic Third World revolutionary style. The FSLN's 1969 program states that the FSLN would establish "a revolutionary government based on the worker-peasant alliance and the convergence of all the patriotic anti-imperialist and anti-oligarchic forces in the country" (Marcus 1982, 13). It was the alliance of the workers and the peasants—and anyone else who wanted to participate—that would overthrow oppression. Not surprisingly, the platforms dealing with agrarian reform and labor legislation were some of the most detailed.

This stance would not directly help women because it did not acknowledge the sexual division of labor or the negative effects of capitalism on women. There was no strategy to deal with either. However, it would benefit women in as much as it presented an economic platform that would benefit poor men. Peasants would not have to migrate in search of work but could work their own plot of land. Factory workers would have a forty-hour work week, unjustified firings would be abolished, and the minimum wage would be enough to support a family. Even if only as a secondary effect, the position of women would be improved.

At a direct level, the program's section on women promised day-care centers, support for abandoned mothers, and maternity leaves, which might give women the necessary support to leave the informal sector. The 1969 program also promised to eliminate prostitution, to regulate domestic service, and to raise the political, cultural, and vocational level of women. This would all be possible through the growth of employment, because unemployment too would be eliminated, directly benefiting women, especially poor urban women. Also, general physical services were promised: medical aid, housing, education, mass transit, and electricity and water.[7] Women could only gain.

AMPRONAC, seeing that the FSLN's economic platform was attracting the most support in the poorer neighborhoods, built on its program, explaining women's economic oppression and expanding on women's economic liberation. An example of the importance given to economics are the seventy-eight lines of AMPRONAC's program devoted to women's economic oppression. In comparison, the section calling on women to participate in the general emancipation of the people runs only thirty-three lines.[8]

Although the FSLN may have been correct to assume that working-class women would participate in the movement in greater numbers than women from the upper classes, it overlooked the generation of young, educated women who were seeking an organization that supported their nascent egalitarian ideals. These women may not have participated in the sheer numbers of their less-educated counterparts, but the nature of their participation in the FSLN fundamentally altered society's understanding of women's roles.

Ideas of equality had spread from America and Europe to the women of Latin America (Chinchilla 1981, 5; Jaquette 1989, 5, 187; Hahner 1980, 78), finding fertile ground in universities, where the rising female populace was questioning traditional roles and values. In the FSLN program, these women found an alternative to women's traditional role of mothering.

The FSLN program, written in 1969, promised dignity and equality through a seven-part strategy. A Sandinista declaration in 1978 promised a "new revolution: a woman's revolution. . . . Women will be put on the same plane of equality with men" (Saint-Germain 1983a, 126). The FSLN's promises were made more attractive by its position as the only viable organization addressing women's issues.

Initially the FSLN did not let women into combat positions, but when women began to die as collaborators, the door cracked open for women's military participation. The Christian-based communities, with their radical interpretation of the Scriptures, allowed women to redefine their roles to include the possibility of fighting back. Female guerrilla fighters made connections with Christian-based communities, using their religious legitimacy to influence the FSLN (Herrera 1994). It helped that Sandino himself had enlisted both his wife and his mistress to fight in his ragtag army. Also, many of the guerrilla fighters had visited Cuba or other nations and were influenced by those countries' debates over gender equality (Chinchilla 1983, 4). Between 1970 and 1974 there was increased recruitment of women as guerrilla fighters.

Women's participation in war inevitably broke down barriers to equality within the army, because women being warriors shattered the concept of women as creators of life and men as destroyers of it. By allowing women access to men's power through warfare, women's power was augmented and men's monopoly broken (Young 1981, 56). Maier (1980, 69) considers the role played by the female commanders as critical in breaking the gender stereotype of women as mothers.

This fundamental change in gender understanding was supported by the FSLN's strict meritocracy, which allowed women to rise to the position of commander. Sandinista ideology insisted on a concept of the "new man," who would treat all as his equals, including women.[9] The possibility of receiving respect from (male) colleagues and subordinates is one possible reason why a higher percentage of young bourgeois women joined the FSLN than young bourgeois men (Chinchilla 1983, 11).

The women in the guerrilla columns may have been accorded equality, but the price they paid was living the life of a man. The women left their children with their mothers and sisters and abandoned any traditional trappings of womanhood.[10] Nonetheless, there was a massive entry of women into the armed revolutionary forces after twenty-five Sandinista soldiers under the command of Dora María Téllez and two men took control of the National Palace during August 1978. Téllez then negotiated with Somoza himself for the two thousand hostages, the release of some key Sandinista political prisoners, and $500,000. Some of the hostages were journalists who reported on Téllez's quiet commanding, obvious military competence, and effective negotiations with Somoza (Maier 1980, 109; Booth 1985, 159).

Educated, middle-class women, straitjacketed by traditional understandings, became *guerrilleras* in such numbers that their entry altered the demographics of the guerrilla group, its political organization pre- and post-1979, and the expectations of Nicaraguan women. The *guerrilleras* shattered the discourse of feminine behavior and created a new one. After the triumph, these women and others influenced by them would become the organizational backbone of the women's movement and thus, by definition, Sandinista, and, by virtue of their experience, committed to an atypical vision of women's roles (Randall 1994; Chinchilla 1983).

These two groups of women, poor and bourgeois, both wished to transform the fundamental norms that underpinned Nicaraguan society. Both groups were attracted to AMPRONAC's and the FSLN's platforms, which promised a new understanding of women's participation in society. While some women joined the armed conflict, many preferred to work through AMPRONAC. How AMPRONAC organized women in the year preceding the final revolutionary triumph demonstrates the praxis of resource mobilization and identity focused on a specific goal of overthrowing the dictator.

AMPRONAC was not the only organization with which the FSLN

had ties. There was a web of shifting alliances as groups jockeyed for position in postrevolutionary Nicaragua. In 1977, the Terceristas made alliances with the agri-industrial class through its umbrella organization, the Broad Opposition Front (FAO), which was also attempting to oust Somoza.[11] The military defeats of the FSLN between 1974 and 1976 lulled the FAO into underestimating the level of organizing and strength of the Frente. The FAO needed the FSLN to bring the working class into a united front, making general strikes coordinated and effective. However, the FAO's agenda was different from the Sandinistas'; the FAO intended to have "Somozism without Somoza," that is, a political opening that nevertheless protected the economic status quo. The FAO had no intention of including the Sandinistas in the postvictory organization of the country. By 1979, the FAO had fallen from its position of influence as the efficacy of strikes proved limited and as negotiations with Somoza proved pointless. This strengthened the FSLN and its affiliated organizations.

The FSLN was also assisted by the 1978 election of Jimmy Carter as president of the United States. Although American financial support for the dictatorship had been one of the two pillars of support for Somoza (the American-funded National Guard was the other) (Booth and Walker 1993, 34), Carter was appalled at the extent of the human rights abuses perpetrated by Somoza's dictatorship. When Somoza could not or would not reduce them, Carter reduced American financial assistance by 75 percent. This had the effect of reducing the Nicaraguan elite's support and the resources the National Guard had available to it (Booth 1985, 128–29).

Once the Sandinistas realized that the FAO was intending to cut them out after the revolution, the FSLN split from it and began to build its own umbrella organization, the United People's Movement (MPU), which was formed by popular groups supportive of the Sandinista agenda (Weber 1981, 23–60).[12] AMPRONAC was instrumental in establishing the MPU in the spring of 1978 with fourteen groups made up of students, youth, trade unions, political parties, and neighborhood defense communities (Maier 1980, 85). Eventually, the MPU included twenty-three groups (Black 1981, 122).

AMPRONAC also worked in conjunction with the civil defense committees, which were local cells of political and later military action. They were built on neighborhood committees that had organized around ad hoc demands for electricity or water (Maier 1980, 72). Later, these committees engaged in general strikes. They frequently worked in conjunction with the Christian-based communities. Thus, civil defense committees were not completely without experience or their own method of organization. Dominated by women, these grass-roots groups were led by AMPRONAC members, trade union leaders, or Sandinista militants. The civil defense committees were the backbone of the MPU, AMPRONAC, and Sandinismo (Murguialday 1990, 47). Women's participation in the MPU, either through civil defense committees, Christian-based communities, or AMPRONAC, highlighted the contradiction between the definition of femininity as passive and subordinate and the reality of women's ability and legitimacy (Maier 1980, 79). Societal norms were being rewritten through action.

The MPU spent the fall of 1978 expanding its neighborhood networks through the civil defense committees and then linking them to a hierarchy of coordination: from the local to the district, from the workplace to the university, from all of these to the FSLN commanders (Black 1981, 12–13). The structure became more centralized using a chain of command, with leaders from each community meeting rather than the entire community. "Under MPU supervision, the mass movement organization had become a well-oiled and genuinely democratic machine" (Black 1981, 139). By the end of 1978, AMPRONAC numbered three thousand members, making it one of the largest groups in the opposition coalition (Murguialday 1990, 46). It was also one of the best organized.

It was well organized because Guido realized, after the failed occupation of the UN buildings, that there were organizational problems in AMPRONAC due to the lack of grass-roots support (Randall 1981, 7). Guido decided that the most effective method of organizing among women was through the grass roots with a high degree of decentralization. Thus, she consciously built or strengthened grass-roots bases and political networks. This form of organization facilitated the development of women's identity with AMPRONAC by allowing personal commentary and participation at the local level with easy entrance into, and exit from, the organization (Melucci 1989, 60). Through the spring of 1978, AMPRONAC ran a number of grass-roots workshops on political analysis, explaining an essentially Sandinista program with the women's element emphasized. These seminars culminated in a conference in July 1978 approving demands for civil and economic rights, equal pay for equal work, and abolition of discriminatory laws (*Central American Women Speak* 1983, 11).

In addition to decentralization, AMPRONAC needed more analysis of women's rights and a communication network to keep everyone informed. AMPRONAC created committees to study law, to establish contact with the base communities, to organize around human rights, and to promulgate its propaganda. According to Guido, only the propaganda (i.e., communication) committee functioned with complete efficacy (Randall 1981, 7). If, as resource mobilization analysts tell us, communication makes or breaks the movement (Klandermas 1992, 90–91; Tarrow 1994, 191), this stage was of critical importance to AMPRONAC's success.

When the final Insurrection began in September 1978, AMPRONAC concentrated its energies on preparing neighborhoods for fighting (Randall 1981, 18). In order to do this, it had to close down base offices and go underground. Clandestinely, it built emergency medical clinics, stored supplies, built bombs and barricades, spied on and harassed the National Guard, carried messages, hid combatants, and joined the armed fight (Murguialday 1990, 48).

In the final Insurrection, members from the MPU engaged in hand-to-hand combat with the National Guard. Women were not merely the support staff for these battles, but they manned the barricades and fought (Schultz 1980a, 38). The difference between collaborator and guerrilla fighter, political activist and soldier, was erased. Approximately one third of the FSLN combatants and collaborators were women. AMPRONAC numbered a further eight thousand to ten thousand (Chuchryk 1991, 144; Murguialday 1990, 48). In the final Insurrection, the activities of FSLN female guerrilla fighters meshed with those of AMPRONAC. Together, they would fundamentally change themselves and the political role and understanding of women.

On July 19, 1979, the FSLN marched into Managua and assumed control of the state. As Leonor Argüello said, the revolution could not have happened without the women (McVey 1995, 112). Women became *guerrilleras*, community and student organizers, collaborators, and, through the first women's movement, activists demanding gender rights. AMPRONAC's actions delegitimized the dictatorship and mobilized ten thousand women to protest, resist, and literally to battle the Somoza dictatorship.

The most powerful impact of AMPRONAC, however, was its very success. The FSLN created a political concept that presented women's reality to women themselves and then organized around that reality.[13] Guido says of AMPRONAC: "We were successful because we learned how to organize women in the national struggle while at the same time organizing around problems specific to women. We always looked at the situation from a women's point of view. If we hadn't, what meaning would it have had for us to organize women? . . . None of the other organizations could provide women with the same kind of political space" (quoted in Randall 1981, 16).

Women linked personal and political emancipation. According to Clara Murguialday, AMPRONAC was able to link the oppression and discrimination that women were experiencing at all levels of their lives with generalized political oppression: "[AMPRONAC] emphasized the necessity that women organize themselves in order to defend their rights and obtain full social and political participation 'because only by doing so are we able to guarantee the total destruction of the system of women's discrimination and oppression'" (1990, 46; source of quote is believed to be an AMPRONAC document). Carrión concurred, suggesting that the experience of helping overthrow the dictator had repercussions within the home, with women refusing to submit to their husbands (Randall 1980, 14).[14] Women had became conscious of themselves, empowered by their participation. They had gained self-respect in the process of organizing to overthrow a dictatorship (Flynn 1980, 30; Chuchryk 1991, 146).

The articulation of a woman's sociopolitical identity may have been semiformed, but it was nonetheless the first step to the full articulation of an autonomous identity. That identity was created through public forums and discussions in which the women themselves analyzed their best direction. The barrier between public and private was immediately broken. A feminist critique of economics was embraced as the logical result of their political action.

In the process, AMPRONAC changed its organizational base and strategy from a middle-class mothers' club seeking reforms to a radical grass-roots paramilitary group fighting to overthrow the public and private status quo. As the identity and needs changed, the organization changed. As the organization changed, the identity became better articulated. Some things nonetheless held constant: horizontal organization, networking, and public forums to discuss directions and approaches. The process of building AMPRONAC reflects the development of a nascent identity-based social movement.

Through their experiences with AMPRONAC, women learned concrete political skills. During the chaos and the repression, women learned how to keep their organization afloat. "Our association learned to function in an emergency situation. We learned how to keep going, keep operating, no matter what kind of situation we found ourselves in. . . . [After the September 1978 Insurrection], we shored up our operational structure, held seminars, distributed a lot of propaganda and re-established national contacts that had been lost. Many people were afraid; some vacillated; others dropped out altogether. But in spite of all this we managed to hold together a dedicated core of women" (Randall 1981, 17, 22). AMPRONAC didn't just keep itself operating, it also passed its organizational knowledge to the masses. According to Guido, this was the organization's single greatest achievement. "I believe that our greatest contribution was helping organize the masses. By this time all our neighbourhood women knew how to organize people. . . . AMPRONAC stood out for its mobilizing and organizing capacities" (quoted in Ruchwarger 1987, 51). Tilly (1978) would agree with Guido that skills can become a repertoire of actions to be passed from one social movement to another. And indeed, the experience that women gained from their involvement in the revolution would be utilized in the 1980s.

AMPRONAC was autonomous but still connected with the FSLN, strategically cooperative via networks with numerous groups to achieve a specific end, led by those with some experience but based on the grass roots, with a preference for workshops and conferences to define its objectives, and democratic in its decision-making. It mobilized its resources in a short time period. A large part of its success was due to the fact that it organized around an identity, first of the mother then of the working woman seeking justice, whether it was economic or social. AMPRONAC had an implicit understanding of patriarchy and women that was profound yet applicable to the moment with a self-defining and changing identity. This combination of autonomous identity, complementary mobilization of resources, and focused goal would not be seen again until the 1990s.

CHAPTER 3

The Glory Years, 1979–1984

BY THE TIME THAT SOMOZA FLED THE COUNTRY and the FSLN declared victory, the anti-Somoza coalition was a complex web of alliances and groups representing all ranges of the political spectrum. Truly, the revolution was "popular"—in both meanings of the word. The unity of the alliance, however, proved fragile in the task of rebuilding a bankrupt and war-torn nation. Somoza had absconded with all the money in the treasury, leaving the incoming government $1.6 billion in debt to various banks, international funding institutions, and countries. As a result of the fighting, damage to property alone came to $470 million. There were approximately 600,000 people left homeless or with badly damaged homes, and per capita productivity fell to 1962 levels. Between the Insurrection and related epidemics, 40,000 to 50,000 people died between 1977 and 1979 (Booth 1985, 183).

As the best organized and most cohesive alliance, and as the group that sacrificed the most while fighting the longest, the FSLN was primed to take over the state. However, it first had to neutralize the elite and other established interests while consolidating its own power base. In an effort to attract legitimacy and support, the FSLN targeted marginally represented political groups. Women, along with peasants and workers, made up one such group. The women's movement became a vehicle for mobilizing and legitimating support for the FSLN (Molyneux 1986).

The strategy was effective. Because the goals of the Sandinista women's organization matched those of the FSLN, because the FSLN offered generous resources for the development of the women's organization, and because the identity of Sandinismo readily adapted to fit women's own yearnings for liberation, the Sandinista women's organization was successful and influential. It increased its membership rapidly and promoted women's participation in the public sphere. It achieved remarkable goals that directly and indirectly affected women. As a social movement under the control of a supportive government, it performed exemplarily. Women showed their appreciation for the government's generosity and for its program of social justice by voting for it in the 1984 general election.

Until that election, there were two public bodies governing Nicaragua, plus the National Directorate of the FSLN. The National Directorate consisted of nine Sandinista commanders, all men, three from each of the splinters. Each of the commanders had responsibility for one of the popular organizations. Tomás Borge was responsible for the women's movement. The National Directorate set overarching policy, controlled key ministerial and bureaucratic posts, and organized national security (Booth 1985, 186). In effect, it operated as a traditional Leninist vanguard (Hoyt 1997, 38).

The National Directorate transmitted its policies through Sandinista commander and Nicaraguan president Daniel Ortega to the Governing Junta of National Reconstruction (JGRN), which operated as the chief executive council. Until 1980, it legislated by decree with its decisions made by consensus and without formal votes. Its body was drawn from all political and socioeconomic sectors of Nicaragua. In the years immediately following the revolution, it was highly active, restructuring the bureaucracy and administration of government and initiating and supporting reconstruction programs. By 1982, it had shrunk in size as non-Sandinista members, unhappy with its policies, left it and as the volume of work it needed to perform also diminished (Booth 1985, 188–90). After 1980, the JGRN cogoverned with the Council of State, a legislative body of forty-seven seats, of which the FSLN controlled twenty-seven and key posts (Booth 1985, 190). One of the seats on the Council of State was given to the Sandinista women's movement. Thus, it was incorporated into the new government and the new governing party.

This system of governing with overlapping and inclusionary legislatures, tolerance for dissent, and Sandinista hegemonic control was corporatist in nature. People belonged to a political, popular, or socioeconomic group that had representation on as many as all three of the bodies, or in the case of women, representation on one and a commandante from the National Directorate representing it on another. With increased mobilization, a group could not increase its representation on the Council of State but might well increase the amount of its influence in attaining access to resources or in changing public policies. For this reason, the FSLN claimed that government was a participatory democracy. As Sandinistas filled bureaucratic positions, and as the opposition weakened or failed to express itself outside the political system, the difference between the mass organizations, the Sandinista Party, the state, the government, and the people became blurred.

Sandinista tolerance for dissent originating within the privileged socioeconomic groups declined markedly after the counterrevolutionary war began in earnest in 1982. The whole of the corporate body was urged to unite to fight the war (Hoyt 1997, 52). The war had a profound impact on the Sandinista women's movement by altering its identity and reducing its resources, although the war also opened up the possibility of new ways of organizing new groups of women.

Before the war began, however, the women's organization had already caused AMPRONAC to develop a new structure and ethos. In 1978, after publicly endorsing the Sandinista program and working with the Popular Unity Movement (MPU), a Sandinista-affiliated mass organization, AMPRONAC finally announced its support for the FSLN. It still maintained its own autonomy, however. After the revolution, the leaders of AMPRONAC abandoned its hard-won autonomy and horizontal structure and joined the Sandinista corporate body as a Sandinista organization. They made this change without democratic vote or even discussion. This quick move from independence to corporate membership happened for several reasons. First, the fervor of the triumph of Sandinista troops rolling into Managua made everyone want to be part of the new state, especially because of its promise of gender liberation mediated by a revolutionary government and by a mass organization. Second, with a corporatist regime, either a political actor is part of the system or must operate outside it altogether: lobbying, confrontation, and individual rights were political tools that did not emerge until the late 1980s. It would not have served women's needs if the women's movement had not belonged. Finally, the leaders of AMPRONAC were already Sandinista, and it probably never occurred to them to maintain their autonomy after the revolution.

The ideology of Sandinismo that successfully unified the disparate protest groups during Somoza was continued under the government of the FSLN and became the reigning ideology (Burbach and Nuñez 1987, 56–59). This ideology of personal and group liberation was modified to respond to the reality of the 1979 revolution. This modified Sandinismo became the framework within which the new women's movement would place itself. The Association of Nicaraguan Women "Luisa Amanda Espinoza" (AMNLAE) was formed in August 1979, a month after the revolutionary triumph. The name reflected the new feminine ideal, the Sandinista alternative to traditional gender roles.

Luisa Amanda Espinoza was the first female Frente member to die in combat (Maier 1980, 50). Espinoza came from the urban poor, had married young, and left her husband because he beat her (Randall 1981, 27). After several death-defying missions, she was betrayed by an informer and killed while en route to a safe house to warn her colleagues of possible treachery.

Naming an organization after her presented her as a new feminine ideal: childless, autonomous, and, above all else, Sandinista. There was very little of traditional feminine content in this new ideal; Espinoza forsook a woman's society for a man's. In 1979, this was the most liberating model available, since the traditional role of motherhood was shunned, leaving only the male model of combatant. However, women could not be told to act like men. Hence they were to act like "persons," that is, like neither women nor men. Espinoza was the ideal because she had attained "personhood" (Mujeres Autoconvocadas 1994, 2). However, personhood was not a reasonable or even desirable goal for most women. This foreshadowed the identity crisis that AMNLAE would experience throughout the 1980s.

AMNLAE's identity of Sandinista personhood produced twin goals of the advancement of women's rights and the revolutionary transformation of society. The twin goals were seen as mutually reinforcing, as evidenced in AMNLAE's slogans. In 1979–1980, its slogan was "No revolution without women's emancipation: no emancipation without revolution" (Molyneux 1986, 288). In 1981, after several successful campaigns, its slogan had become "Building the new homeland, we are shaping the new woman" (Association of Nicaraguan Women 1983, 17). AMNLAE obviously felt that it was advancing on both fronts simultaneously. And by all accounts, it was.

In general, the FSLN supported AMNLAE's goal of gender liberation. Although the strong moral inspiration that governed Sandinista policies should not be underestimated, it must be pointed out that there was a gap between many of the commandantes' rhetoric of gender liberation and their actions. Both of the commandantes of the National Directorate who were in charge of women's issues, Tomás Borge and Bayardo Arce, had terrible reputations for womanizing and sexism (Schultz 1980b; Randall 1994, 57).[1] Daniel Ortega, who is married to noted intellectual Rosario Murillo, and whose previous marriage was to Leticia Herrera, the famed guerrilla commander and later speaker of the National Assembly, did not support a woman's right to an abortion. The gap between the Sandinistas' theory of gender liberation and their actions necessitates a political analysis of the reasons why the FSLN so strongly supported AMNLAE.

The FSLN supported gender liberation for three reasons. First, the women had earned equality through their extensive military participation in the Insurrection (Association of Nicaraguan Women 1983, 15; Nuñez 1988, 142; Murguialday 1990, 102). Political rights result from military glory because the ability to risk life and limb for the state requires a devotion to the public realm. "Courage therefore became the political virtue par excellence, and only those men [sic] who possessed it could be admitted to a fellowship that was political in content and purpose" (Arendt 1958, 36).[2] Women have always risked their lives in military battle, especially nationalist struggles. However, never before had the participation of women been based on their personhood rather than on their kinship (Fraser 1989), and never before had the sheer number of participants been so large. A combination of the two allowed all Nicaraguan women the right to demand participation in the public realm on the basis of their personhood (Women's International Resource Exchange 1985, 30).

Second, women's emancipation would consolidate their support for the revolution because, as the assumption went, all women were unhappy under patriarchy and would be grateful for their liberation. Third, a change in gender relations would restructure the family to reproduce the new social values that the Sandinistas were promulgating (Molyneux

49

1986, 296). To a certain extent, the FSLN created AMNLAE with its Sandinista personhood identity to achieve the FSLN's short-term political goals.

The first two goal-oriented projects that AMNLAE endorsed were the Literacy Crusade and the immunization campaign. Then, at a level that the FSLN supported less, was the goal to improve women's legal status. All three of these goals coincided with women's demands for education, health care, and equality. All three goals coincided with the FSLN's and women's desire to increase women's participation in the public sphere. All three of these goals were focused and helped to create a Sandinista identity of female personhood. With some legitimacy, Carrión could say in 1980, "Now women's specific demands are the Revolution's demands" (quoted in Randall 1981, 34).

The first goal around which AMNLAE mobilized was the Literacy Crusade, which served an important need in creating identity by showing women how to analyze their lives based on their own subjective understanding. In Nicaragua, 33.6 percent of women were illiterate (*World's Women* 1991, 52). However, they were concentrated mostly in rural areas where the illiteracy level was much higher (Ruchwarger 1987, 198). The Literacy Crusade began two weeks after the triumph of the revolution and used the Sandinista networks to mobilize people to teach and learn through a critical analysis of their reality (Black 1981, 315; Women's International Resource Exchange 1985, 16). Hence, at the beginning of August 1979, AMNLAE called up its old AMPRONAC membership to assist the crusade.

AMNLAE threw itself into the Literacy Crusade in an organizational capacity. Given that it was also in the process of organizing and creating itself, the extent of its involvement was impressive. Two out of three AMNLAE members participated (Murguialday 1990, 107). Four hundred members of AMNLAE were coordinators for the Popular Education Centers where the literacy classes would meet. Sixty-seven percent of AMNLAE members, those who had a lower level of education (and thus couldn't teach), helped in the support tasks. Twelve percent of AMNLAE members worked as teachers. AMNLAE also organized 196 Mother's Literacy Committees to provide logistical support (food, clothing, etc.) for the young brigade workers, and built forty-two minilibraries in rural areas (Association of Nicaraguan Women 1983, 31).

There were three results of the Literacy Crusade. First, the illiteracy rate dropped to 12 percent, earning Nicaragua an award from United Nations Educational, Scientific, and Cultural Organization (UNESCO). From the Literacy Crusade itself, AMNLAE won an award for its involvement. Second, the Literacy Crusade was an unsubtle tool to demonstrate the benefits of Sandinismo to the population, predominantly directed at and via women (Collinson 1990, 122). Finally, it empowered women by breaking the silence on women's reality (Women's International Resource Exchange 1985). "Literacy for women is not only about learning to read and write: it is about finding a voice after centuries of invisibility, building a sense of dignity and self-confidence, and participating in the political process at an equal level with men" (Collinson 1990, 123).

After the Literacy Crusade, AMNLAE's goal was to improve the health of the Nicaraguan people. Women are the primary caretakers of health in Nicaragua.[3] By improving health care, AMNLAE directly benefited women, thereby encouraging their support for the FSLN. The Health Campaign strengthened AMNLAE's organizational skills.

Before the 1979 revolution, health care was available only for the wealthy. A 1974 study showed that the Social Security Institute (INSS) spent 50 percent of its health budget on 8 percent of the population; an estimated 90 percent of the health care resources benefited 10 percent of the population; and only 28 percent of the population had access to health care. Infant mortality was 120 per 1,000 live births; two of three children under five were malnourished; six of ten deaths were from preventable diseases; and less than 20 percent of both children under five and pregnant women received health care (Collinson 1990, 97–98).

With limited resources, the FSLN government had to establish a national health care system. Based on the strategy of the literacy brigades, the health care brigades moved throughout the urban neighborhoods and rural areas teaching sanitation, giving vaccinations, and encouraging community participation.

AMNLAE was once again in the thick of the organizing. Emerging from community organizations and resulting from the positive experience of the literacy brigades, 80 percent of the health care workers and 75 percent of the health brigade coordinators were women (Association of Nicaraguan Women 1983, 21). AMNLAE and Christian-based communities made possible the incorporation of health brigades into the community. AMNLAE also facilitated the connection between health at the grass roots with national programs presented by the National Health Council. Coordination between the groups improved as a result of the campaign (ibid., 24).

Programs and institutions that directly benefited women included midwifery, health clinics, and a women's hospital in Managua. The effects were undeniable. By 1983, infant mortality had dropped to 80 per 1,000 live births, malaria cases dropped by 50 percent, polio was eradicated, and 80 percent of the total population had access to health care (Collinson 1990, 98–99).

Through alliances that stretched horizontally across the nation and vertically to the Ministry of Health, through grass-roots involvement with skilled trained workers, the Health Campaign was another success. It would not have been possible without AMNLAE (ibid., 107). The Health Campaign consolidated women's support for the revolution. Furthermore, it taught more women community organizing skills. Women learned from action but also from their contact with the more experienced and trained workers in other ministries. The high degree of cooperation between AMNLAE and the other ministries facilitated a sharing of political skills and knowledge. These skills, like many skills, are difficult to forget and flexible in their application. Women would use them again and again, although in the future against recalcitrant governments and their policies.

While the Literacy Crusade and the Health Campaign may have directly benefited the lives of women, neither project was explicitly focused on women's needs alone. This was not the case with legal reform. Laws make excellent goals around which to mobilize because laws are public statements of societal norms. There appeared to have been an awareness among legal activists that there was an opportunity to change laws and society and create a new ethic (Murguialday 1990, 127; Women's International Resource Exchange 1985, 4). As a result, women's organizations have constantly used law as a tool to force social reform from 1979 to the present. It was in the struggle over legal reform that AMNLAE's conundrum of affiliation with the Sandinista Party first became apparent. The FSLN supported some but not all of AMNLAE's proposed legal reforms, so AMNLAE had to mobilize women against the Party to achieve its legal reform goals.

The Sandinista Women's Movement, 1977–1990

52

The FSLN's support for women's legal status is evident in the Statute of Rights and Guarantees. The JGRN decreed the statute in 1979 and it "portended significant new roles and possibilities for women" (Booth 1985, 236). Article 7 declared the unconditional equality of all Nicaraguans. Article 30 declared all equal before the law and barred discrimination on the basis of birth, race, color, sex, religion, language, opinions, origins, economic status, or any other social condition. It also stated that "it is the duty of the State to remove, by all means at its disposal, the obstacles that prevent equality among all citizens and prevent them from participating in the political, economic, and social life of the country."[4]

All of these measures were fairly well accepted by the populace (Murguialday 1990, 126) until AMNLAE decided to enact this new ideal proposed in the statute with 1981 reforms to the *Patria Potesdad* law.[5] *Patria Potesdad* gave men almost unlimited rights over women and children. In comparison, AMNLAE's proposed reforms were to create equality in the family (Relations between the Mother, Father, and Children) and make a man responsible for all his children, including those born outside marriage (Nurturing Law) (Close 1988, 160–61). AMNLAE's proposed reforms did not get passed until 1982 (Relations between the Mother, Father, and Children) and 1983 (Nurturing Law). According to a former Nicaraguan Supreme Court judge, these reforms to the family code were the greatest achievement of the revolution because they created, at least in principle, a horizontal power structure within the family (Brenes et al. 1991, 35).

Not surprisingly, the reforms were popular only with women (Ruchwarger 1987, 190). Initially, the FSLN refused to pass the reforms. However, AMNLAE fulfilled its function as a voice and vehicle for women's demands and would not allow the FSLN to back away from the legislation. In order to generate the necessary support for these reforms and overcome resistance from both the public and the FSLN, AMNLAE organized 75 assemblies to discuss "Relations between Mother, Father, and Children" and 210 assemblies to discuss the "Nurturing Law." Through these public forums, women developed a strong consensus in support of these legal reforms to *Patria Potesdad*, which AMNLAE then used to force the FSLN to pass the legislation.

The use of public spaces to inform the grass roots while mobilizing them in support of social change began with AMPRONAC and continues today. Due to the shorter time frame it had to organize and the nature of organizing under a dictatorship, AMPRONAC had fewer public forums to discuss, propose, mobilize, and lobby than AMNLAE had. AMNLAE developed the skill of informing and mobilizing the grass roots in massive shows of public support. It was assisted by having the time, the support from the FSLN, and the financial resources to do so. It was also assisted by geography and demography. With a population of three million and the majority under eighteen years of age, it was physically possible for the leaders, rank-and-file members, specialists, and bureaucrats to meet in one room, albeit a large one.[6] Furthermore, the majority of Nicaraguans live within the same geographical area, western Nicaragua, an easy commute to the only city, Managua. Thus, it was neither expensive nor time-consuming for AMNLAE to go the communities outside Managua or to have people come to Managua for organizational meetings. These two advantages certainly facilitated the usage of public spaces as an integral part of the Nicaraguan women's movement.

To reform *Patria Potesdad*, AMNLAE had to choose between grassroots demands and its party affiliation. AMNLAE's mobilization at the grass-roots level was so successful that it forced the new Sandinista government to align itself with AMNLAE (Brown 1990, 53; Association of Nicaraguan Women 1983, 11). Temporarily at least, the integration of the two identities—gender and Sandinista—remained viable. From this, one might conclude that AMNLAE had sufficient autonomy from the National Directorate to formulate its own gender-based demands and possibly even develop a gender-based identity. However, this freedom to mobilize and operate at a critical distance from the hierarchy of the FSLN evaporated with the start of the counterrevolutionary (contra) war.

With the war, AMNLAE's goals and identity changed, reshaping the relationship between the FSLN and women. AMNLAE's primary goal was now resisting the counterrevolution rather than improving women's lives. AMNLAE's identity, as a result, shifted from a social justice ethos focused on women's liberation to a defensive approach focused on mothers. In addition, the FSLN sharply reduced the availability of resources to meet women's needs.

In November 1980, Ronald Reagan was elected president of the United States. By the winter of 1981, he was funding training camps for disenchanted Nicaraguans, predominantly but not exclusively members of Somoza's National Guard. Reagan also suspended the $75 million American aid package that Carter had promised, including a $30 million loan to business development. By 1982, the counterrevolutionary war was in full swing with the counterrevolutionaries (contras) trained in economic sabotage and terrorism aimed at civilians. In 1983, the United States invaded Grenada and increased its already large joint U.S.–Central American army exercises in Honduras. Nicaraguans felt that they were next. In 1983 as well, the United States made sure that loans from conventional multilateral agencies such as the International Monetary Fund, the World Bank, and InterAmerican Development Bank were blocked (Burns 1987, 30). In January and February 1984, the United States sponsored a covert action against Nicaragua. The United States mined the only major shipping harbor in Nicaragua, damaging five international ships, four Nicaraguan patrols, seven fishing boats, and killing eight Nicaraguans (ibid., 56).

By 1984, the United States was sponsoring war on two fronts, on the northern border with Honduras, where the one contra camp was based, and on the southern border of Costa Rica, where the other camp was based. The contra army numbered between 10,000 and 15,000 soldiers (Gorman and Walker 1985, 106).[7] The Nicaraguan army numbered between 60,000 and 100,000 (ibid., 113). Unlike the Nicaraguan army, which was trying to militarily defeat the contras, the contras' goal was terrorism directed at the Nicaraguan populace (Burns 1987, 58), which made it difficult for the Sandinistas to effectively combat the contras, although as the decade progressed, the contras made fewer incursions into Nicaragua. In 1985, the United States began a trade embargo against Nicaragua, closed its Nicaraguan consulates, and withdrew landing rights for the Nicaraguan airline.

The military, called the Sandinista Popular Army (EPS), allowed women as soldiers. After the role played by female guerrilla fighters, how could it not? In 1980, the female quotient of women in the EPS was 6 percent of the officers and 40 percent of the rank and file. Although the mobilization of women into the EPS continued, gradually women were shifted into noncombat roles or into the Sandinista police force (Gorman and Walker 1985, 101). Over the protests of the women, the professionalization and modernization of the EPS meant that women's role was adjunctive rather than essential. Women were fully aware that much of their right to equality derived from their participation in the Insurrection, and they were apprehensive that their secondary status in the EPS would be reflected in society at large.

Women had reason to be apprehensive. The war changed the relationship of AMNLAE and the FSLN. AMNLAE's goal of simultaneously promoting the revolution and women thinned to promoting just the revolution. Furthermore, the demilitarization of women from the ESP gave lie to women's new identity of personhood. Even if women embraced personhood as an ethos, they could not use it to become a soldier. This forced women to abandon pure action as a means of achieving equality and seek their status, identity, and ethos in political arenas.

The FSLN was concerned that the counterrevolutionary movement could use the symbol of the grieving mother to erode support for the FSLN and the revolution in much the same way that the FSLN used the grieving mother to erode support for the Somoza regime. So AMNLAE shifted its focus from individual projects and "the women's question" in general to women's role as mothers of fighting or fallen sons.[8]

AMNLAE organized the Mothers of the Revolution—Heroes and Martyrs (Madres H-M) in 1980 as a support group for the mothers of those killed in the Insurrectionary War of 1977–1979 and in continuing skirmishes. With the beginning of the counterrevolutionary war, the FSLN redirected resources to this group. Madres H-M in turn publicly endorsed Sandinista military actions. AMNLAE also provided logistical and material support for the troops (Chinchilla 1990, 382–3; *Central America Report*, November 14, 1986: 348; Bayard de Volo 1995).

The Sandinista feminine ideal shifted from personhood to its diametrical opposite, motherhood, with the ever-mutable Sandinismo as the supporting political creed. Idealized motherhood, like idealized personhood, lacked the range and nuance to adequately express women's reality and needs. Neither ideal was self-defined, democratically chosen, or politically sustainable. In the short run, however, dissent from female activists was muted. Conscious of how dissent could be used against the FSLN during the war, women kept their complaints private for several years. One high-ranking female Sandinista called this "self-censorship" (Randall 1994, 59).

Those women without male children or those who felt that gender liberation should continue apace were asked to postpone their demands and to disregard their own needs until peace had been achieved (Murguial-day 1990, 138). As a result of its new focus on motherhood, AMNLAE lost its ability to create an alternative identity for women.

Not only was the opportunity to create a new understanding for women reduced but the Sandinistas' successful meshing of women's and the revolution's needs was diminished. To fund the war, by 1982 social expenditure for social justice programs was reduced, and by 1984 programs that were the bread and butter of the Sandinista platform were cut (Booth 1985, 259). For example, a 1985 study done by the Nicaraguan Institute for Social Security and Well-being (INSSBI) estimated that only 10 percent of the urban need for day care was being met (Woroniuk 1987, 7). Fully half of the budget went to defense (Hoyt 1997, 111).

To a certain extent, foreign aid mitigated the impact of the cutbacks. Foreign aid supported AMNLAE by building a women's reference library, setting up women's centers, and contributing material (interview Stewart). Foreign sources of money could also have been used to increase its autonomy from the FSLN, allowing AMNLAE to continue to pursue women's needs (Brenes et al. 1991, 171). However, development aid did not increase AMNLAE's autonomy because AMNLAE supported the Sandinista goals and priorities. Right or wrong, AMNLAE believed that women's equality was inextricably tied to the viability of the revolution. Because foreign aid supported AMNLAE and its premise, foreign aid also supported the FSLN, thereby reinforcing the legitimacy of the FSLN and its approach to gender equality.

Obviously war alters every society, especially its goals and its economy. Nicaragua and AMNLAE were no exception. AMNLAE's identity, goals, and resources became more conservative, reflecting the needs of the government rather than of women. Thus, AMNLAE's claim to represent both women and the Sandinista vision of social equality was no longer valid.

By the time that the contra war was an unpleasant reality for many Nicaraguans, AMNLAE discovered that it had another problem: its organizational structure. Paradoxically, this "problem" had also been responsible for AMNLAE's remarkable success in mobilizing women for the Literacy Crusade, the Health Campaign, and legal reforms. AMNLAE was organized like a pyramid with its leaders appointed by the FSLN. The building blocks of AMNLAE's structure were groups, or chapters, of thirty to one hundred women from every town. The cities had more than one chapter. Each chapter was made up of work committees of several women from every factory, farm, school, state institution, market, hospital, and neighborhood. Each chapter elected a representative to attend municipal and regional meetings. These representatives elected an executive committee, who in turn reported to the national headquarters on a biweekly basis (Association of Nicaraguan Women 1983, 3).

AMNLAE had special days to stay in contact with the grass roots. In other words, grass-roots participation was not an integral part of AMNLAE's daily happenings. Not surprisingly, there were complaints that AMNLAE was not hearing women's voices.

From twenty activists in Managua and Matagalpa at the time of the revolution (Murguialday 1990, 102), AMNLAE grew in little over two years to 25,000 women in 802 chapters (Ramirez-Horton 1982, 154–55), and by 1984 to 85,000 women (Booth 1985, 236). This vertical structure allowed AMNLAE to respond quickly to government-sponsored campaigns, to disseminate information, and to mobilize and train participants, and thereby to achieve its short-term goals.

On a longer time frame, though, this hierarchical and antidemocratic internal organization contradicted AMNLAE's identity of equality and freedom for all. "The new organizational form of contemporary movements is not just 'instrumental' for their goals. It is also a goal in itself. Since the action is focused on cultural codes, the *form* of the movement is a message, a symbolic challenge to the dominant patterns. . . . The medium, the movement itself as a new medium, is the message" (Melucci 1985, 801).

AMNLAE was aware of the problem, and in 1981 and continuing every few years until 1994, AMNLAE was restructured in order to maintain participation and to attract new members (Women's International Resource Exchange 1985, 24). However, the hierarchical structure was never abandoned. As a result, the problem of declining membership, commitment, and legitimacy was never resolved.[9] The lack of a hospitable environment suggests that organizational structure is one of the primary resources that must be correctly mobilized (McCarthy 1996, 149; Clemens 1996, 207).

The organizational breach between AMNLAE and the grass roots was widened by the competition for participation from other Sandinista organizations. Due to successful mobilization by other mass organizations, women belonged to multiple groups. To women's triple burden of job, child-care, and housework, add two or three political organizations that were competing for a woman's time. For example, a female factory worker belonged to the Sandinista Workers' Committee (CST), the Sandinista Defense Committee (CDS), and AMNLAE (Brenes et al. 1991, 175). AMNLAE was losing the competition. According to one AMNLAE member, the group abdicated recruiting women in the rural areas and the factories because it could not compete with the local unions (Murguialday 1990, 120–21).

While AMNLAE competed with some Sandinista organizations for members, it simultaneously cooperated with other Sandinista organizations to achieve its ends. Between 1979 and 1981, AMNLAE had to work cooperatively with several ministries, with committees to coordinate policies on women, and with the Council of State (Flynn 1980, 31). These ad hoc alliances were reminiscent of AMPRONAC's methodology and like AMPRONAC were helpful in assisting women with little experience to learn from more experienced colleagues in other ministries. As the memories of AMPRONAC's ways faded, and as the war dissolved the possibility of enacting Sandinismo, this cooperative work declined, isolating AMNLAE with a vertical and alienating structure.

According to Molyneux (1981, 1986), under revolutionary governments women typically make great advances in the first few years of the new regime. However, because the government's goal is political consolidation rather than women's emancipation per se, the goals that women tend to achieve are those that correspond to the broader goals of the revolution. As the government consolidates its power base, it no longer has to appeal to the dispossessed for support and legitimacy, and women's ability to achieve concessions from the government is reduced. AMNLAE's identity, goal, and resources may have altered with the onset of the counterrevolutionary war, reducing AMNLAE's legitimacy to speak for or respond to women, but the election of 1984 truncated any leverage that AMNLAE may have had within the FSLN because the election consolidated the government's power.

The FSLN moved slowly and hesitantly into agreeing to the election. With a participatory democracy directed by a vanguard party during a time of civil war, an election, to many Sandinistas, seemed not merely unnecessary but potentially disruptive. To appease the growing discontent within the FSLN and within Nicaragua, to garner legitimacy both abroad and domestically, and to fulfill the requirements of Sandinismo, an election became politically necessary (Hoyt 1997).

Women decided the 1984 election because they were the majority of the voters and the most undecided. Women formed 62 percent of the electorate and, according to the preelection polls, were less supportive of the FSLN than were men.[10] The FSLN responded by shifting its campaign to reflect women and their needs. The entire campaign was a frank acknowledgment of the constraints of the times but also of the gains that women had achieved through the revolution. The election obliged the government to talk to women about women's needs in a language that women could understand. Murguialday (1990, 139) summarized the campaign: "We have advanced but still there remains a lot of ground to cover." This was the highest instance of political articulation of women's needs and wants.

Women elected the FSLN into power and through this election—that is, through the election campaign that targeted women for support—the Sandinistas consolidated themselves as a legitimate political power. According to most independent observers, the election was clean and fair given the situation of war.[11] The FSLN won with a 67.9 percent majority, affirming its legitimacy in the minds of the international community (with the exception of the Reagan administration) and the Nicaraguan populace. Of the representatives elected, 19.6 percent were women. Only one out of the thirteen elected women did not belong to the FSLN.

All of these statistics are even more impressive in the context of women's roles as single parents in a tightening economy and with lower levels of education and training. Few of the women elected came from a stereotypical middle-class background. One third had six years or less of education. Among the occupations of those elected were peasant, market vendor, beautician, teacher, journalist, dentist, and military commander (Morgan 1990, 22). All of the elected representatives explained their political activity as a result of their participation in overthrowing Somoza. All twelve of the FSLN female representatives had strong ties to AMNLAE (Saint-Germain 1993a, 129). There were obvious advantages to be derived from having such a high percentage of women representatives. "In this framework it promoted the development of women's consciousness in a socio-political context and at the same time it projected the problem of her emancipation into the national arena" (Olivera et al. 1992, 73).

In addition to the elected representatives were women appointed to positions of authority. In the mid 1980s, women held 21 percent of the positions in the Ministry of the Interior, considered by many to be the most powerful ministry, and 15 percent of ambassadorial and international positions (Saint-Germain 1993a, 125). As well, Doris Tijerino was minister of police, the first woman in the world to hold that position, and Dora María Téllez was the minister of health. Women were visibly in power, proving that they could be capable actors in the public realm. Similar to the female guerrilla fighters, these highly visible and effective women continued to shatter the image of women belonging only to the private sphere.

During the next few years, however, the FSLN took advantage of its consolidation to remove women from positions of power and to return those positions to men. The famous and high-profile women were kept in visible positions of power, but the female leaders in the second tier were slowly eased out. "Little by little, they took away upper management positions from women. Why? Because of machismo" (interview Herrera). Thus, the numerical shape of women in the public sphere had an hourglass figure: impressively top heavy, waisted in the middle, and spread wide at the base.

Gioconda Belli, a Nicaraguan poet, FSLN commander, and feminist puts the change earlier than 1984. She suggests that it started as soon as the revolution was at hand (Randall 1994, 175–76). It may be that the commitment to gender equality was scaled back that early. But it was inevitable that women's public participation and the effort to achieve gender equality would be reduced after the 1984 election and the consolidation of the FSLN in power.

The decline in women's status under a freely elected Sandinista government was in marked contrast to the growth of women's status under the Sandinista guerrilla force before the revolution and the increase of women's goods, services, and rights offered during the first few years after the revolution. The overt change in Sandinista attitude began after the election. Until then, AMNLAE had been an effective and efficient organization because women's interests coincided with those of the revolution. In this situation there was no conflict between the mobilization of women for women's rights and the mobilization of women in support of the revolution. To guarantee women's support, the FSLN opened a political space for women and espoused some of the concerns of women activists. The FSLN supplied sufficient resources to make AMNLAE effective. Thus, AMNLAE was successful in achieving its twin goals.

As Molyneux predicted, however, after the revolutionary government consolidated its power base, it no longer had to pander to the politically marginalized in order to guarantee support. After winning the 1984 election, attention to women's issues diminished. Political support, public policies, and even rhetoric favoring women declined (Molyneux 1986).

In addition to the postelection decline in support, the contra war itself altered the women's movement. The war changed AMNLAE's ability to mobilize. After the counterrevolution began in 1981, the supply of economic goods available to the women's movement diminished. Simultaneously, the counterrevolution meant that the FSLN had a different sociopolitical group to consolidate: mothers. AMNLAE's attention shifted to mothers, organizing and articulating around their needs. The political space for AMNLAE to speak for an alternative understanding of women's role in society was consequently reduced. AMNLAE and the FSLN lost the opportunity to create a gender-based goal of social justice.

In addition to the external factors that undermined AMNLAE's ability to continue to fulfill its goal, AMNLAE's internal structure was alienating to women. A social movement must choose a correct mobilizing structure to respond not merely to external constraints but also to the demands and needs of its own participants. In other words, the internal organization of a movement is a resource that must be correctly utilized or the social movement will suffer.

The problem of internal structure stemmed from AMNLAE's inability to distinguish itself as either a social movement espousing a liberatory ideology or a Party organization achieving specific partisan goals. AMNLAE was supposed to lead and even to personify the women's movement. However, without an autonomous, self-created identity and control over its own resources, AMNLAE could not be a mass movement, much less personify one. As a result, it could not accurately reflect women's needs, including the need for a decentralized, horizontal, and democratic organization. This inability to distinguish between a party organization and a popular movement was an important lesson that AMNLAE taught future activists. Nicaraguan women learned from this experience and improved later organizations.

In addition, AMNLAE made two other important contributions to the women's movement. First, AMNLAE introduced women to the concept of women organizing as women and the concept of gender equality in a nonthreatening manner. The ease of acceptance of this idea can be traced to the accessible ideology of Sandinismo that AMNLAE embraced and the beneficial projects it carried out. Through its projects, AMNLAE spread the idea of gender equality to areas that had previously not been politicized. With the spread of a gender-based Sandinismo throughout Nicaragua, AMNLAE left in its wake the expectation of gender-based justice. Future women's groups would build on the groundwork that AMNLAE left them.

Finally, from AMNLAE women learned organizational skills later used by other women's groups to attain the goods and services for which AMNLAE refused to fight. Indeed, through strengthening women's organizational skills, AMNLAE left itself vulnerable to disgruntled women activists. Despite the success of the Sandinista women's movement, the seeds were sown for future conflict: the battle between the women and the FSLN for control over the identity, goals, and resources of the women's movement. This conflict would dog the women's movement into the 1990s, when it finally achieved autonomy from the FSLN.

CHAPTER 4

The Confused Years, 1984–1987

DEMOCRATICALLY LEGITIMATED AFTER THE 1984 ELECTION, but with a thinner purse due to the war, the Sandinista government began to back away from gender equality. Without direction from the National Directorate or clear social justice projects, AMNLAE's identity became confused. AMNLAE was trying to respond to women's needs without acknowledging that revolutionary Nicaragua remained patriarchal; was mobilizing mothers for partisan ends while claiming to represent all women; and was pursuing the betterment of society in general in the hope that this would improve the lives of women as a secondary impact. Because identity understandings have a drive toward implementing its alternate ethos, a confused identity inevitably produces unfocused goals. What projects AMNLAE did undertake were hampered by the war effort. Due to these contradictions within the Sandinista women's identity, by 1987, AMNLAE had lost the legitimacy necessary to represent women. Since women were frustrated at the slow pace of change for women's rights, the political opportunity to involve women in the corporatist structure of the Party declined (Oberschall 1996, 94). AMNLAE's membership decreased, and there was a growth of new groups which responded better to women's needs and expectations (Síu Bermúdez 1993, 2, 7).

Activists built on women's discontent in order to create new women's groups. The new groups were successful because they had an identity created at the grass-roots level with a degree of autonomy that AMNLAE lacked, focused goals, and the resources to achieve them. As a result, they were able to attract participants and influence both AMNLAE and political activities. The fulcrum of the women's movement shifted from AMNLAE to these groups. Nonetheless, these new women's groups lacked complete autonomy from the FSLN, and thus there was a limit to what they could achieve. Due to their hybrid status, neither fully controlled by the FSLN nor fully free to define themselves as they wished, I have labeled these groups "semiautonomous."

Sidney Tarrow (1990, 1991, 1994) offers a mechanism by which we can understand why a semiautonomous group was able to achieve what the party faithful could not. He suggested that new political arrangements within the party allowed for the rise of internal criticisms that had been previously muted. In other words, the party itself produced its own insurgency. The internal insurgent group acted like any other social movement organization and tried to attract resources and attention, to change policies, and to persuade supporters to their perspective. The group utilized the changed opportunity structure to influence the party until it responded to the discontent. The difference between internal party insurgency and an autonomous social movement was that the former repeated the themes, techniques, origins, and alignments of the mother party. Once changes were produced within the political party, the renegade group was welcomed back to the fold or withered away. Tarrow called the process of inclusion-exclusion-inclusion of these renegade groups a "cycle of protest" (1990, 271).

The rise of semiautonomous women's groups came from an internal power realignment: AMNLAE abandoned women's issues to concentrate on the mothers of soldiers. Unions stepped into that vacuum, creating women's secretariats to respond to the unique situation of women. The unions were indubitably Sandinista, and the women's secretariats were geared toward Sandinista goals of increasing economic productivity and securing political support. To achieve their goals (critically important during a war), women's secretariats were allowed greater latitude during mobilization than were other mass organizations, inadvertently creating a semiautonomous identity. The productivity goal was quite specific, and the FSLN was able to respond to many of the secretariats' demands, strengthening the FSLN's legitimacy. In turn, the institutionalization of the demands legitimized and strengthened the semiautonomous groups until the women's secretariats became powers unto themselves and developed more autonomy from the Party than did the other mass organizations. With some autonomy and with the mobilization of resources around specific goals, the women's secretariats became vehicles for criticisms of patriarchy. The semiautonomous women's groups used their success and ideology of equality to pressure the Sandinistas to reform policies and approaches.

The problem with Tarrow's analysis of the cycle of protest is not that the FSLN would not reform or take back the renegade groups. Rather, the women did not want to return to the fold. This is because the semiautonomous groups created a semiautonomous identity. If Melucci (1989, 46, 115) is correct, it would have been unusual if women, reflecting together in a public space on their own bodies and lives and then using this knowledge to analyze their reality, did not create some form of identity. An identity suggests that the purely strategic mobilization of resources around a grievance has been altered to include an ethical element; there has been a transformation within the social movement organization which was nonnegotiable. In creating this new identity, the semiautonomous groups were assisted by the ability to speak freely in semiautonomous public spaces, an arena mostly free from Sandinista control and influence, an ad hoc, fluid, temporary space that permitted women to not recognize Sandinista norms and needs and instead focus on their own. It appeared as if the semiautonomous groups liked defining their own reality and their own identity. They liked creating their own institutions, symbols, and analyses. They liked their autonomy. The Party could offer them nothing to entice them back. As a result, the semiautonomous women's groups neither devolved nor withered away. Instead, a degree of cooperation had to be established between the branches of the women's movement and the FSLN, which finally happened by the 1990 general election.

The impetus for the creation and development of the first semiautonomous women's organization was the dire economic situation. When Somoza and his cohorts fled the country in 1979, they left behind a $1.6 billion debt, a manufacturing sector in irretrievable decline (Weeks 1985, 282), and substantial agricultural holdings. These lands were transferred to the new government and became state farms with production continued for the export market.

The industrialization of Nicaragua under the Central American Common Market (CACM) may have increased the percentage of gross domestic product gained through manufacturing from 12.6 percent in 1960 to 20.2 percent in 1978 (Dunkerley 1988, 202); however, Nicaragua was and remains a predominantly agricultural economy. Approximately 70 percent of the population earned its income from the land, and 80 percent of foreign earnings came from agricultural products (Colburn 1986, 4). Agriculture (including livestock) occupied an increasingly large percentage of Nicaraguan exports, mostly because of the decline in mining and industry but also because of the Sandinista's restructuring of the economy. For example, in 1981 agriculture comprised 60 percent of the nation's exports. By 1989, it was close to 79 percent (Close 1995, 21).

In addition to the economic importance of agricultural production was its political importance. Two thousand large landholders owned half the agricultural land in Nicaragua. The FSLN tailored agreements with those large landowners who stayed. The agreements were inconsistent, as well as inconsistently implemented, leading to suspicion and resentment among the wealthy (Colburn 1986; Spalding 1990). In comparison, 70 percent of total farmers were small landholders with less than seventeen acres, yet their holdings amounted to only 4 percent of cultivated land, much of it of marginal fertility. The contras recruited predominantly from the rural dispossessed. The rest of the land was owned by medium landholders. This group could have swung its support either way. Since the rural areas were the terrain of the civil war, at a minimum their livelihood was interrupted if not their lives threatened or lost. Therefore, consolidating power bases in the rural areas and increasing production were critically important to the government.

By 1984, it was evident that productivity was falling, which was due to several factors.[1] The Insurrection interrupted the sowing of seeds, which in turn did not generate enough seed for the following year's planting. The postrevolutionary *campesino* ethic seemed to entail truncated work days. In addition, flooding one year and drought the next reduced the harvest. The prices of export crops fell in the international markets, resulting in reduced planting. The contra war destroyed approximately $50 million per annum of the economic infrastructure (Hoyt 1997, 110) and interrupted farming, especially in the bread basket of Nicaragua—the Jalapa valley and the Matagalpa region. The American embargo on Nicaraguan exports and the depression in the rest of Latin

America reduced markets for Nicaraguan goods.[2] The conscription of young men for the war effort and low wages reduced labor for harvesting crops. The uncertainty that accompanied rapid changes, such as the agrarian reform, undermined efficient production. Finally, the government's own economic policies significantly contributed to the low productivity and rural discontent.

The FSLN's economic policies were part of the ideology of Sandinismo. The economic goal was to create a mixed agricultural economy by increasing the number and size of small landholdings. This policy promised the possibility of not merely redistributive justice but also breaking the power of the agricultural elite by creating a more politically equitable citizenry (Booth 1985, 241). In 1981, the Agrarian Reform Decree took idle, abandoned, or poorly managed farms of more than 850 acres and gave titles to farmers generally in the form of cooperatives.[3] By 1982, there were 3,000 cooperatives with 60,000 members, and by 1984 small landowners, both with individual title and cooperative affiliation, increased their productivity to 27 percent of total agricultural productivity (Hoyt 1997, 110).

There were, however, some economic problems with the agrarian reform program. Tenant farmers had their wages increased, their rents lowered by 85 percent, and their eviction banned. These policies eliminated any incentive to rent land, leaving farms of less than 850 acres to lie fallow. Agricultural credit was available but poorly administered: if a peasant, for whatever reason, was unable to pay back a loan, the debt was forgiven (Hoyt 1997, 108). In addition to the unsustainability of this kind of economic organization, farmers complained that they could not set prices for their produce. Because the urban popular demand for cheap food led the government to depress prices, there were consistent supply problems for domestically consumed produce (Gilbert 1988, 95). Finally, farmers demanded the right to own land in their own names and not in the form of a cooperative. By 1984, rural support for the FSLN was noticeably falling (Dijkstra 1992, 186).

In response, the government changed its agrarian reform policy, increasing its pace and doubling the amount of land distributed. In 1981–1982, just before the war intensified, titles were issued to 6,500 individuals and members of cooperatives (Close 1988, 92–93). In 1982–1983, the number rose to 13,000. In 1983–1984, 25,000 families received land. In

1984–1985, 35,000 families received land. In the three weeks leading to the fifth anniversary of the revolution, as many families received titles as during the first two years of the revolution (Collins 1986, 151–52). By 1989, 62 percent of peasant families (120,000 families) had received agrarian reform titles, half in individual holdings (Hoyt 1997, 112). Most of the land came from state farms.

In addition to the increase in the number of titles the government handed out, in 1984 the FSLN also reformed its economic policies. Food subsidies ended, basic grain prices floated, and credit became somewhat more restricted.[4] In general, small producers responded by increasing their productivity, or at least slowing the rate of their declining productivity. "Agrarian reform had come to the defense of the revolution" (Close 1988, 93). Defending the revolution allowed women to start defending themselves.

The war changed the political opportunities available to women. There was a need for increased food production and women's labor in nontraditional areas. Furthermore, the war helped the development of women's consciousness by offering women greater domestic control. "There is a cruel but truthful thing to say: the longer the war lasted, the more opportunities women had" (quoted in Murguialday 1990, 218). Because one's understanding of the self and society depends on experience and self-reflection, the opportunities afforded to women changed their appreciation of their own abilities. When this understanding was shared and agreed on in a public forum, it became an identity.

The 1981 Agrarian Reform Decree and Cooperative Decree changed the laws to allow women to own land, join cooperatives, and receive equal pay for equal work.[5] However, few women, farm managers, or cooperative support personnel were aware of women's new legal rights, and, even if they were, there were no sanctions for noncompliance (Padilla, Murguialday, and Criquillon 1987, 131). There was no discussion of methods to overcome the barriers to women's inclusion in agrarian reform (Collinson 1990, 42). In addition to more overt sexism, such as women being prohibited from leaving the house, there was also the problem of simply not recognizing women's labor. Most *campesinas* raised chickens and livestock and planted vegetables, which might or might not be sold on the market. They also helped with weeding or harvesting. All of this, with the exception of harvesting, was considered women's work and thus was of minimal value and did not require wages. Of course, women also had other duties, such as cooking, cleaning, and child-care.

Despite these forces, women did take advantage of their changed legal status, especially single mothers who had no other source of income. Women rural workers and farmers worked within the cooperatives (Padilla, Murguialday, and Criquillon 1987, 129). A 1982 census showed that 43.8 percent of 2,846 cooperatives had at least one woman member. Women made up 6 percent of the total membership of all cooperatives, but only 19 percent of the cooperatives had more than 10 percent female membership (Williams 1986, 9–10). When this study was repeated in 1986, the percentage of women workers in the total cooperative membership had risen to 7.3 percent from 6 percent, and still only 19 percent of the cooperatives had more than 10 percent women membership. By 1987, 44 percent of the cooperatives had at least one woman member (Chuchryk 1991, 150).[6]

The Center for Agrarian Reform (CIERA) traced the lack of growth of women's inclusion in agricultural production to sexist attitudes on the part of many men. CIERA's 1984 study of five cooperatives discovered that, contrary to law, women had been denied membership in some cooperatives, which used excuses such as land scarcity or a shortage of male full-time employment to justify their discrimination. Another method of dissuading women to join was making restrictions on women's memberships more rigid; for example, to join a cooperative women had to already own land (Padillo, Murguialday, and Criquillon 1987, 129). If allowed membership, women were assigned a lower share of the profits. Generally, the larger the cooperative and the more land it controlled, the lower the percentage profit that women received (Centro de Investigaciones, 80–82). Both men and women tended to undervalue women's work, and women were paid less (Padilla, Murguialday, and Criquillon 1987, 129). The 1989 CIERA collection of life stories of rural women in cooperatives concluded that "the traditional sexist attitudes that continued to thrive among peasants were in part responsible for the marginalization of women in the cooperative movement."

State farms, being highly regulated by the government, were more inclusionary of women workers (ibid., 130). A detailed study of a state tobacco farm in 1989 showed the sexual division of labor: certain functions (supervisory and technical) were male dominated; certain jobs were held by men only; there was not equal pay for equal work; and the same duties were called one name when performed by men and another when performed by women. Nonetheless, changes were being made. Women were moving into nontraditional areas and were working their way into supervisory positions. Day care and a noonday meal were provided, lightening the load for women considerably. In addition, women were salaried for the entire year, giving them economic stability (Ruchwarger 1989, 88).

Due to the labor laws, the creation of cooperatives, the economic needs of single mothers, and the labor shortage (Ruchwarger 1987, 256), more and more women became involved in economically productive rural activity. By 1983, women's membership in the Association of Rural Workers (ATC) had reached 40 percent. This worried the upper echelons of the ATC (Collinson 1990, 44). By 1983, declining productivity was a critical issue. The ATC leaders had to not only increase productivity but decide how to do so with almost half their workers being women. "It was then that the ATC realized how little was known about the situation confronting rural women" (Collinson 1990, 44).

The (male) leaders of the ATC called a meeting of *campesinas* in 1983. Jointly with AMNLAE, it organized a National Assembly of Rural Women Workers, attended by one hundred women. Although it was supposed to bring women together to jointly discuss and solve the problems of women in agriculture, the outcome was a frank acknowledgment of the dearth of information concerning *campesinas.* Therefore, the men and women formed a women's secretariat (in operation in 1984) to investigate the life of *campesinas* (Collinson 1990, 44–45; Chinchilla 1990, 384; Padilla, Murguialday, and Criquillon 1987, 139). It took a year and half to do so using ten researchers who were themselves rural women (Murguialday 1990, 119). AMNLAE did not participate.

The researchers started by acknowledging the importance of having an arm of a union to fight for women's rights. Said Heliette Ehlers of the women's secretariat in 1987, "We [the union] looked particularly at the situation of women in Canada after the war [WWII] when women had to go back into the home and give up the jobs they'd been doing. We noticed that although Canadian women were involved in trade unions at that time, there hadn't been any organisation strong enough to put its foot down and prevent their return to the home. So, in contrast, we women are aiming to be represented in all the different power structures" (quoted in Collinson 1990, 43). The women's secretariat would fight for women within the ATC, and the ATC would fight for the rights of *campesinas* within the FSLN, an idea predicated on the assumption that there is only one system in which they all operated and which had to respond to the needs of women and peasant men.

This assumption was reasonable for the corporatist organization of Sandinista Nicaragua. The FSLN had an inclusionary political and social organization integrated into its economic organization. As a result, there was no way to communicate with powerful people except through this structure. The benefits of the system were well-established lines of communication between the ATC and the government, which the women's secretariat could access. Furthermore, with the support of the government already secured, changes could be enacted quickly. In the case of increasing productivity, the FSLN was already committed to any necessary change. As a result, the political opportunity and the means existed for women's new demands to be institutionalized as government policy (Tarrow 1990, 271).

The women's secretariat began an investigation focused on the problem of "work norm," that is, what is considered normal for the workday. Examination of women's normal workday allowed the ATC women's secretariat to raise the issue of the sexual division of labor and then to relate it to productivity. By placing its critique in a definition of what was considered normal behavior for women, the women's secretariat avoided the destructive and dismissive label of "feminist" and thereby guaranteed the full support of the union.

A series of workshops was held at the grass-roots level and at the regional level using a photoessay to present an aspect of women's work norms, for example, the problem of sick or injured children. Approximately eight hundred women participated.[7] Consensus about women's issues was reached at this level.

From these stories, a discussion of women's reality emerged and included issues such as sexual harassment, rape, birth control, day-care centers, maternity leave, communal sinks, potable water, and the lack of corn mills. Women continuously complained of men's macho attitudes that resulted in widows and pregnant women being denied access to land (Murguialday 1990, 175). These stories served as a basis for the formation of a gender identity by acknowledging the barriers that individual women faced.

"A *collective identity* is nothing else than a shared definition of the field of opportunities and constraints offered to collective action" (Melucci 1985, 793). The women shared an understanding of their opportunities and constraints and activated that understanding through connections via the ATC women's secretariat's group meetings. Women demanded equality of opportunity (Murguialday 1990, 168–69), basing that demand on the women's understanding of the injustice of their lives.

These grass-roots sessions were so successful in articulating women's opportunities and constraints that a second National Assembly was convened in September 1986. It was attended by hundreds of women, who formally passed resolutions calling for what they had already agreed on in local meetings. Included in the resolutions was a demand that the ATC incorporate the women's requests into any agreement signed with the state and Ministry of Development and Agrarian Reform (MIDINRA). Another resolution called for the printing of a double page written by and for *campesinas* in the National Union of Farmers and Ranchers' (UNAG) newspaper. The reporters were volunteers. The experience was so educational for women reporters that it not only radicalized them and empowered them but also compelled them to encourage other women to become reporters (Collinson 1990, 47). It is a nice example of the positive spiral of praxis.

There were immediate material results from the Second Assembly. By 1986–1987, five hundred new farm day-care centers were operating, as well as more laundry facilities and corn mills (Collinson 1990, 46).[8] As for productivity, it too increased significantly, turning many men from skeptics to cautious supporters. This support in turn led to a greater support for women's resolutions (Collinson 1990, 48). By 1988, women held 28 percent of union positions versus 1 percent in 1983 (Collinson 1990, 48), and 89 percent of women attended union meetings (Chuchryk 1991, 149).[9] The result of these material and political changes was an increase in the number of the hours that women could work. By 1988, 90 percent of female workers surpassed previous work norms (Murguialday 1990, 169).

The second impact of the women's secretariat and the benefits it brought to women was the consolidation of support for the government (CIERA 80). Women, as heads of households and previously heavily discriminated against members of society, greatly appreciated the opportunity to own land, either individually or communally, a measure of security hitherto unheard of. As a result, their commitment to the cooperative was higher than men's. Women were self-affirmed through work, acquiring new skills, and participating in decision-making (Padilla, Murguialday, and Criquillon 1987, 128–29). This positive experience also enhanced the connection between the FSLN and the *campesina.*

The third impact of the articulation of women's needs was the changed understanding within the ATC. Women's demand for equality of opportunity extended to include its own union. The ATC instituted the principles that all issues should be examined from a perspective of the sexual division of labor (Collinson 1990, 45) and discarded the idea that women were only temporary, wartime substitutes for the missing men (Murguialday 1990, 169). Analyzing agricultural productivity from a woman's perspective had evolved by 1987 to acknowledge that women's issues needed to be understood within a wider social context of inequality and structural discrimination and thus could not be adequately examined separate from the broader political process (Chuchryk 1991, 150). These internal changes in the ATC were considerably more progressive than those that the FSLN instituted for itself.

The final and most influential impact to emerge from the ATC women's secretariat was the capacity of women to name their own reality. The act of naming the system and men *"machista"* had implications for the possibility of consciousness. As women's discussions continued and a second series of grass-roots meetings was initiated, the very act of naming a reality affected the reality of that topic (Escobar 1992, 62). Women's understanding of the sexist reality in which they lived became better accepted, and their understanding became more sophisticated, as was evident in the extent of the changes that the women's secretariat was able to make in the ATC itself. Tilman Evers (1985, 51, 59) suggests that by creating collective social spaces and new patterns of practices at the micro-level (such as the women's secretariat grass-roots meetings), new basic values and assumptions are created. Through reconstructing fragments of autonomous identity by sharing experiences and understandings, the individual and the group can become conscious. This consciousness is then injected back into the society through other networks, such as the family, unions, political parties, and mass media.

According to the ex-director of the Nicaraguan Institute of Research on Women (INIM), the ATC women's secretariat opened the discussion on patriarchy. The women's secretariat's frank discussions about reproductive health, sexual abuse, and job constraints had repercussions throughout Nicaragua. These discussions fundamentally changed the direction and profundity of the national dialog on women's issues (interview Siú).

Despite the influential activities of the ATC women's secretariat, its success is, at least in part, due to the initiative and support of a sympathetic, experienced, and powerful institution, the ATC, and the economic and political opportunities at the national level. It was the male leaders of the ATC who first brought women together. The men listened closely to the emerging women's voice and mobilized resources around that voice, including organizing a second assembly, providing access for women to use the media, and supplying requested material needs. The support of the male elite of the ATC influenced the support of the FSLN in responding rapidly with material goods. The experience, skills, and connections that the male elite of the ATC offered the women's secretariat were critical to its ability to mobilize resources.

An opening in the political opportunity structure was also critical to the ATC women's secretariat's success. The government wanted to increase production; the women wanted the equality of opportunity to do so. The government wanted political support; the women wanted a different organization of labor. The government wanted a political solution to its economic problem; the women wanted justice. The two complemented each other. At least in the short term, the government and the women both got what they wanted.

Because of the mobilization of resources, focused goals, and the creation of identity, it might be tempting to call the ATC women's secretariat a social movement. In fact, it was not, for the simple reason that it lacked autonomy. The ATC women's secretariat was restricted by the nature of the corporatist system of control of social groups. This lack of autonomy from the political system had implications for the goals chosen, the resources available, and the identity created.

When goals were being developed, fundamental issues were not placed on the table for discussion, regardless of whether these issues were a source of conflict. For example, support for the Sandinista revolution in the rural areas was muted, especially in the rural departments (provinces) of Matagalpa and Jinotega (interview Vega). Yet neither the value of the revolution nor the value of agrarian reform as a topic for discussion was broached. Thus, women could not choose goals antithetical to those of the Sandinista Party.

Resources were supplied at the government's largesse. Once the opening in the political opportunity structure for addressing women's needs closed, the ability of women to attain access to resources was diminished. Indeed, after 1987, once the government supplied rural women with as much as it was prepared to, the ability of the ATC and its women's secretariat to obtain more goods was curtailed.

The scope of the articulation of women's understanding about patriarchy was controlled by the government. Women had to direct their understandings into a context of economic productivity. That economic productivity had to be phrased in the contours of the Sandinista ideology of social justice. Thus, women's identity, while created by women, was nonetheless automatically Sandinista as well.

The government's control over goals, resources, and identity demonstrates the natural limits of a semiautonomous women's group in Sandinista Nicaragua. This group nonetheless became a crucible for change within the existing system.

AMNLAE was impressed by the mechanism through which the ATC women's secretariat was able to attract new participants, reach new understandings, and lobby for new goods and services. AMNLAE decided that it too should go to the grass roots and have them define their needs and concerns. AMNLAE then planned to use this new understanding as its new identity. The strategy unfortunately did not take the FSLN into account and hence was doomed to failure. In the process, however, the discussion of women's reality was broadened to include urban areas and was widely publicized. This may not have helped AMNLAE, but it did help more semiautonomous women's groups to emerge.

In 1985, AMNLAE held a series of six hundred town hall meetings to listen to women's concerns. AMNLAE intended to collate the various responses for public presentation at two different forums. The first was in preparation for the constitutional negotiations, and the second was for its own Second Assembly. The organizers were astonished by the attendance of nearly 400,000 women and by the content of their complaints. Despite the war, their concerns centered on attaining access to birth control, halting sexual harassment at work, domestic violence, and rape, and guaranteeing paternal support (Collinson 1990, 143; Morgan 1990, 23 n. 78).

If the attendance at and the content of the town hall meetings were surprising, then the constitutional negotiations were shocking, spurring AMNLAE into a more combative stance with the FSLN. The negotiations publicly shattered any vestige of Sandinista control over women's politicization by demonstrating the gap between women's expectations and AMNLAE's offerings, by articulating the authentic power of an unmediated women's voice, and by giving women the language of civil rights. AMNLAE was eclipsed. Although the constitutional negotiations may have shattered AMNLAE's increasingly untenable conflation of "women and the revolution," the negotiations left women with no new identity.

The constitutional negotiations deepened Nicaraguans' understanding of how institutions produced and supported a democracy and citizens' participation in it. The constitutional negotiations brought women's consciousness of their inequality into full articulation because "the constitutional process became a stage for airing women's concerns and produced heated debates among women themselves" (Morgan 1990, 19). In other words, women were given the public space to jointly state their political needs and desires, their definitions of equality and justice. Furthermore, the debates pushed the government and the women's movement into a language of civil rights, which gave women a powerful theoretical framework with which to explain themselves. Sandinismo, as a concept, proved not as useful as civil liberties and was abandoned. Women redefined their roles as citizens, which not only had an immediate effect but also empowered them to shape their political world in a way that a thousand union meetings and literacy campaigns had not. Nonetheless, women could not have been as coherent, critical, and informed about their concerns if AMPRONAC, AMNLAE, and the ATC women's secretariat had not organized for the previous eight years around issues of women and politics.

The constitutional negotiations were divided into four stages. Stage One (August to October 1986) involved presentations from mass organizations and groups about their special concerns. During this stage,

AMNLAE presented to the constitutional subcommittee a ten-page document on women's needs based on its six hundred open forums convened in 1985 (Collinson 1990, 144).

Stage Two (November 1986) consisted of the presentation of the draft of the constitution to the public. The constitutional subcommittee printed 150,000 copies of the draft, which were distributed throughout the nation and debated in seventy-three *cabildos abiertos,* or public town hall assemblies, constituting Stage Three. Several *cabildos* were allotted to the topic of women, but women took the floor whenever they could. Stage Four was the August 1986 presentation of the second draft, which incorporated some of the concerns raised in the *cabildos.* This draft was debated in Congress beginning November 1986 and was proclaimed January 9, 1987.

At each stage there was an incremental increase of demands for women's rights and for an improved legal language for expressing those rights. Questions of the legality of such issues as rape, abortion, and battery of wives produced further discussion. The articulation of women's rights that emerged was an organized interplay between women's everyday reality and the theoretical framework of civil rights. It was a process of clearer articulation of each. Through this articulation, women heard one another speak, expressed the same concerns, and became empowered through finding their own voice. A consensus emerged from finding this voice, or, as one writer called it, "a notable coordination in their approach" (Murguialday 1990, 203).

Yet the lack of contact between the leaders of the women's movement and the women at the base was such that AMNLAE was surprised by the independence and sophistication of women's criticisms. Sofia Montenegro, then editor of the editorial page of the Sandinista newspaper, *Barricada,* and feminist intellectual, admitted that she and a small group of other feminists had planned to prompt discussions at the *cabildos* but discovered that there was no need; women were giving a critical women's perspective without encouragement. "When we got to the *cabildo,* we found other women had already very carefully read the whole damn thing and they came up with the same positions" (Morgan 1990, 25). The ability of women independent of AMNLAE to articulate their demands during the constitutional debates demonstrated to all AMNLAE's failure to understand the grass roots and to represent them to the government.

Even more, it indicated that women did not need AMNLAE to express themselves but rather that they could organize outside the FSLN and Sandinismo. It is not accidental that after the constitutional debates many more semiautonomous women's groups emerged.

Legal reform had always been one of the goals around which AMNLAE had successfully mobilized. However, AMNLAE's strength was more in reforming existing laws than in creating an alternative organizing framework in which to place the demand for women's rights. However, with the constitutional debates, a new framework was based on two international declarations of human rights, the Universal Declaration of Human Rights and the American Declaration of the Rights and Duties of Man; and three treaties, International Covenant on Economic, Social, and Cultural Rights, International Covenant on Civil and Political Rights, and American Convention on Human Rights. This pushed the government from a social justice ideology with individual liberation as a secondary feature to an ideology with an emphasis on civil rights. Although it was not intended to be an entry for women's rights, women applied civil rights to their own life experience and found their rights notably lacking.[10] Consequently, civil liberties were applied to private issues, introducing women's reality into law.

The issue of violence against women was probably the clearest example of the violation of women's civil rights in the private sphere. Vargas extended basic civil rights to the private sphere and explained why: "We believed that we had to talk not only about our physical integrity in the face of the state but also the physical integrity of one citizen with respect to another citizen, and we had to advance this conception. Why? Because the state can protect my physical integrity against it, that is to say, against the police, against the army. But it is not just this respect for physical integrity that interests me; I am interested in the state protecting me from the aggression of other men or women citizens" (quoted in Morgan 1990, 48).

Another example of the consideration of civil rights in terms of women's reality that arose from the cabildos involved the definition of equality. Women asked that equality of rights between men and women be specified and extended to all spheres of society. Montenegro said, "Democracy is not an abstract thing, you build it according to what appears to be a necessity. Now [it] appears to be a necessity, but democracy two years after the revolution? Nobody understood what it was all about because it was not known. But now women are beginning to say, O.K., these are the political expectations in the public life, I want them reflected in my house. The revolution and the constitution and the laws are finally getting into the private kingdom of men" (quoted in Morgan 1990, 38). A fuller articulation of political rights and equality was in the second draft of the constitution (article 27).

How did such a coherent voice emerge so suddenly? Barrington Moore suggests that for an unjust situation to be recognized and used to create a viable and effective political movement, at least three things have to occur. First, the situation has to be identified as unjust (1978, 459). By 1986, enough information about the structural inequality of gender had been circulated that the idea of a gender injustice held currency.[11] Women knew this from eight years of Sandinismo.

The second factor is the need to overcome the psychological dependence that accompanies subjugation (ibid., 467). Women had to overcome the idea that patriarchy was natural, to break down the isolation between women, and to allow women to find their own voice. At the beginning of the debates, women's issues were called "nameless problems" (Murguialday 1990, 203). By the end of the debates, the problem had a name and the name was *machismo*. Women accused the laws of being macho and therefore discriminatory. The constitutional debates broke the public silence on patriarchy. The women were aware of the psychological shift that accompanied the constitutional debate. "They have come to understand the process of empowerment involved in becoming active subjects in the construction of the reality of their society and their daily lives" (Morgan 1990, 70).

The third factor in overturning a situation of injustice is the need to create a social and cultural space in which these new ideas can be discussed. The resource mobilization theorists consider this to be an opportunity in the political process. The *cabildos*, indeed the entire debate, from newspaper articles to legislative responses, were spaces created to discuss overarching concepts of justice. The Sandinistas, to their credit, allowed the people, including women, to control that space. It is inconceivable that women's concerns could have been so influential if the *cabildos* had not been an open, accessible, and traditional forum; if the language of the draft and the commentators had not been open, accessible, and typically Nicaraguan; and if the issues were not seen as life and death and yet commonplace. The success of the constitutional debates is a testimony to the integrity of the FSLN in this process.

Despite the relentlessly positive commentary from all regarding the constitutional debates, it is important to recognize that the two topics that were the most discussed during the *cabildos* and long after were sex education and abortion, in other words, reproductive information and control. Yet when the constitution was finally ratified in 1987, neither of these two topics was written into it (Association of Nicaraguan Women 1987, 15). Although the opportunity to discuss ideas may have been available, the opportunity to codify them was more limited. The limits of women's ability to implement their rights heightened their awareness of gender inequality.

One of the instructive features of the development of the women's movement between 1984 and 1987 was the critical role of public spaces. These spaces resided on the boundary between civil society and the state, incorporating, in varying degrees, elements and actors from both and thus encouraging actors to speak more freely than usual. The capacity to hear others speak developed women's own awareness. Then, the same public space gave women a forum from which to promulgate that awareness, persuading other women, groups in society and the state, of the value of their new principles. The use of public spaces to better women's legal and political status in Nicaragua was not the planned and directed handiwork of some social movement but the spontaneous and natural result of women hearing one another's stories after years of haphazard consciousness-raising.

The creation of awareness of an injustice is the forerunner for the creation of a new political movement. Since justice is an artificially created and commonly held understanding (Moore 1978, 497), it must be created somewhere and somehow. The constitutional debates, preceded by the approach of the ATC women's secretariat (which AMNLAE then mimicked), and preceded even earlier by AMNLAE's and AMPRONAC's campaigns, created a new understanding of justice by and for women. That concept of justice was codified into the new constitution, extending women's civil rights into new avenues and strengthening existing rights.

With a new understanding of citizenship and a new language, a new identity for the women's movement outside the purview of the FSLN became feasible.

As the largest, most established, and most diverse women's group, AMNLAE hoped to be the organization that expressed that new identity (Murguialday 1990, 194). Despite the National Directorate's reduced commitment to women's issues, women activists had reason to be optimistic after the ratification of the new constitution. After so many meetings dominated by the grass roots, not merely were women's demands clearer, so were AMNLAE's. The FSLN proved capable of responding quickly and positively to a previously unorganized group of the women, the rural workers. AMNLAE proved capable of recognizing its own failed strategies and approaches, and instead learned from the ATC how it was to be done. As an ideology, Sandinismo proved capable of supporting spaces free from partisan politics in which women could discover their own voices. And the corporatism of the Sandinista regime proved flexible enough to integrate new visions, a new language, and new techniques of organizing. The confusion and uncertainty that had bedeviled AMNLAE—and hence the women's movement—since the 1984 election appeared resolvable.

CHAPTER 5

The Limits of Autonomy, 1987–1990

AMNLAE's WISH TO REGAIN its hegemonic position in the political sphere was not to be. The opening of public spaces had awakened women to their own needs. Women's collectives led by top-ranking Sandinista women spontaneously formed and began speaking out. Unions that did not yet have a women's secretariat formed one. The women's secretariat of the Nicaraguan Confederation of Professionals—Heroes and Martyrs (CONAPRO H-M) became the major new voice of gendered Sandinismo. The slow and inevitable emergence of a semiautonomous gender identity fragmented the Sandinista women's movement. The emergent ethos demanded a supportive structure and new goals, which the new groups had. As a nationwide women's movement emerged in Nicaragua, AMNLAE struggled to regain its constituency. The group articulated its new understanding at the 1987 Second Assembly and met considerable resistance from the FSLN. The failure of the Second Assembly and the recent peace negotiations prompted the FSLN to take notice of women's increasing disillusionment with the FSLN and AMNLAE. As a result, the movement was reorganized, patriarchy was acknowledged, and AMNLAE received a new identity. However, that identity was not freely formed, AMNLAE was still vertically organized and nondemocratic, and the FSLN still controlled the resources. Nonetheless, with the 1990 election looming, women from all organizations united to assist the FSLN in its reelection.

AMNLAE's Second Assembly in 1987, where it unveiled its new approach, was a watershed. AMNLAE presented to the FSLN and Nicaragua the demands that women had made in the previous years.

AMNLAE's theme was motherhood, or rather changing the understanding of motherhood. The slogan of the assembly was "We don't want to just give life, we want to change it." AMNLAE presented its stance in a paper titled "The Right to Motherhood," which included demands for legalized access to abortion, birth control, sex education, and sterilization (Morgan 1990, 55). All of these actions implied that AMNLAE wanted to change the role of motherhood, one of the bedrock institutions of society and of its own policies.

Some high-ranking members of the FSLN publicly resisted these new demands at AMNLAE's Second Assembly, instead accusing AMNLAE of being discriminatory because it excluded men and suggesting that female emancipation was inherent within socialism. These accusations were met with boos from the women in the audience. For rank-and-file Sandinistas to boo the elite of the FSLN was unheard of, especially given the extent to which the Party had supported women's rights. This spontaneous and guttural rejection of the Party line spoke clearly about women's impatience with the FSLN, their awareness of their own rights, and an identity increasingly growing autonomous from the Party. The hostility of women to Sandinista control shocked the Party (Collinson 1990, 144; Murguialday 1990, 142–43).

The assembly was such a debacle that a week later one hundred women activists met with the leaders of the FSLN to discuss the continuation of AMNLAE. The FSLN, rather than trying to understand the source of antagonism, sought simply to reestablish control over the women. According to one intellectual-activist, the FSLN never understood the organic nature of social movements, viewing them instead through a strictly utilitarian lens (Síu Bermúdez 1993, 2).

The meeting lasted all day and was dominated by men. It was finally decided that a women's organization was needed but it would have to be reorganized to respond better to women's needs within the context of society's needs (Collinson 1990, 145; Woroniuk 1987, 17). In other words, AMNLAE's attempt to respond to the grass-roots demands for reproductive rights was denied because the needs of the revolution still took priority. As a result, according to Ana Criquillon (1995, 211), the remaining years of the Sandinista regime, 1987–1990, saw a crumbling of a myth, the belief that there could exist the female revolutionary who struggled in support of the interests of all of the oppressed, including women.

Criquillon's statement reflects the failure of the Sandinista identity for female activists. The contradictions between the nongenderized revolutionary modeled after Luisa Amanda Espinoza and the needs of women collided at the Second Assembly and the subsequent meeting. The contradictions within the identity ultimately eroded its legitimacy, producing apathy and a declining membership within AMNLAE (Síu Bermúdez 1993, 1).

Without an identity, there is a loss of effective and complementary mobilization of resources. An identity offers an overarching ethos, guiding principles that automatically set priorities (goals) and means to achieve them (resources). As the previous chapter demonstrated, a confused identity or an identity with contradictions within it leaves a social movement organization struggling to determine what its next move should be. Without any identity at all, a social movement organization has no raison d'être, no reason to even struggle. In addition, without an identity, there is a loss of the state's legitimacy, that is, a loss of women's moral acceptance of the state's authority, which weakens the state's ability to control social movement activists and erodes the citizens' loyalty to the state (Oberschall 1996, 94). With the public criticism of the Sandinista hierarchy at the Second Assembly and then the inability of the FSLN to respond to women's demands, the Sandinistas lost legitimacy. This loss significantly reduced the political opportunity for the FSLN and AMNLAE to bind women closer to the Party. Instead, the loss of legitimacy helped to pave the way for the rise to dominance of the semiautonomous women's groups in the late 1980s.

In 1987, high-ranking Sandinista women created a women's collective called the Party of the Erotic Left (PIE) in an attempt to poke fun at the FSLN as much as to offer a political message. Technically speaking, it was the first fully independent group, although, given that every member was a Sandinista, the reality of that autonomy must be questioned. Furthermore, it had no detailed platform for change and did not actively engage in mobilizing women. In 1988, the first women's health clinic, *Ixchen*, opened in Managua. Led by another high-ranking Sandinista woman, it offered an alternative approach to women's health care. Women were encouraged to take ownership of their own bodies by participating in the decision-making of their care and by being informed about health issues, including reproductive health. Women's groups were springing up throughout Nicaragua to discuss concerns and problems. From one semiautonomous women's group in 1984, the number grew by 1990 to ten women's secretariats in unions supported by sixty *Centros de Servicios Alternativos Para la Mujer* (Centers of Alternative Services for Women), which offered concrete ways in which women could solve their problems; twenty-three research and education centers, which incorporated women's studies and issues; eight women's collectives; eleven foundations or associations; plus intergroup alliances and coordinators (Síu Bermúdez 1993, 9–10). Of those, it was the women's secretariat of the Nicaraguan Confederation of Professionals—Heroes and Martyrs (CONAPRO H-M) that took semiautonomy to its logical end. Its identity was still broadly Sandinista and not fully autonomous, yet CONAPRO H-M consciously set out to create an identity as an end in itself. CONAPRO H-M women's secretariat used this identity to engage in a sustained criticism of Sandinista policies, and it organized around women's constitutional rights. It chose its own goals and organized itself through women's groups, horizontal networks, and public spaces. As a result, CONAPRO H-M women's secretariat became the most powerful and most public critic of the government's position on women.

CONAPRO H-M was a more sophisticated version of a semiautonomous organization than the ATC women's secretariat because CONAPRO H-M more closely resembled a social movement. According to Alberto Melucci (1985, 797), social movements do not merely fight for material goals or for greater participation in the system but also for symbolic goals, "for a different meaning and orientation of social action." This was the goal of CONAPRO H-M. In order to attain its goal, it behaved similarly to a fully autonomous social movement organization. It acted with effective independence, built on the grass roots, created new public spaces, lobbied the national government, and participated in international meetings. It independently mobilized its resources of political opportunity, alliance building, communication, leadership, new constituents, and access to funding around the conflict of women's legal rights in the new constitution. By successfully mobilizing around that issue, CONAPRO H-M encouraged the Party to pass legislation supportive of women's rights and to discuss women's reproductive rights. However, its identity was not fully autonomous from the Party.

Even its name, CONAPRO H-M, was a complex symbol of affiliation and autonomy. There already was an existing CONAPRO, begun after the revolution by disgruntled professionals who were conservative and anti-Sandinista. In comparison, the new CONAPRO was a group of disgruntled professionals who were reformist and Sandinista. For this new group to copy the name CONAPRO was an indication of its class allegiance. The addition of H-M was a symbol of their Sandinista political beliefs. However, the obvious absence of the word *Sandinista* from the name reflected their critical distance as well. Their name was a symbol of their stance, neither revolutionary nor counterrevolutionary. In the highly polarized wartime society, there was little room for nonpartisanship. CONAPRO H-M operated in as wide a space as possible.

To stress the importance of semiautonomy and the difficulty in finding the appropriate balance between the two opposing sides of the war, it is useful to compare CONAPRO H-M women's secretariat with a women's theater group. In the same year that the women's secretariat of CONAPRO H-M began, 1988, Marta Magali Quintana began a theater group in the mountain town of Matagalpa to bring awareness of women's reality to women in a nonpolitical and entertaining way. This evolved into a radio show called *Ya Ahora Tenemos La Palabra* (Now We Can Speak). This program had an explicitly feminist content but also dealt with the lives of the local peasant women, discussing such issues as abortion and domestic violence. Its slogan, "Every child should be a wanted child," was radical in a country and an area where children were considered given by God. As a result, the FSLN censored the radio show in both 1988 and 1989, once threatening to take it off the air (O'Donnell 1991, 132–33).

Quintana was not Sandinista. In fact, she had no political affiliation whatsoever. As a result, her group was fully autonomous but also had no protection from the government when threatened. By not aligning itself to the FSLN, by not skillfully manipulating resources and spaces, the women's radio program could barely operate. CONAPRO H-M women's secretariat was cleverer and used spaces and topics that the FSLN had already approved.

The National Directorate opened a space to criticize patriarchy within the confines of the corporate body: AMNLAE got a new general secretary, Lea Guido, and a new mandate to forge a more inclusionary and genderized Sandinismo. Always careful never to antagonize, and yet always pushing to broaden the definition of women's roles, Guido showed how women's rights related to Sandinismo and the newly completed constitutional negotiations. She wrote of the new understanding of women, "The enemy is not men; the enemy is the system" (quoted in Association of Nicaraguan Women 1987, 6). The downfall of patriarchy would liberate the sexes to full emancipation through a strong and viable women's movement, from which happiness and a new kind of love would emerge. Guido continued: "In this sense, the [women's] movement takes in the profound humanism of the Revolution, its democratic essence, which is to liberate all oppressed sectors of society. The movement brings democracy to the home where it should really begin, and to everyday life. In the end, all the important tasks of the Revolution are carried out in daily life, and that is how concrete advances of the Revolution must be measured" (quoted in Association of Nicaraguan Women 1987, 7). This was the newest Sandinismo, embedded in the personal, which women could evoke to support their cause. AMNLAE's understanding of women's rights was firmly and thoroughly grounded in the unique event of the revolution and its ideology of Sandinismo, combined with the language of civil rights and democracy. AMNLAE could now criticize the patriarchal system with the explicit intent of changing it through a public sphere struggle (ibid.).

AMNLAE, under Guido's handling, was sufficiently persuasive at articulating this new identity that it was able to shift the FSLN's stance on women. On Mother's Day 1988, the FSLN issued a major revision of its stance on women's issues and public policy. The FSLN admitted that patriarchy was the reason for women's subordination and that women should not have to wait for the end of the war to attain their rights. These sweeping statements delighted most women activists, although they tended to grumble about the lack of reproductive rights. Known as *La Proclama*, the FSLN's revised stance was the platform for a new relationship between women and the FSLN.

The FSLN may also have shifted its position on women because of two further factors. First, the Central American Peace Treaty was nearing completion and the war was winding down, although fighting did not fully cease until 1990. Nonetheless, the FSLN no longer needed the heavy emphasis on mothers to politically safeguard itself. Second, the FSLN was losing support among women of all ages. According to a June 1988 survey of 1,123 randomly selected Managuans, 63 percent of women and 55 percent of men did not identify with any political party. Furthermore, of the women who did identify with a political party, a lower percentage affiliated themselves with the FSLN: 27 percent of women versus 30 percent of men (Morgan 1990, 67). More women than men were disassociated from the political process, and fewer of the women involved were Sandinistas. *La Proclama* was an attempt to make the FSLN more attractive to women.

Given that women were already asserting their demands outside the purview of the FSLN, and given that there was the frank admission that the war and the economic crisis fully absorbed the energies of the Sandinista leaders (Randall 1994, 250), *La Proclama* might be considered little more than tokenism. However, *La Proclama* must also be seen as a symbol. Identity-based social movements place great importance on symbolic struggles due to their emphasis on ethics and morality. *La Proclama* was a moral and ethical triumph outlining the rights and duties between the government and women. As such, it had significant value. Women could use the document strategically to lever public policy and to legitimate their own arguments (Vargas 1993).

As well as revising its stance on women, the FSLN decided to reorganize AMNLAE's internal structure to make it more in touch with its grass-roots base. Thus, in 1988, AMNLAE was officially changed from an "association" to a "movement" in order to reflect the broad-based nature of women's needs. AMNLAE's leaders started organizing at the grass roots through *"casas de mujeres"* (women's centers), which were legal and medical clinics, and through hostels in the urban informal sector (Chamorro 1989, 137).

Not only did AMNLAE have these new tasks, but also it had a reformed internal structure. Instead of AMNLAE committees in the workplace, women's interests were represented by semiautonomous women's groups or unions. These unions (or women's groups) would voice complaints to the local AMNLAE organization. It was hoped that in such a way everyday problems within the women's context would naturally emerge, be heard, and be addressed. At the executive level, representatives from the semiautonomous women's organizations were included.

However, AMNLAE's internal structure was still hierarchical, with the top positions appointed by the FSLN. Thus, the reorganization did not resolve the fundamental problem of AMNLAE's structure.

Through *La Proclama* and the reform of AMNLAE, there was a small but critical opening in the Sandinista political structure. CONAPRO H-M's superb mobilization of resources widened that opening (Tarrow 1990; 1991; 1994). The resources it mobilized were leadership, internal structure, communication, autonomous funding, alliances, and public spaces.

CONAPRO H-M had one priceless advantage: its president. The president of the women's secretariat was Milú Vargas, member of one of Nicaragua's most prestigious families and wife of Commander Carlos Nuñez, a member of the National Directorate of the FSLN. She had been active in AMPRONAC's initial meetings. She was named head legal counsel for the Council of State just after the revolution, and was then named to the tribunal writing the constitution. Vargas was renowned for her commitment to women's rights, her intelligence, and her charm. She should also be known for her organizing skills, since the women's secretariat during her two-year leadership (1988–1990) organized two international conferences on law and gender. With her leadership, CONAPRO H-M had instant legitimacy and complete protection from the FSLN and from the rest of the women's movement. The combination of intelligence, legal training, experience, and connections widened the space for CONAPRO H-M to criticize the government and patriarchy more than other groups could.

CONAPRO H-M women's secretariat had a horizontal structure. As demonstrated with AMPRONAC and AMNLAE, internal organization is a resource that must be appropriately used. An organization's structure must reflect its values, or it will lose legitimacy and support. CONAPRO H-M women's secretariat had twenty-three chapters throughout the country and elected an executive by secret ballot. Unlike AMNLAE's pyramid, CONAPRO H-M women's secretariat had only two tiers: the chapters and the executive. This horizontal structure was also financially efficient—a necessity given how little money CONAPRO H-M the group had. It received no funding from the Party, but it did receive some external assistance.[1] This lack of Sandinista funding had the benefit of increasing CONAPRO H-M women's secretariat's autonomy from the Party.

As a strategy, Vargas explicitly called for the creation of alliances because collective action by an alliance of women's groups was, she believed, the only method to achieve goals. This included working with women who may not have shared CONAPRO's values. According to Vargas, action creates its own consciousness, which may simply be lacking articulation (Vargas 1989a, 28, 29). "To comply with the principal objective of social transformation asks that men and women participate in a simultaneous process of personal change. That is a political action as well" (Vargas 1989a, 30). Presumably this is an explanation for colluding with AMNLAE. The alliance not only strengthened joint actions but also kept CONAPRO H-M operating within a Sandinista framework. Jane Jaquette (1989, 186) suggests that this sort of cooperation, even the right to criticize one another, is typical of women's movements and is necessary to achieve their goals.

Alliances were strengthened between various groups within the Nicaraguan women's movement because members of each semiautonomous women's group sat on AMNLAE's executive board. These meetings ensured that the women's groups cooperated on some issues and avoided unnecessary duplication on some projects. For example, AMNLAE's newspaper folded in 1988, and CONAPRO H-M began a more radical newspaper later that same year. AMNLAE targeted policy formation with the FSLN, while CONAPRO H-M targeted Supreme Court interpretations of the constitution and existing legislation. AMNLAE offered training seminars to women without job skills. CONAPRO H-M organized international conferences on women and the law. CONAPRO H-M was vociferous in its criticism of the entrenched patriarchy of the FSLN and of the revolutionary society it was attempting to create and AMNLAE's role in this process. AMNLAE was more mainstream in its criticisms and thus was perceived as the voice of reason (Bouchier 1979).

In addition to institutional networks, CONAPRO H-M used mass media to reach the rest of society and its own members. In addition to its newspaper, it had a radio program and access to the Sandinista information network. Given how focused and esoteric the group was, its quantity of news outlets appears excessive. However, CONAPRO H-M needed this many news outlets to discuss new ideas, for example, the possibility that women can be fulfilled without being mothers, and to attract more members and funding. The complex use of mass media reflected the members' experience working both in grass-roots politics and with the means of communication.

CONAPRO H-M women's secretariat was also able to attract a new constituency of women with nominal affiliation to the FSLN. As Vargas explained when talking about recruiting members, "CONAPRO was the product of the necessity of representing a sector of women [that was not being represented]" (interview Vargas). These women tended to care less about class revolution than about sexual revolution. The necessity of keeping all these women in contact with the organization was also one reason for its extensive media outlets.

The ability of CONAPRO H-M women's secretariat to successfully mobilize its resources was obvious in its utilization of public space. In August 1988, it organized a three-day national seminar on women and the law. The purpose of the conference was to apply pressure on the National Assembly to make good on its own constitution and pass laws reflecting its values. This would be a difficult topic even for lawyers. But Vargas managed to make it comprehensible by focusing on women's experience. In her opening speech, she wove together women, law, and politics, articulating the possibility of a new identity: "To do politics is to fight against oppression, whether it be class, sexual, social . . . It is to want to transform relations of domination or subordination that are expressed in a form of specific oppression in the private sphere as much as in the public. . . . It is the full intent to transform unequal relations" (Vargas 1989a, i).

The statement of general intent and specific goals suggests the Sandinista element of CONAPRO H-M women's secretariat. Women's political actions were a just fight against oppression, domination, and subordination. It was presented as a fight to attain a new human identity, to reach together with men a new and better category, that of the person (ibid., 2). Vargas evoked the Sandinista ideal of the new men and the new women—only instead of just women achieving the status of personhood, so too would men. This was the language of Sandinismo extended to the sexual and the social with the public and the private explicitly collapsed. Vargas called on women to be aware of their legal reality after reflecting on the social organization of daily life. The speech was both clearly Sandinista and critical of patriarchy.

Vargas took one more important step in the creation of woman's identity. She attempted to define women's identity outside the context of the FSLN. In her introductory statement, she called on women to reflect on the historical role of women's political participation. In one of her speeches she went into considerable depth about the role of the suffragettes in England and the United States and their battle for citizenship and civil rights. She then turned to Nicaragua and the role women played and were playing at the time for national sovereignty, citizenship, and the reform of the constitution (ibid., iv, 3–18).

With this presentation of history, Vargas entered into the contested ground of constructing history, a global woman's history of civil rights. She melded the international women's movement with the historical specificity of the Nicaraguan Revolution. This was the ground upon which she had attempted to found CONAPRO H-M women's secretariat. The identity was to be Sandinista with a global awareness of gender inequality. One feature of social movements is their global awareness (Melucci 1989, 185). People in one nation are capable of recognizing similar patterns of domination in other countries. Because the oppression is seen as global rather than national, the goal of the social movement is limited to opening small spaces of freedom rather than in overthrowing a government (Cohen 1985, 664). By positing the Nicaraguan women's movement within a framework of global patriarchy, Vargas was unwittingly shaping CONAPRO H-M women's secretariat into a social movement organization rather than a government-controlled union, such as the ATC women's secretariat.

In 1989, CONAPRO H-M organized a second conference on women and legislation in Latin America. International in scope, it attracted a number of speakers from other countries. This conference's global scope strengthened the legitimacy of CONAPRO H-M's ideas and approaches, thereby increasing its influence. After the conference, CONAPRO H-M began working toward the 1990 election, producing analyses of party platforms from the perspective of women's rights.

The goal of CONAPRO H-M women's secretariat was to reform the legal status of women by organizing around the constitution. Specifically, CONAPRO H-M women's secretariat wanted issues such as reproductive rights codified. In order to attains its goals, it had to present an alternative understanding of women's role in society, which it did through presenting an alternative understanding of women. Thus, the creation of its identity was also its goal.

Despite its short existence, it seems reasonable to assume that CONAPRO H-M had an impact on the discussion of women's rights and the creation of women's identity. The discussions and the conclusions of its conferences were well covered by the local press and the women's networks. Transcripts of some of the speeches were reprinted as a supplement in *Barricada*. The conferences also received international attention, which would further legitimize it and help with future external funding (interview Vargas). Nonetheless, it is difficult to trace CONAPRO H-M women's secretariat's impact on the shifts in the debate and understandings about women in Nicaragua.

It seems reasonable, however, to suggest a connection between CONAPRO H-M's lobbying and proposed legislation. For example, one month after CONAPRO H-M's conference on women and legislation in Latin America, Carlos Nuñez, husband of Milú Vargas and speaker of the National Assembly, promised that legalized abortion would be discussed in the next legislative assembly (Morgan 1990, 80).[2] It is easier to draw the connection between CONAPRO H-M and other pieces of legislation. In January 1989, for example, AMNLAE and CONAPRO H-M presented a detailed submission to the National Assembly on reforming the laws pertaining to crimes such as rape and sexual harassment (ibid., 86 n. 393). This document would be the basis for legal reform to the 1992 penal code. Finally, CONAPRO H-M broadened the understanding of Sandinista identity, strengthened the application of civil rights to women, and validated strategies for achieving goals such as strategic alliances and semiautonomy from the FSLN.

Emboldened by the semiautonomous women's groups represented in its national executive, and in an attempt to reclaim its leadership status from the semiautonomous women's groups (Chamorro 1989, 137), AMNLAE became more aggressive in the Nicaraguan National Assembly. As the only women's organization that had a seat in the Congress, AMNLAE was uniquely situated to present the women's perspective to a formalized and permanent public forum. Although AMNLAE had always had that political opportunity, it had been hesitant to use it in the past. However, on September 30, 1988, AMNLAE too demanded decriminalized abortion and free and available contraception (Morgan 1990, 81).

Again, however, AMNLAE appeared to have pushed the FSLN too far. The FSLN reneged on its promise, made in the 1989 Assembly, to democratize AMNLAE. The demand for democracy stemmed from the issue of AMNLAE's autonomy from the FSLN. The lack of autonomy continued to confuse and frustrate feminists who perceived democracy as the solution to AMNLAE's lack of control (Vargas 1993).[3] The FSLN instead suddenly appointed the minister of police and famed guerrilla commandante, Doris Tijerino, as general secretary. This was done against the wishes of the AMNLAE rank and file and of Tijerino herself (Randall 1994, 211). Tijerino was parachuted into AMNLAE to control the rumblings and grumblings of the women's movement. Members within AMNLAE suggested that the Frente was using its top police officer to try to police the women's movement (ibid.). Simultaneously, the FSLN canceled the Latin American and Caribbean Feminist Meeting, scheduled to be convened in Nicaragua at the end of 1989, because the convention included topics such as autonomy (Criquillon 1995, 224). AMNLAE was none too subtly being disciplined.

Tijerino strengthened AMNLAE with her political skills. As a highly experienced political organizer, she was well aware of what needed to be done to make AMNLAE stronger. She brought to the forefront women's private sphere concerns and then created the means through which their voices could be heard, the creation of alliances.

Tijerino's skill at political organizing was most evident at AMNLAE's March 1989 conference. It was well attended by seven hundred women from all the related women's organizations, including women from the Atlantic Coast.[4] The topics spanned both the public and the private sphere in a continuing attempt to break the division between the two spheres (Chamorro 1989, 138; Association of Nicaraguan Women 1989, 7–8).

The forum also marked the first time that AMNLAE consciously and publicly formed alliances with the other women's groups. Alliances, integral to the success of AMPRONAC and AMNLAE's early years, had been eschewed in later years. However, the new alliances that Tijerino negotiated were not as loose as those of the AMPRONAC years or as ad hoc as those of the early years of the revolution. Rather, alliances were now seen as fundamental for the success of breaking the division between public and private spheres, and of changing the relationship between men and women by including men in the alliances. Although partisan, the alliances nonetheless allowed for the emergence of criticism of the government. With criticism came the possibility of creating a woman's identity.

In 1989, a year before the Sandinistas fell from power, one could see the possibility of the emergence of women's issues as defined by women and organized through a loose network. The loose network allowed semiautonomous women's organizations, with their unique demands and critiques, nonvertical structure, and complex identity, to be heard and integrated into Sandinismo. The new identity may have been grounded outside of the specificity of the Nicaraguan revolution, preferring instead a global context, but the semiautonomous organizations and AMNLAE nonetheless shared broad goals of equality and freedom.

In the last year that AMNLAE enjoyed access to the upper echelons of power, the group was better organized and more in touch with its base. It began to deal with the semiautonomous women's groups in a coordinated fashion in order to construct a unified and powerful voice. Once its resources were mobilized in a mode that might have allowed it to create and hear women's voices, the possibility of creating an autonomous identity emerged. An autonomous identity would have allowed it to choose its own goals. This scenario, however, is speculative. The fact is that in 1989 AMNLAE's primary goal was to assist in the reelection of the FSLN. The semiautonomous women's organizations joined AMNLAE to help in the election campaign.

Despite the role of any number of organized women's groups, it is difficult to suggest that the FSLN deserved to win. It badly bungled the election campaign for the simple reason that it did not address women's issues, and, according to more than one commentator, it was women who decided the results of the 1990 election (Chinchilla 1990, 291; Saint-Germain 1993b, 80; interview Herrera). Women's anti-Sandinista vote was the result of three factors.

First, the choice of party leader, always a key component of an election, was skillfully used to get women to vote against the FSLN. The FSLN was running Daniel Ortega again as president. In opposition, the United States cobbled together an opposition alliance, the National United Opposition (UNO) with Violeta Chamorro as its candidate. Chamorro promised peace, and she was probably the only person who could deliver it (Saint-Germain 1993b).[5] Nicaragua lost 50,000 people in overthrowing Somoza and another 30,000 (from both sides) during the contra war, figures that do not include those permanently damaged emotionally and physically.[6] Nicaragua had been at war at varying levels of intensity from 1978 to 1990. Although the Esquipulas Peace Treaty reduced the amount of fighting, it did not halt it. In fact, contra leaders before the 1990 elections stated that they would refuse to lay down their arms if the FSLN won. Hence the FSLN could not promise with any kind of credibility that peace would reign if it won and that it could therefore end the highly unpopular conscription. A vote for the FSLN was a vote for seemingly endless bloodshed. As women's greatest status lay in their sons, the ongoing loss of life negatively affected women's lives more than it did the men's.

Second, the FSLN created the conditions for a traditional woman to be elected president with its concept of a politically active mother. The extensive changes that the FSLN undertook on behalf of women in the public sphere meant that the idea of women's political activism was accepted (Saint-Germain 1993b, 80–82). Yet AMNLAE's ability to articulate an alternative understanding of women's roles in society was sufficiently curtailed that the strongest public role for women was still the mother. The UNO used this image of the mother/activist to its advantage, referring to women as mothers and wives rather than as women. It wanted to stop sex education, access to birth control, and family planning. The family was to be organized into a hierarchy which revolved around the man (Vargas 1989, 25–31). For example, on being asked if she was a feminist during the 1990 election campaign, Chamorro replied, "I am not a feminist nor do I want to be one . . . I am dedicated to my home, as [my husband] taught me [to be]" (*Barricada International,* January 20, 1990: 11). On another occasion, she was reported as saying that women should be happy to stay at home, that she had been, and that she bears "the Chamorro brand" (i.e., her married name had branded her) (Randall 1994, 259). AMPRONAC, AMNLAE, and the semiautonomous women's organizations had been successful in getting mothers into the public sphere but unsuccessful in persuading Nicaraguans to reject the image of women solely as mothers.[7]

Third, the economy was in such a crisis that the socialist government of the FSLN was forced to embrace rigid structural adjustment policies in 1988 and again in 1989, which they optimistically presented as "stabilization with justice." While protection for health care, education, and the poorest of the poor was guaranteed, without the support of the international banking community, the programs were even more stringent than usual. The currency was devalued by 3,000 percent in order to eliminate the black market (Stahler-Sholk 1990, 62). The system of indexing wages to inflation was abolished in June 1987 because the government intended to have inflation under control. However, price controls proved untenable with the elimination of an overvalued currency. Inflation continued to climb. In 1988 it reached 33,600 percent while real wages dropped (Dijkstra 1992, 140). As well, the government began massive layoffs equivalent to 2 percent of the labor force (Ocampo 1991, 356). The informal market doubled as it absorbed the unemployed (ibid., 359), and at the same time the regressive distribution of wealth in the country increased.

Women were more economically disadvantaged by structural adjustment policies than were men. Men returning from war replaced women workers (Collinson 1990, 90). State workers, overwhelmingly women, were laid off in the structural adjustment. Some suggest that women were targeted for layoffs (Collinson 1990, 33). Reductions in services such as health care and transportation also hit women the hardest. Food subsidies were heavily cut. The economic crisis negatively affected women, as those responsible for feeding their family, more than men.

By election time 1990, even Sandinista supporters had a hard time defending the FSLN's economic management. The Sandinistas blamed external circumstances, which made it difficult to believe that the economy would significantly change with reelection. If the UNO won, on the other hand, the economic embargo would be lifted, and U.S.-blocked credit to the Nicaraguan government would be lifted. As well, American aid money would flow in, presumably followed by investment capital. Thus, voting for the UNO was presented as an act that would produce tangible economic benefits.[8]

The FSLN should have responded to the needs of women who were not incorporated into the formal economy, as these women were the UNO's greatest source of support. A poll just before the election showed that 51 percent of all men supported the FSLN. Women who worked outside the home in the formal economy had the highest level of support for the FSLN at 59 percent, while women who did not work outside the home had the lowest level of support for the FSLN at 46 percent and the highest level of support for the UNO (28 percent versus 22 percent for men). There was also a difference between the men, housewives, and working women among the undecideds (20 percent of housewives were undecided compared to 16 percent of men and 12 percent of working women) (Chinchilla 1990, 391). Norma Stoltz Chinchilla (1990, 392) suggests that as a result of the pronounced difference between working women and housewives, there were three genders voting in the 1990 election.

The results of the election shocked all. The UNO won a solid majority with 54.7 percent of the popular vote, with a turnout of 86 percent of registered voters. The FSLN won 40.8 percent of the popular vote. The UNO alliance had fifty-one of the ninety-two seats in the National Assembly, and the FSLN won thirty-nine seats.

The profile of women in the Congress changed dramatically. Surprisingly, more women were elected to the Congress, although fewer of them were from the FSLN. The number of female representatives rose from thirteen to fifteen, nine of whom were from the FSLN, and, of them, five were incumbents. The new FSLN representatives were middle-class professionals, were older, and had ties to AMNLAE. Although the FSLN had lost a number of seats, female Sandinistas increased their representation from 19.6 percent to 23.1 percent of the total number (Saint-Germain 1993a, 133).

The remaining six representatives were sent by five different parties, all more conservative than the FSLN. These women were professionals, older, but had no ties to the women's movement. Perhaps the most important difference is that the women from the non-FSLN parties considered politics as a profession. Unlike the FSLN female candidates, who were active in military or grass-roots resistance and who therefore lacked legislative skills, the non-FSLN female candidates came from political families or from a background of political organizing within a party. As a result, they tended to hold more traditional values (Saint-Germain 1993a, 129). The election of Chamorro and the makeup of the new legislative assembly would have a profound influence on women and the women's movement in the 1990s.

Nicaraguan women would be capable of responding to the new government because of the emergence of the semiautonomous women's movement during the latter years of the Sandinista regime. The semiautonomous movement emerged firstly because of the failure of AMNLAE to adequately represent women's needs. Between 1985 and 1990, AMNLAE vainly attempted to redefine its identity so that it could regain its leadership position and the successes that it had enjoyed in the early 1980s. It was unsuccessful for three reasons: lack of an autonomous identity based on women's voices, lack of resources, and lack of a focused goal.

AMNLAE became aware of women's demands during the ATC women's secretariat's grass-roots meetings, the constitutional negotiations, and its own preparatory meetings for the 1987 Second Assembly. Consistently, women demanded reproductive rights, paternal support, and a cessation of sexual abuse. AMNLAE attempted to incorporate these concerns into its own goals and identity, but the FSLN would not allow it to do so. Instead, the FSLN insisted that AMNLAE assume the Party's goals and identity, and not women's. To an immeasurable extent, the decisions of the FSLN and the leaders of the women's movement were influenced by the reality of war and an economic blockade. Nonetheless, without autonomy, AMNLAE could not construct its own identity, expose patriarchy, and offer an alternative to the dominant role of motherhood for women. This failure eventually hurt the FSLN during the 1990 election, when Chamorro and the UNO capitalized on the politicized image of motherhood, legitimizing Chamorro's candidacy.

AMNLAE's second major problem was its lack of resources. Dependent on Sandinista largess, it could not mobilize resources as it saw fit. This was clearest with its organizational structure, which women found alienating. Although AMNLAE was aware of the problem, it could not reorganize itself horizontally. The best it could do was streamline its hierarchy. However, even that restructuring proved ineffectual. Under the guidance of Tijerino, the organizational structure was slowly evolving to a more horizontal, alliance-based movement to achieve common goals.

The final problem that AMNLAE had between 1985 and 1990 was the lack of a focused goal. Its goal was the general emancipation of women within the context of the Nicaraguan revolution, simply too broad a task around which to organize. A goal is an organization's locus of conflict, yet AMNLAE's conflict was primarily with the FSLN and its control over AMNLAE rather than with patriarchy. Thus, its locus of conflict and its focused goal excluded rather than mirrored each other.

Despite its lack of horizontal structure, focused goals, and autonomous identity, AMNLAE was remarkably successful in accomplishing as much as it did. AMNLAE consistently demonstrated that it could organize women around campaigns and issues, train new staff, pinpoint problems, and extend itself into new regions.[9] These skills and the knowledge gained about how to organize a social movement were used by the semiautonomous women's movement in the mid to late 1980s. AMNLAE also taught women the value of autonomy from partisan politics, a lesson also used by both the semiautonomous and autonomous women's movements. What began with such promise in 1979 and what continued to show potential through the 1980s dwindled into a cross that AMNLAE still bore as the century ended.

AMNALE's failure spurred frustrated women to search for alternative organizations. Initially, however, it was the decline in economic productivity that led the FSLN to actively promote new women's groups. As corporatism weakened due to the 1986 constitution, the space for groups to operate semiautonomously widened. CONAPRO H-M women's secretariat was considerably more critical of the FSLN than was the women's secretariat of the ATC. With greater autonomy came a clearer definition of women's identity. As was evident from Vargas's speech, CONAPRO H-M had a much clearer understanding of its relationship to Sandinismo, history, the state, and equality than did the ATC women's secretariat.

Semiautonomous women's groups can be best understood as a hybrid phenomenon of internal party insurgency and identity-based social movement organization. Groups such as CONAPRO H-M women's secretariat performed like identity-based social movement groups by consciously creating an identity for themselves. That identity was based on shared experiences of women's reality, which were then extended into an analysis of the broader forces that worked against women. This meant that the identity was not overtly political but, rather, integrated public criticisms with private concerns.

Identity was created through a reflective process in groups trying to understand the nature of the problems women were confronting. This process turned group participation into an identity (Melucci 1989, 35). These groups used broad Sandinista concepts such as equality, freedom, and human rights to criticize patriarchy. Yet these groups operated under the protective shield of the Party. The ideas may have been broadly Sandinista, but the Party did not explicitly outline the content of the new women's groups. This space of freedom allowed the new women's groups to define themselves as they saw fit. They created an identity that was Sandinista in tone and content but not dictated by the Party. This identity was then used to mobilize resources.

The strategy of creating identity was an innovative technique that characterized the semiautonomous women's groups. According to Tarrow, innovative techniques of mobilization also characterize groups engaged in a cycle of protest. According to Tilly (1978), these techniques can then become part of the strategic knowledge of women activists and used widely. This certainly was the case with identity; the mechanism by which it was created was replicated extensively in the rest of the decade and into the next one as well.

Another innovation of the semiautonomous women's organizations was their decision-making mechanism. It began with the ATC women's secretariat, when the leadership in 1984 approached the rank and file to request priorities and needs. The frank discussion that this method generated and the success of the ATC women's secretariat in attaining its goals led many groups to copy its mechanism. AMNLAE used it in 1985 to prepare for the 1986 constitutional negotiations and in 1987 for the Second Assembly. It was used again in 1991 when the autonomous women's movement first began mobilizing. The method entered the repertoire of mobilization strategies available to women activists.

The final innovation practiced by the semiautonomous women's groups was a more horizontal internal structure organized through alliances. This internal structure matched its semiautonomous identity. CONAPRO H-M in particular demonstrated how to produce an effective social movement organization with a horizontal internal structure. This knowledge would also be used by the autonomous women's groups in the 1990s.

These innovations in strategies reflect the fact that the mobilization of resources is not merely a calculation of what is externally available for a social movement organization to utilize but also that a social movement organization must recognize and define resources and, thus, that resources can also be in the eye of the beholder. The semiautonomous women's groups demonstrated with equal clarity that the strategies used to mobilize resources affect the identity created.

The conflict that each group had was also its goal. That conflict/goal was very focused. It ranged from specific problems with the Sandinista Agrarian Reform Program to critiques of the new constitution. Criticizing patriarchy was a secondary but broader theme of the semiautonomous women's groups.

The semiautonomous women's organizations altered women's perspectives of their lives and society's understanding of patriarchy. Semiautonomous organizations, such as CONAPRO H-M and the ATC women's secretariats, were able to radicalize and politicize issues beyond what the government wanted and to keep alive issues long after the government had tried to shut the discussions down. They forced the government into formal decision-making and activated resolution mechanisms on issues that the government would have preferred not to deal with. This pressure by semiautonomous organizations was most obvious with the inability of the government to control discussion on the issue of abortion and reproductive rights. CONAPRO H-M kept the issue in the public eye, influencing the democratic conservative party to raise the issue in the National Assembly in 1988 (Morgan 1990, 77). Although the government refused to deal with the issue before the 1990 election, the president of the National Assembly did acknowledge that women's mortality from illegal, botched abortions necessitated the reexamination of the legalization of abortion in the next legislative assembly (ibid., 80). However, the FSLN ultimately did not change its stance.

Other semiautonomous social movement organizations built on the breakthroughs made by the ATC women's secretariat and utilized new techniques of mobilizing resources. Tarrow, in his research on Italian internal party insurgency, documented the same phenomenon. Some of the other state-controlled unions and semiautonomous organizations (e.g., UNAG) were content to simply absorb the connections made between economic productivity and the sexual division of labor. Others, such as CONAPRO H-M, built on the achievements of the ATC women's secretariat to broaden the understanding of gender and inequality.

Tarrow also suggests that the insurgent elements could work jointly to push through reforms to benefit both the government and the insurgent groups. This is what happened with the Nicaraguan semiautonomous women's groups. The groups built on one another and created alliances to reinforce their positions. The government gained by appeasing the disenchanted and critical activists while still controlling the extent of the reforms.

There are natural limits to the gains that a party insurgency can make, because it must operate within an existing system. The identity of the semiautonomous women's groups was still too closely tied to the FSLN to allow criticism of the basic structure or to allow too harsh a criticism of Sandinista policy. For example, the peasant women's group did not criticize the agrarian reform program, and the legal rights group did not criticize the Sandinistas' 1990 sexist campaign strategy. Once the reforms were made, the insurgents are supposed to be reabsorbed into the mainstream of the party, the purpose of the insurgency having been achieved. The rise and fall of insurgent groups should not be considered a failure but rather a natural evolution. The semiautonomous groups, however, refused to devolve or be reabsorbed into the Party. The ethic of a semiautonomous identity meant that social movement organizations refused to reintegrate themselves into the FSLN.

The semiautonomous women's groups paved the way for the creation of fully autonomous women's groups in the 1990s by clearly showing the limits of autonomy, broadening the space within which women could organize (Síu Bermúdez 1993, 7), creating a semiautonomous identity, and educating women on techniques of resource mobilization.

PART 2

The Post-Sandinista Women's Movement, 1990–1996

CHAPTER 6

Under Chamorro, 1990–1996

ALL SOCIAL MOVEMENTS RESPOND TO, are shaped by, and focus their goals on the external environment. Therefore, to understand the women's movement during any one time period requires an analysis of its external environment, its field of conflict (Melucci 1996, 4). During the Sandinista years, the government constrained the Nicaraguan women's movement by controlling the goals, resources, and identity of the women's movement. Simultaneously, the FSLN offered women the dazzling possibility of equality, freedom, and power. These two factors of constraints and opportunities became the women's movement's field of conflict, the external environment affecting it.

The Chamorro government equally affected the Nicaraguan women's movement, although more through constraints than through opportunities. The Chamorro government privatized the economy through a harsh neoliberal economic program. Furthermore, the Chamorro government implemented a number of policies aimed at returning women to a more traditional status. The combination of economic liberalization and the introduction of policies influenced by strong Catholic values eliminated many of women's options. The increase in absolute and relative poverty and unemployment combined with a loss of reproductive freedoms created extensive hardships for the vast majority of women in Nicaragua. These factors made the government an easy target for the women's movement, although the increase in women's economic hardship made it problematic for women to organize due to lack of free time and difficulties leaving the home, as well as the erosion of the legitimacy of women's rights due to the triumph of neoconservative values with its female ideal

107

of motherhood. Nonetheless, the women's movement became so influential that it was able to force the Chamorro government to make at least rhetorical promises, to cooperate with the women's movement internationally, and to pass some important pieces of legislation concerning women. This chapter will focus on the macropolitical and macroeconomic trends of the Chamorro mandate and how they affected women.

The political/economic structure of Nicaragua changed as profoundly under Violeta Chamorro and her coalition government, the UNO, as it had under the FSLN. While the intent of the incoming government may have been to create a neoliberal state with sufficient macroeconomic and macropolitical stability to accumulate capital, the reality of post-Sandinista Nicaragua made that task daunting (Robinson 1994, 251). Chamorro's coalition was unable to maintain its unity, forcing Chamorro and her prime minister, Antonio Lacayo, to create an alliance with the single largest party elected to the National Assembly, the FSLN. In July 1990, workers and peasants staged a three-day national strike, which threatened to topple the government. In August, the Transition Protocol was announced. It stipulated that the FSLN would continue to control the army and the police and that the incoming government would respect the 1986 constitution. Also in August 1990, the government publicly negotiated an economic *concertación* with the FSLN party, Sandinista unions and groups, and business organizations. In exchange for protection of the Sandinista agrarian reform and some worker-owned businesses, the Sandinistas agreed to keep civil unrest to a minimum while the economy was undergoing its structural adjustment. This alliance of Chamorro supporters and Sandinistas, which was to deepen throughout the following four years, was dubbed "cogovernment" by supporters and critics alike. The alliance crumbled in 1994 as the FSLN officially distanced itself from the Chamorro government in preparation for the 1996 election. Few bills were passed in the remaining two years of the Chamorro mandate. "Effective governance of the country stopped" (Dijkstra 1996, 10).

Cogoverning officially ended at the May 1994 Sandinista Extra-Ordinary Conference. Convened to resolve the split within the FSLN between those who supported the cogoverning and the concomitant structural adjustment policy and those who wanted to agitate against the UNO and its structural adjustment policy (Patterson 1997, 222), the conference was also to resolve complaints of the FSLN's dictatorial style. The conference thus saw the Sandinista's first democratic election for party leadership. Although Daniel Ortega, the Nicaraguan president between 1979 and 1990 easily won, the election divided the party. The winning group then purged the FSLN of all those who had stood against Ortega and those who had been critical of his platform. By January 1995, disenchanted and purged Sandinistas created a breakaway party called the Sandinista Renewalist Movement (MRS). Although it had the backing of many intellectuals and top Sandinistas, it lacked grass-roots support.

Cogoverning did not assist women for the simple reason that the FSLN did not put women's interests on the negotiating table. The Chamorro government, to attain some level of political harmony and economic consensus, produced an inclusionary and integrative approach to forming and implementing public policies. Within this process, women's needs were clearly not represented. At the *concertación* negotiations, the FSLN sacrificed women's labor interests to safeguard men's (Wiegersma 1994, 203).

In addition, the FSLN legitimated the undermining of women's labor rights when it refused to support these rights, such as equal pay for equal work, during the rewriting of the labor code, and failed to support the head of the women's secretariat of the Sandinista Workers' Committee (CST), Sandra Ramos. In April 1994, Ramos attempted to protect funds earmarked for women's programs from being diverted to existing programs that did not specifically benefit women. When Ramos attempted to separate the women's secretariat from the control of the CST, she was arrested and accused of absconding with CST funds (*Barricada*, June 17, 1994: 4). The accusation was an attempt to control her and, by extension, the women's secretariat and its money (Jubb 1996, 2; interview Beaudoin). Ramos was later found innocent.

Without an entrée into the governmental structure from their traditional patron, the women's movement had no option but to embrace Chamorro's vision of a liberal democracy with its competitive and confrontational organization of civil society. Cooperation with the government to achieve mutually beneficial ends no longer appeared to be a possibility.

With structural adjustment, there were no mutually beneficial ends. The neoliberal economic policies were harsh. These conditions rapidly eroded the gains that women had achieved under the FSLN. Their standard of living fell, their employment opportunities diminished, and their access to remaining government-funded programs and services was reduced.

When Chamorro took power the economic situation was dire (Arana 1997, 85). Inflation was 13,492 percent, the debt stood at $10 billion (four times the gross domestic product), and underemployment and unemployment was 45 percent (Ocampo 1991, 331; Arana 1997, 86). The Chamorro government implemented a plan to stabilize the Nicaraguan economy by privatizing industries, cutting government expenditures, and imposing monetary stability. The stabilization plan promised to bring hyperinflation to zero within the first hundred days of office by devaluing the Nicaraguan currency 116 percent and then fixing it at parity with the American dollar. After a year, inflation dropped to 865 percent, and the currency was devalued a further 400 percent. In January 1993, it was devalued a further 20 percent and transferred to a crawling peg. Despite devaluations, by 1994 the currency remained overvalued by at least 50 percent, hampering exports. Nonetheless, inflation dropped to 12.4 percent.

The structural adjustment policy also tightened the supply of money, reducing credit from the Central Bank to the commercial banks by 36 percent in 1991 and a further 50 percent in 1993 (*Envío* 12, no. 150 [January 1994]: 7; Dijkstra 1992, 193). Some suggest that these actions adversely affected small and medium-sized producers more than larger ones (Dijkstra 1992, 193; Stahler-Sholk 1997, 91; Babb 1996, 43). The macroeconomic structure was further stabilized by massive foreign aid (Avendaño 1994, 9). Between 1990 and 1994, Nicaragua received more aid per capita than any other developing nation (*Envío* 14, no. 166 [May 1995]: 5). The United States alone transferred $541 million in the first two years of the government (Robinson 1994, 242).

The debt, however, continued to grow at a rate of $520 million per annum, and by 1994 was eight times the gross domestic product (*Central America Report*, December 15, 1994: 4), despite the government's significant reduction of its expenditures. The prices of subsidized goods such as food and electricity were raised to market value. The size of the military was reduced, as was the public workforce (Spalding 1994, 166–69). State-funded medical care was reduced, and the best hospitals were privatized. Prescription medicine was no longer free. Funding for education was reduced at all levels of the school system, and children who attended public schools had to pay tuition, even at the primary level.

None of these measures served to reactivate the economy. The government hoped that liberalizing the economy to allow free-market mechanisms to dominate would promote business. Thus, the structural adjustment policy privatized state companies, which accounted for 30 percent of the country's gross domestic product (Arana 1997, 86); deregulated the economy; ceded control of foreign trade and banking to the private sector; and dropped tariffs from 43 to 15 percent (Dijkstra 1992, 17; Stahler-Sholk 1997, 90). The government encouraged wages to be cut to promote exports and, in 1994, reformed the Labor Code to "flexibilize" labor, that is, to erode labor rights (Stahler-Sholk 1997, 92).

The economy did not show any growth until 1994. Between 1990 and 1994, per capita gross domestic product contracted 12.4 percent, with a cumulative growth rate over the same period of 1.9 percent (*Envío* 13, no. 151–52 [February/March 1994]: 6). The increase in exports in 1994 came primarily from an unanticipated frost in Brazil, which improved the terms of trade for Nicaraguan coffee (Stahler-Sholk 1997, 94). Exports increased again in 1995, raising per capita gross domestic product for the first time since the revolution. However, underemployment and unemployment still pushed 70 percent (Arana 1997, 92). If the economy does continue to grow, as some independent economists have predicted, then the benefits will likely not be distributed through the population. With the economic restructuring, "the Chamorro administration's naive and uncritical faith in market forces and its general disregard for market imperfections injected a bias which—by default, if not by design—favoured large business and strengthened the positions of monopolies, oligopolies, and the business elite of the government" (Arana 1997, 84).

In particular, the structural adjustment policy eroded women's standard of living. "Typically of orthodox adjustment, the distributive impact fell heavily on women" (Stahler-Sholk 1995, 9). Of female-headed households, 72.5 percent were below the poverty line, compared to 67.5 percent of male-headed households; 81.3 percent of female-headed households reduced food consumption, compared to 75 percent of male-headed households (Fernandez 1996, 56).

Unemployment and underemployment as a result of the structural adjustment policy rose to 45 percent in 1992 and 60 percent in 1994, with formal sector employment dropping 18 percent between 1990 and 1992 alone (Babb 1996, 32). Unemployment and underemployment rates for women were higher than for men (Stahler-Sholk 1995, 10; Metoyer 1995, 19) because women dominated public sector employment (Collinson 1990, 32). Up to 70 percent of government layoffs were women (Wiegersma 1994, 201). In addition, the recession also forced women from private-sector employment because they were the first to be laid off (Fernández 1996, 52).

Nonetheless, women had to work to feed their families. It was estimated that 65 percent of urban families and 82.6 percent of rural households were headed by women (ibid., 55). Women responded to the economic crisis by actively searching for alternative means of earning money. In comparison, men adopted a posture of resignation to or avoidance of the family crisis (ibid., 56). Thus, even with a male head of the household, there was no guarantee that the family would be supported.

Women were the hardest hit from not only the economic downturn but also reduced social infrastructure spending. Social services that predominantly affected women were reduced or withdrawn. Government-sponsored training initiatives and community programs, such as day care, were eliminated. The lack of training left women unable to alter their skill level, trapping them in poverty. The lack of community programs increased women's child-care concerns and reduced their ability to leave the home in search of paid employment.

In addition to the economic restrictions, women also had to overcome the attempt by the Chamorro government to return women to the home, to define themselves within the family, and to be cared for by men. The value of women's work, whether inside or outside the home, was undermined. Work outside the home would be viewed, at best, as supplementary and nonessential both to the maintenance of the family and to the personal development of the woman, and, at worst, unfeminine and detrimental to the family. Sexual relations were to be heterosexual and within a Church-consecrated union, clearly defining the ideal as both natural and moral. Through public policy, Chamorro's government restricted women's access to reproductive control. The birthrate, maternal mortality, and illegally induced abortions increased, compounding the difficulties women faced in escaping poverty.

These neoconservative values were articulated and implemented through state mechanisms such as law and education, through the Catholic Church in a complementary campaign, and through the media. Combined, the impact on women was a decrease in the legitimacy of women acting in the political arena, demanding women's rights.

First, the government used the educational system to inculcate the new ideal. In 1990, the government removed primary school texts donated by the Norwegian government, apparently because the texts included information on the human reproductive system and sexuality. The books were replaced with ones that presented "family values," that is, nuclear families with mothers working without compensation within the home and fathers working at salaried jobs. The new texts emphasized consecrated marriage as the only form of marriage, the Ten Commandments, and the sin of abortion (Kampwirth 1996, 73). This ideological shift to lay Catholicism was recognized as such by an official at the Ministry of Education who explained that the goal was to open the educational system to Christian values (ibid., 83).

Law was the government's second mechanism to encourage its feminine ideal. In 1991, even though female-headed households comprised 65 percent of urban families and 83 percent of rural families (Fernández 1995, 7), the government opposed a law enforcing paternal child support. In 1992, an odd alliance of Sandinista and laissez faire feminists did move the legislation through the National Assembly, despite the resistance of the Chamorro government (Kampwirth 1996, 76–77).

In 1992, the government reformed the Penal Code through Law 150, which regulated previously unregulated sexual behavior. Law 150 created definitions of licit (moral and legal) and illicit (immoral and illegal) sexual behavior. Only sexual activity identified with procreation was sanctioned because the will to procreate was inherent in every species and thus was natural. What was natural was moral and hence legal. Sexual activity not identified with procreation was unnatural and hence immoral and illegal. In such a way, "morality becomes an important mechanism for disciplining and regulating the social" (Alexander 1991, 133).

With Law 150, rape became a public crime for the first time. This meant that the state could charge an alleged rapist rather than leaving the victim to sue for private redress. The new legal concept of rape nonetheless protected the inviolacy of the family and the reproductive basis of the male-female relationship. Thus, a man could not be charged with rap-

113

ing his wife, including his common-law wife, and rape victims who be-came pregnant as a result of rape were not allowed an abortion. Instead, the pregnant victim was forced to maintain contact with her rapist in or-der to receive child-support payments (Vega Vargas 1993). Changing the legal status of rape allowed the government to define the meaning of vio-lence against women as existing only outside the family, and of second-ary importance to procreation.

The primacy of procreation as the basis for sexual relations was fur-ther emphasized with the criminalization of homosexuality for the first time in Nicaraguan history. When the clause banning sodomy was taken to the Supreme Court on the basis that it contravened the constitution, the justices decided that the entire purpose of the sex act was to procreate and the purpose of procreation was to increase the population and thereby to build a state. Therefore, a sex act that could not include the possibility of procreation was a crime against the state (Supreme Court decision #18, March 7, 1994, II:iii). Since crimes against the state were ille-gal, legislation banning homosexuality was constitutional. The Supreme Court decision clearly articulated the intersection of the state definition of "natural" with the state definition of legal.

Control over sexuality was heightened as well by including, again for the first time, a legal punishment for procuring or performing abortions. Doctors and midwives were explicitly denied the legal right to provide an abortion (*Barricada International* 359, no. 3 [March 1993]: 19).

In Law 150, the Chamorro government further articulated the ideal of the heterosexual family by not modernizing aspects of the original penal law that supported a paternalistic and heterosexual family. For example, a woman was still defined as belonging to her parents while she was sin-gle. Once married, she became the possession of her husband. The bill also refused to criminalize spousal abuse, which remained a private or civil crime (Blandón 1994, 99).

The newness of the discourse was reflected in the National Assembly by the heated debate over the government's definitions of adultery and morality, and over the illegality of abortion and homosexuality. The bill narrowly passed by a vote of 43 to 41 (*Central America Report* 19, no. 23 [June 26, 1992]: 4), suggesting that, within the National Assembly, there was no consensus about the new moral code.[1]

After Law 150 was passed, the government moved against abortion clinics that insisted on staying open, jailing a doctor and a woman for respectively performing and receiving an abortion (Agurto Vílchez 1992, 14).

The government used the legal system to create a new morality again in 1994 when it codified the heterosexual nuclear family as the legal ideal in the Family Law (*La Prensa*, June 21, 1994, 16).

The traditional Catholic Church supported these legal changes with a complementary campaign to strengthen the heterosexual nuclear family and to ban birth control and abortion. The traditional Catholic Church in Nicaragua, politically active since the mid-1970s, had become increasingly concerned with sexuality (Lernoux 1989, 368–69). The Church legitimized the government's public policies, serving as the government's third mechanism for creating and solidifying its stance toward women.

The connection between the president and the Catholic Church's cardinal has been so close that "she is perceived by some as a surrogate for the Cardinal Miguel Obando y Bravo" (Saint-Germain 1993, 91). In addition, many of the president's top advisors belonged to the neoconservative sect, the Charismatics (McVey 1995, 191; Lernoux 1989, 400–401).

Bolstered by its close connection to the government and the pope's designation of 1994 as the "Year of the Family," the Catholic Church in an "unprecedented move" organized a march for life on the National Assembly to strengthen laws against abortion (*Central America Report*, July 1, 1994: 4). The Church organized it as a celebration of Father's Day, the significance of which was not lost on the population: if abortion and contraceptives were legal, then men could not be fathers. If men were not fathers, then men could not be men (Fauné 1994). The Church "intensified its campaign against abortion and 'unacceptable' campaigns which encouraged the use of contraceptives" (*Central America Report*, July 1, 1994: 4).

The alliance between the government and the Church to change legal definitions of moral and licit behavior had grown so strong that by 1994 the minister of education, Umberto Belli, attempted to overturn Article 124 of the constitution, which guaranteed a secular public education, and to replace it with one that Catholicized the public school system. Although the Catholic Church again mobilized a march in support of Belli, the outcry against Belli's proposal was so vociferous and widespread that the president abandoned it (*El Nuevo Diario*, May 20, 1994: 1, 5).

Finally, the Chamorro government used its own newspaper, *La Prensa*, to promulgate the new understanding of women's roles in Nicaragua. Owned by the Chamorro family, *La Prensa* was one of three dailies. A respected voice for dissent during the 1970s and 1980s, in the 1990s the newspaper became the voice of the government. An editorial in *La Prensa* on International Women's Day issued this clarion call: "The most special, important, and urgent place that a woman should occupy today and in the future is the family, the fundamental base of society. The woman is the fundamental axis of the family, its formative base, and its stability, and it is the family that is the nucleus of society and the nation" (March 8, 1994: 10). In a signed editorial, Christina Chamorro, editor of *La Prensa*, daughter of Violeta Chamorro, and wife of Antonio Lacayo, the prime minister, also supported the concept that the family was the core of society and that the family was the woman's responsibility (ibid.).

The government's public policies resulted in a reduced role for women in the public sphere. Women were encouraged to return to the home and to be mothers, wherein their greatest value lay. Schools taught this role, laws codified it, the Catholic Church demanded it, and one of the three major dailies promulgated it. State, social, and bureaucratic means articulated and enforced an ideology of gender roles so that motherhood and female passivity were reified. Women were increasingly isolated in the home with a declined status to their work in the domestic sphere. This shift in women's status was justified through evoking Christian morality and women's "natural" predisposition to maternal care, and through controlling and reducing women's reproductive options. "Thus, there are a number of forces in play that try to limit the participation of women in public spaces" (Babb 1993, 17).

One result of these government initiatives about women was a decrease in health standards. Health care spending was slashed in half from the 1989 level of $137 million to $67 million (the average for the years 1991–1993). In per capita terms it dropped from forty-five dollars in 1990 to fourteen dollars in 1992 (*NICCA Bulletin*, January/March, 1993: 7). "Few studies have been published to date which examine trends in women's health since the UNO government came to power, but those that do exist point to a general deterioration in the quality and extent of public health services available to women" (Morgan 1995, 67).

Despite the general decline in health care, the greatest killer of women remained in the area of reproductive health. According to the Nicaraguan Ministry of Health (MINSA), for one thousand live births there are 160 maternal deaths (Ministry of Social Action 1997, 9).[2] However, that official number is dubious.[3] Statistics on maternal mortality are suspect because of the lack of reporting. It has been estimated that only 47 percent of pregnant women were registered by the health-care system (Pizarro 1993, 3), meaning that less than half the births and deaths were known to the system. However, it was reported that every thirty-six hours, a woman died as a result of being pregnant (*Barricada*, May 27, 1994, 4). Women died from lack of proper health care before, during, or after a pregnancy. Women had to pay for the use of gloves, medicine, instruments, food, and sheets, yet many lacked the money to do so. Thus, there was a high degree of septic infections (interview Ríos).

In addition to poor maternal health care, women also died from an increase in the number of abortions. This also stemmed from economic liberalization and conservative Catholicism. Seventy-five percent of women who aborted said they did so because they lacked the money to raise children (*La Gente* 227 [July 29, 1994]: 4). Women, however, eschewed therapeutic abortions because of the Chamorro government's strong religious pronouncements and the enforcement of antiabortion laws; women's requests for therapeutic abortions dropped to 3 percent of requests made in 1989 (Morgan 1995, 70). Instead, women aborted outside the health care system, risking their own health. One third of all maternal deaths, it has been estimated, were from self-induced abortions, although again it was difficult to confirm this because the fear and shame of discovery ran high (Wessel 1991, 541–42).[4]

Despite these conditions, women continued to get pregnant. There was little information about birth control and even less access to it (Ministry of Social Action 1997, 7). According to one study, only 12 percent of sexually active women of fertile age practiced birth control, including the rhythm method (Pizarro 1993, 4). Yet one 1992–1993 study showed that 72 percent of married women did not want to get pregnant and 55 percent of women who already had one child did not want more, with that statistic rising to 67 percent for women without education (Ministry of Social Action 1997, 7). The government's response to women's demands for birth control was to advocate abstinence (*Barricada*, February 6, 1994, 7).

In addition to maternal mortality, the result of unfettered procreation was a population growth rate of 3.2 percent per annum. This was the highest birthrate in Latin America and one of the highest in the world (Fondo de las Naciones Unidas 1993, 15). Large families further impoverished the Nicaraguans.

The implementation of Catholic values as public policy changed the nature of state intervention in the private lives of its female citizens. Although the Sandinista government interfered for its own purposes, its intervention consisted of reforming the social structure to increase the economic and political options available to women. Ironically, the Sandinistas offered women so much freedom that they chaffed at the restrictions imposed on their own organization. In comparison, state intervention under Chamorro was subtler. The state did not directly manipulate civil society organizations, leaving the impression of a civil society autonomous from state machinations. Yet the options for women narrowed. The state placed a primacy on women's procreative role within the home, and then reinforced this role through the educational system, penal reform, Supreme Court directives, health care cutbacks, and religious mobilization. The number of paths from which women could freely choose was reduced to one as the state shepherded women into the private sphere of child-rearing.

Simultaneously, women were propelled from the home and into the marketplace in order to feed their families. Economic liberalization reduced the standard of living and economic options of most Nicaraguans, but it especially affected women. Neoliberalism also reduced access to the mechanisms through which poor women improved their standard of living: education, training, and social services such as day care and health care. Thus, women's opportunities to alter their economic position were also reduced. This reduction of women's economic position meant that women had insufficient money to afford the private health care necessary to replace public maternal health care. This had deadly consequences for women, especially given that the government limited their control over their own reproduction. In this context of economic liberalization and neoconservatism, women's options and rights, both economic and personal, were significantly constrained. Indeed, the government's state and public policies threatened the very physical survival of women.

The women's movement, now based in civil society, was able to target the government as its locus of conflict with the focused goal of over- turning specific policies and laws. The women's movement was able to expose the contradictions inherent in the government policies and in so doing undermine the persuasive power and legitimacy of Chamorro's ideology. Slowly, the Chamorro government allowed for dialog with the women's movement, culminating in 1996 with the passing of Law 230, which reformed the penal code to criminalize domestic violence.

In 1993, the Chamorro government gave the defunct Sandinista women's organization, the Nicaraguan Institute for Research on Women (INIM), a new name, the Nicaraguan Institute for Women, leaving the fa- miliar acronym unchanged. With the redubbing came a new mandate to organize with the women's movement to reconcile it with Chamorro's ideal of the family. INIM was to "promote the participation of Nicara- guan women in conditions of equality of opportunity within the eco- nomic, social, cultural, and political development of the country" (Insti- tuto Nicaragüense de la Mujer 1996, 21). In 1994, it held consultations with sixty-two women's groups to prioritize actions and issues. The final draft of the plan defined patriarchy, sexism, and gender stereotypes, and set the goal of reducing inequality in three distinct areas: education, work, and violence. Nonetheless, INIM has been accused of being under- funded, of having nonfeminist and inexperienced leadership, and of try- ing to coopt the growing women's movement by training non-Sandinista women leaders and by refusing to discuss the issue of power—all the while currying for international legitimacy (Jubb 1997, 13–14).

While this might be a harsh indictment, INIM's new level of activity did coincide with the emergence of a powerful and articulate autono- mous women's movement and began the shift in Chamorro's political approach to women. On the one hand, Chamorro promulgated an ideal of motherhood through indirect and direct means. On the other hand, she slowly opened spaces for negotiation with the women's movement, both domestically and internationally.

The best example of the complexity of Chamorro's approach was with the issue of violence against women. Two prominent ex-Sandinistas, María Lourdes Bolaños, the leader of *Ixchen*, and Aminta Granera, the ex- ecutive secretary of the police, approached Chamorro in 1992 and sug- gested implementing Women and Children's Police Stations as a polic- ing/social services response to violence against women and children.

Chamorro agreed, so long as INIM was the head of the organizational structure and controlled the funding. The first such station was established in 1993, and the concept spread throughout Nicaragua during the next four years. By the time Chamorro finished her mandate in 1996, there were ten Women and Children's Police Stations.

The reality of how the stations functioned belied their seeming success. First, 42 percent of women did not return to the station after initially contacting it. Second, of the women who did return, approximately half opted for "extrajudicial" settlements, in which both parties agreed to get along better. These settlements legitimized the prevalent idea that women are at least partially responsible for the violence committed against them (Jubb 1997, 18). Furthermore, there was no cooperation with the women's movement's organization, the Women Against Violence Network, until 1996. Finally, a social worker within the pilot station admitted that they encouraged women to stay away from the court system (interview Palacios 1994), a policy that supported Chamorro's structural adjustment policy and its reduced spending on social infrastructure, as well as reinforced the ideology that domestic violence was a private issue.[5]

The limit to which the Chamorro government was prepared to negotiate with the women's movement was brought into sharp relief with the 1994 Cairo Conference on Population and Development. The Ministry of Social Action (MAS) was charged with organizing the Nicaraguan government's stance in cooperation with the women's movement, specifically with an ad hoc network, Women's Voices, of thirty different women representing seventy-five women's groups and NGOs (*ICPD Watch*, September 10, 1994: 1). As women's reproductive rights became more notable in the draft document, and as the forces against those rights became more vocal, especially the Vatican, the Chamorro government began to back away from its commitment. At the final preparatory meeting in New York, the government sent the minister of education, Umberto Belli, a member of the Catholic right. Belli informed the assembly that maternal mortality was "natural" to the female condition as ordained by God (*El Nuevo Diario*, June 19, 1994: 1). The international outcry was such that Belli was recalled early. However, the government's machinations about the Cairo Conference reached its apogee at the conference itself, when William Baez, the minister of social action, was summarily withdrawn from the conference and sent to Belgium and a representative of an antiabortion Catholic civil society organization took his place as the government's representative. With the support of the Holy See and a handful of Central American and Islamic states, she then refused to sign any clauses of the Cairo document that referred to women's reproductive rights. This switch in the government's approach shocked Women's Voices and created some animosity.

INIM, organizing for the Fourth Congress on the World's Women 1995 sponsored by the United Nations, popularly known as the Beijing Conference on Women, had to overcome the women's movement's distrust of the government. The Beijing Conference was less controversial than the Cairo Conference, both domestically and internationally, because Beijing was seen as being about women in general whereas Cairo was interpreted as being about reproduction. The international realignment allowed the Chamorro government to support a space for negotiation with the women's movement about women's role in society. Auxiliadora Matus was the director of INIM at the time, and many credit her fine leadership as an important factor in the success of negotiating an agreement with the representatives from twenty-two civil society organizations (Feingold 1998). Although there were divisions over the word *gender* (which was imputed to mean lesbianism) and over issues such as abortion and reproductive health, there were fewer contradictions between the women's movement's demands and those of INIM than with the Cairo Conference and fewer than within other countries. Also, Nicaragua was one of the few countries that included civil society organization's members in the government's official delegation. Matus claimed that the conflicts lay not with the Chamorro government per se but rather with conservative civil society organizations and the Catholic Church. Matus was being willfully naive. There is a strong correlation between the rise of neoliberalism and of state-sanctioned fundamentalism. The two ideologies, one economic, one sociopolitical, legitimated and reinforced each other (Isbester 1998). Together, neoliberalism and conservative Catholicism made such an effective tag team that only with difficulty was the women's movement able to slow it.

The delegation signed the Beijing document, although it also supported the bracketing of the word *gender* throughout.[6] Unlike the Cairo Conference, however, the government's actions were of no surprise to the rest of the delegation, and the involvement of the women's movement in the delegation broke Nicaragua's alliance with the other conservative Central American states (notably Honduras and Guatemala) and the Holy See (interview Blandón).

The Beijing process was perhaps the highlight of the government's interaction with women. According to Matus, "We [INIM] were able to reach a type of synergy between the NGOs and the government" (interview). Women who participated in the Beijing process felt that one of its notable achievements was sharing information and strategies with the government in a space that the government itself initiated. It must be noted, however, that neither the Chamorro government nor the next government of Alemán implemented a single clause of the Beijing document. With the women's movement too distracted by the upcoming 1996 election and too exhausted from organizing for international conferences to lobby for implementation, the Chamorro government was not held accountable (interviews Matus; Pasos; Blandón). Thus, the prevalent optimism that surrounds the Beijing Conference on Women must be tempered by the hard reality that Nicaraguan women's lives were not affected in either the short or long term.[7]

This situation of profound commitments made internationally while little was done domestically was reinforced by the 1994 Miami Summit of the Americas, where Chamorro was much lauded for introducing into the draft a text promoting women's political rights and ability to increase earnings, protection against violence, and international aid for women's issues. "But the summit plan of action set no targets and established no monitors, nor did it ensure women's reproductive rights." It also lacked adequate funding, clear priorities, and follow-up (Feinberg 1997, 121, 171). According to the International Center for Research on Women, the text made an impression mostly at the level of statements rather than of action (ibid., 171).

Due to the complexity of the Chamorro government's approach to women, it would be unfair to consider her ideology nothing but a papal-induced backlash against Sandinismo. Indeed, the range of approaches that the Chamorro government undertook from the 1990 election campaign to 1996 obscures the impact on women her government actually had. At best, INIM was empowered, halfway through Chamorro's term in office, to act for the government both locally and internationally and did so through cooperating with civil society, strengthening both in the process. Some progressive laws and programs, almost exclusively to do with violence against women, were initiated during Chamorro's tenure. On balance, however, the Chamorro government was a setback for women's status and for the women's movement. The government's public policies that explicitly addressed women idealized motherhood and the nuclear family, refused women their reproductive rights, and reduced information about and access to women's rights. Implicitly, many public policies were even more damaging to women. The cutbacks to education, health care, and social services severely constrained women's options, livelihood, and even survival. The rise of the Catholic Church to a position of political influence created an atmosphere hostile to women's equality. In regards to the women's movement, the Chamorro government guaranteed that its ideology of the housewife and mother would make a clear target for sustained criticism, thereby assisting the women's movement to develop an equally clear alternative; her public policies made a useful foil against which to mobilize; and her support for developing spaces within civil society helped to integrate a diverse and decentralized social movement.

CHAPTER 7

Nadir and Rebirth, 1990–1992

THE RESULTS OF THE 1990 ELECTION WERE UNANTICIPATED. The women's movement performed ignobly in the immediate aftermath of the Sandinista electoral loss, unable to quickly respond to the change in government. Although the women's movement would eventually reinvent itself to tackle the Chamorro government, it first had to go through the painful process of evaluation and restructuring. The evaluation focused on critically understanding the history and meaning of the relationship between the women's movement and the FSLN. The understanding that individual women and groups reached dictated their approach toward the restructuring of their movement. Unfortunately, there was little agreement, and feelings ran high. The depth of animosity between members and groups of the women's movement fragmented it. During this period, the women's movement was sufficiently disarrayed that it was as ineffectual and unproductive as a social movement can be.

The women's movement had lost its Sandinista identity and support. Some of the women's groups wished to retain both that identity and support. Others did not. This sparked an internecine battle over the fundamental direction of the women's movement. It was resolved in favor of an identity fully autonomous for the first time from the FSLN.

While the conflict over identity dominated the agenda, women's groups did manage to choose their own goals. However, due to the loss of leadership and poor choices made by the remaining leaders, frequently the goals were inappropriate and ultimately destructive. Other women's groups weathered well the internecine conflict by focusing on the issue of health rather than on affiliation with the FSLN. However, most of this latter grouping lacked experienced leadership and the knowledge of how to organize themselves into a coherent movement.

There was a loss of other resources besides leadership skills. Without the support of the FSLN, it was difficult to obtain funds. Some resources, such as membership, were not well mobilized during 1990–1991, which weakened the movement overall. Other resources, such as the media and the FSLN's approach to the women's movement, were mostly outside the control of the women's movement. Finally, some resources, such as the use of public spaces and the organization of the autonomous women's groups, worked in favor of one side of the women's movement and against the other. Of course, the mobilization of resources involved discussions of identity, making it difficult to separate the two issues.

The internecine conflict resulted in a loss of membership in established groups, especially the women's secretariats of the unions, redubbed "mixed" organizations because they had both male and female membership. The shrinking of mixed organizations was mostly due to increased unemployment, as in the case of the Sandinista Workers' Committee (CST), which lost half of its membership between 1990 and 1995 from this cause (Picado and O'Grady 1995). The ATC women's secretariat lost 7,000 of its 15,000 women, and of the remaining 8,000, 5,000 had only temporary employment (*Envío* 10, no. 119 [June 1991]: 40). By 1992, nearly 80 percent of the female members who had been in the union in 1989 were unemployed (Rusmore 1994, 13).

Leaders of the women's movement were incapable of responding to the membership decline due to their inability to cope with the rapid change from the Sandinista to the Chamorro governments. All of the leaders of the women's movement had been Sandinistas, and many had joined well before the revolution. There was a profound process of adjustment following the loss of power after the election. Dora María Téllez, the famous Commander Two of the National Palace takeover in 1978 and the ex–minister of health, spoke about the confusion and the impotence created by losing power.

So on April 26 [the day after the new government assumed office], which was a work day, I got up, I showered, I dressed, and then I sat in a chair. I read the morning paper. And that's when the other part of it hit me. Here there were all these problems, but I no longer had the power to do anything about them. What resources there were, were in someone else's hands now. Even finding out what's going on by reading the paper: that wasn't something I was used to. So that was what it was like for me, a total and absolute change. Now all of a sudden we were on our own, people who were accustomed to our party telling us, "You do this. . . . You go there. . ." We didn't know how to think about what we might want, as individuals. That whole internal process was very difficult. (quoted in Randall 1994, 253–54)

Amparo Rubio, captain in the Sandinista army and leader of Frente Nora Astorga, the first female-only guerrilla group, had an equally shocked reaction: "My first reaction was to look for a gun. I went running to look for my rifle. I was full of rage. Then I started crying. Everything I had given: my youth, my sacrifices. It was a fatal blow, a horrible fatal blow. . . . For me it was like my world had ended" (McVey 1995, 186).

Even if leaders could cope, some of them shifted their focus. For example, CONAPRO H-M women's secretariat, the foremost proponent of women's rights in the late 1980s, effectively disappeared because it lost its leader, Milú Vargas. She was elected as an alternate representative to the National Assembly and assigned as legal advisor to the Ministry of Health. Technically speaking, CONAPRO H-M women's secretariat continued to operate. Every two years there was to be a general meeting to draw up an agenda, but there was no agenda at the general meeting in February 1991. Amanda Lorio was elected secretary of women's issues for a three-year mandate (*Hoja Informativa*, February 20, 1991, 9). However, she did not put in an appearance at CONAPRO H-M for some time, and her assistant had no idea where Lorio was and doubted that she would know in the foreseeable future. Members of CONAPRO H-M women's secretariat never showed up at any of the women's meetings, and Lorio never made statements or public appearances. Once Vargas was gone, so was the vitality and strength of CONAPRO H-M women's secretariat.

With the extent of the leaders' confusion, grieving, and shifting of focus after the electoral defeat of the FSLN, leadership of the women's movement was weakened at a time when it was most needed. Without effective leadership, poor decisions were made. Women activists wasted energy fighting irrelevant legislation, union reorganization, and Sandinista restructuring.

The CST women's secretariat wasted considerable energy fighting its own union, other unions, and the FSLN over legislation concerning the writing of the Labor Code. The CST women's secretariat fought with the rest of the labor organizations to have its demands included in the new legislation: equal pay for equal work, equal access to jobs, and equal treatment on the job. After a long battle, a prohibition on sexual harassment was also included in the new Labor Code, although it did not include a punishment for its contravention. Regardless of what women gained legislatively, with unemployment skyrocketing and with unions forbidden in the rapidly expanding export processing zones, the influence of the Labor Code on women's economic situation was minimal.

The ATC women's secretariat wasted its time fighting its own organization over internal restructuring of the union. The women fought within their own organization to ensure that there was a space for women's needs to be heard (Rusmore 1994, 13). This case of the failure of leadership to choose correct goals validates Joe Foweraker's assertion (1995, 52) that the role of leadership is underappreciated in social movement theory.

The rise of effective leadership was further hindered by the FSLN's actions. First, the FSLN blocked the rise of women to powerful positions within the Party. Then it appointed Gladys Baez to the position of secretary general of AMNLAE.

While women expended their time and energy in an attempt to restructure the FSLN so that women's voices could be heard, the male leadership of the FSLN blocked the inclusion of women in the upper echelons of power through internal electoral manipulation. Because more women than men voted for the UNO and thereby assisted the FSLN's fall from power (Chinchilla 1990, 39; Saint.-Germain 1993a, 133; Criquillon 1995, 226–27; interview Herrera), women activists within the FSLN wanted the Party to reflect on why it had lost the women's vote.

The male leadership of the FSLN felt no need to reflect on this issue. Instead, the FSLN blatantly excluded women from the National Directorate in its 1991 leadership Congress. Voters could not vote for individual candidates, only the entire slate of candidates. One of the people put forward was Dora María Téllez, who was initially rejected because the National Directorate stated that it was not ready for a woman. When it became obvious that Téllez had strong support from the public and from within the Party, rumors that she was a lesbian were broadcast over Sandinista radio stations in order to turn the public against her. Sandinista leaders knew that although the public may have been able to accept a woman in a position of power, it could not accept an unapologetic lesbian. This public humiliation of Téllez in order to keep her out of power brought the long-simmering tensions between the Party and the women's movement to the boiling point.[1]

Milú Vargas explained the nature of the tension between the female members and male leadership of the Party: "It was as if we'd [women] given birth to ourselves in the Party. So, for some, there was also this sense of betrayal, the fear that maybe we were somehow betraying our political selves. . . . This fear of betrayal is something that's been used against us, that's been manipulated, no question about it. Another idea with which they've tried to manipulate us is the accusatory 'Be careful, you'll divide the Party!' At this stage of the discussion, it's pretty clear to most of us that we're not dividing anything. We're strengthening the real Party [i.e., grass-roots movement]" (quoted in Randall 1994, 140–41).

For the first time, there were public pronouncements by female leaders that women's future lay wholly in the grass roots and not in the Party, which would call for the creation of an identity autonomous from the Party. Even those who could not turn their backs on the Party after a lifetime of service recognized that the two identities were mutually exclusive. Doris Tijerino said, "Women have to find a way of wearing both hats [i.e., being a Party Sandinista and being a feminist]" (quoted in ibid., 1994, 217). Given the exodus of members from AMNLAE and the growth of the autonomous women's groups at this time, apparently many women could not find a way to wear both hats and chose to wear one, autonomous identity.

Just before and after the FSLN's leadership Congress, tensions between members of AMNLAE were at a boiling point over exactly the same issue: Where did their identity lie? In a perfect collapse of means and ends, identity and resource mobilization, the identity question revolved around the very structure of AMNLAE. As Melucci said, the movement is the message (1985, 801).

The identity question became a factor in AMNLAE's democratic restructuring, and the question became who should be a member and for what reason. Without an identity, these organizational questions could not be resolved. As Sofia Montenegro, then editor of the *La Gente*, a supplement of the Sandinista newspaper *Barricada*, put it: "We didn't even know if an election with the same old structure was what we wanted. It seemed to us that other questions had to be answered first: what kind of movement do we need? What do we need it for? And who should be a part of it?" (quoted in Randall 1994, 309).

These questions reflected the recognition that identity, goals, and strategies were closely interrelated. The reorganization of AMNLAE and of the women's movement was impossible without deciding who would be the members. And it was impossible to see who would be members without understanding why there was a movement. It was impossible to understand why there should be a movement without appreciating what the movement was for, that is, recognizing specific power inequalities working against women. Rectifying power inequality required the development of strategic reasoning to organize around the movement's goals, which then decided who would be members. The mobilization of resources (the "what") mixed with an understanding of the goals and identity (the "why"), eliminating any easy separation between the strategic and the ethical, that is, the mobilization of resources and the creation of identity.

A group of ten women wrote a proposal suggesting that AMNLAE's internal election, planned for March 8, 1991, be postponed until there had been a nationwide discussion and resolution of these questions. The organizing committee was composed of eleven volunteer women who consulted with Sandinista organizations, then with other groups, and then with the grass roots. Once again the women's movement asked for input from the rank and file, building on its grass-roots meetings of 1987. In fact, without the mobilization of preexisting resources, there could have been no creation of identity. As theorists from the resource mobilization school suggest is the norm, a new movement was built from an existing one.

The leaders asked the grass roots the same questions that they asked themselves: "the *what*, the *why*, and the *how* of the movement in order to define a strategy born where there will be declarations about these fundamental questions" (*La Gente*, 57 [February 15, 1991]: 10).

This process of reflection was integral to the creation and recreation of identity, and was recognized as such at the time. "All [the leaders] tried to instigate a process of reflection" (Blandón 1994, 100). "We have lived in 'activismo' for ten years without reflecting" (quoted in Thayer 1994, 12). In order for an identity-based movement to emerge, identity has to be more than merely reflective: it has to be consciously created through group relationships (Melucci 1989, 35). Whereas the reflection might have begun during the constitutional negotiations and AMNLAE's preparatory grass-roots meetings, the conscious creation of identity as a goal in and of itself did not occur until 1991. The leaders initiated the role of reflection and then supplemented the process with the unabashed promotion of the acceptance of difference. The awareness of the natural and nonthreatening nature of difference came from the experience of the activists within the FSLN, which had placed a premium on unity.[2] The acceptance and even the cultivation of difference would become one of the key tenets of the women's movement.

Nonetheless, collective identity cannot be created through a top-down process, but must be created through sharing experiences and clashing over the meaning that can be derived from history (Foweraker 1995, 13). An individual telling a story of her own experiences within an organization or group requires a critical stance and a judging eye. The sharing, thinking, and judging creates a common sense, a meaning or understanding, which all individuals need in order to reconcile the paradoxes and contradictions of society (Arendt 1961, 8). This meaning, or identity, creates a sense of belonging, of judging and being judged. This identity transcends all "truths" but, due to its judging component, has an inherent ethos or morality.

This created understanding of an individual's and a group's history allows the group to search the past as the only legitimate source of knowledge for solutions to immediate confusions. This process, however, could obviously easily produce more than one understanding of what happened, that is, more than one history. For this reason, identity is constantly shifting. Thus, Jane Jenson (1994) says that historicity is the primary locus of the battles of social movement organizations. Nicaraguan women attempted to create this sense of historicity during 1990 and 1991, and the process and resultant stories became the battle between AMNLAE and the emergent autonomous social movement.

Women's response after extensive reflection was clear. A document was written about the future of AMNLAE, calling for a democratic, horizontally organized structure driven by the base. One of the clauses of the document declared that AMNLAE must recognize that its dependence on the FSLN had limited its own development and that this dependency resulted in its inability to represent the interests of the women of Nicaragua (*La Gente* 57 [February 15, 1991]: 10). With the conscious creation of an identity, AMNLAE's historical lack of autonomy was considered detrimental to the women—even if this had not always been true. Identity insists on autonomy.

For some women, the document did not go far enough. According to Olga María Espinoza, who was one of three women to spearhead the ATC women's secretariat in 1983 and who left the ATC in 1990 to join a women's think tank, the document did not fully utilize the accumulated experience of the grass roots, and it did not suggest how women could profoundly democratize the home, the movement, and society. It treated the democratization of AMNLAE as an end rather as than an interim goal. The document, according to Espinoza, did not recognize the extent to which leadership had emerged from the grass roots rather than filtered down from above (ibid., 10). Despite such criticisms, Espinoza accepted the document as a step in the right direction.

The National Directorate of the FSLN, however, could not accept it, and made it clear at the 1991 General Assembly that the only item on the table was the election of the general secretary (that is, Doris Tijerino's position). According to Montenegro, the democratic demands of the masses scared AMNLAE's top echelon, which stopped the process of democratization, in other words, the process of creating identity and mobilizing resources (Randall 1994, 310). The rank and file of AMNLAE accused the leadership of being interested in only cosmetic change. Said Espinoza, "Some women felt tricked by this decision" (quoted in *La Gente* 57 [February 15, 1991]: 11).

Approximately six hundred women attended AMNLAE's March 1991 conference despite the boycott by most of the women's secretariats and a number of unaffiliated women, who claimed that their voices could not be heard, that the delegates had been preselected, and that the leadership of AMNLAE hadn't the legitimacy to lead the women's movement (*Envío* 10, no. 119 [June 1991]: 40).[3]

While there was discussion of a number of women's concerns at the conference, there was no identity formation. Identity formation posed too great a danger, with its potential ability to criticize the FSLN through reflection, analysis, and shared experiences. In addition, identity formation inevitably leads to autonomy from partisan political parties, a phenomenon that the FSLN wanted to avoid. Conference leaders thwarted identity formation by discouraging participants from discussing leadership, history, or organizational structure, implying that such a discussion would be tantamount to public criticism of Doris Tijerino (*Barricada International*, April 1991, 21). By preventing the examination of the organization, the leadership of AMNLAE denied its members the opportunity to tell their own story and to critically judge their own history, thereby halting the creation of a new collective identity. The denial of the right to create identity became the central source of conflict between the women who refused to attend the conference and the women who did attend it. Denying women the right to create their own identity was not a wise decision on the part of the upper echelons of AMNLAE and the FSLN, because dissident women left AMNLAE to create their own movement. This error was compounded by the appointment of Gladys Baez as general secretary (later approved through a vote).

Baez was another of the top Sandinistas who had joined the FSLN long before there was any hope of attaining success. Like Doris Tijerino before her, Baez had never before participated in the women's movement. Also like Tijerino, she was famous for her heroic actions and knew her identity as a Sandinista before all else.[4]

Under the leadership of Baez, AMNLAE turned against those within the organization who questioned its hierarchical structure and Sandinista goals. Unlike Tijerino, who had been brought into AMNLAE to police it but ended up negotiating alliances and appeasing fractious disputes, Baez cracked down on the dissidents. After the FSLN Congress in July 1991, Baez blasted the dissident leaders and rank-and-file members. Recalls Montenegro, "She called us every name in the book: lesbians, prostitutes, feminists, CIA agents, counterrevolutionaries—you name it. She even revived that old accusation that we were trying to divide the FSLN" (quoted in Randall 1994, 310). Baez overplayed her hand. The people she was accusing had too frequently risked too much to be Sandinistas for these accusations to be anything but insulting and absurd. The fight was so bitter and public and the divisions were so deep that Baez had to go to the National Directorate and ask it to resolve the problem. "And the male leadership of the FSLN, in its wisdom or cowardice, washed its hands of the whole affair. . . . The leadership responded, 'You wanted autonomy. Deal with it'" (quoted in Randall 1994, 310). After that, both AMNLAE and the autonomous women's movement got what it had long requested: autonomy. However, the attacks widened the breach between AMNLAE and the emerging autonomous women's movement.

To be fair to Baez, she was doing what had been successful in the past: imposing a command structure in order to create unity, which in the process denied any identity other than Sandinista. She insisted that the leadership could not move faster than the community it represented, a convenient explanation, which was abandoned or embraced depending on the need of the FSLN. She never raised the issue of abortion with political parties, the state, or the general populace. Nor were women allowed to raise it in AMNLAE, despite the internal demands for a discussion. On the other hand, Baez initiated a program to make the structure of AMNLAE more horizontal, included the environment as a critical component of the debate, defended the autonomy of the Atlantic Coast, and lobbied political parties for inclusion of women's issues in their platforms (*La Gente*, April 10, 1992, 21). In other words, Baez operated on an older understanding of politics that no longer applied: unity at all costs, lobbybased actions aimed at the government to attain goods and services, strategy over identity, material over ethical. In Nicaragua in the 1990s, Baez was the wrong person in the wrong place at the wrong time. And she was reviled for it. Baez abruptly resigned from AMNLAE in late 1992 without completing her mandate.

While AMNLAE organized itself along traditional lines, another group of women was using new understandings of organization and needs to gain greater strategic influence. The women, who refused to attend the 1991 AMNLAE conference, organized their own conference to run simultaneously with AMNLAE's. These women called their conference the 52 Percent Majority, an evocation of the power of democracy. Approximately two hundred women attended the 52 Percent Majority Conference, a younger and more critical crowd that tended to take for granted the rights gained through the revolution (*Envío* 10, no. 119 [June 1991]: 40).

AMNLAE considered the 52 Percent Majority Conference a threat not because of anything it produced but rather because it challenged the existing power system. The new group of women activists, by coming together and mounting an alternative conference fully autonomous for the first time from AMNLAE and the FSLN, demonstrated a viable alternative outside Sandinista control. The 52 Percent Majority was a threat because it ruptured the existing ways of operating.

As a result of the rupture embodied in the conference, the Sandinista media were vitriolic. A Sandinista radio station called the participants of the 52 Percent Majority "lesbians and prostitutes" (*Barricada*, March 9, 1991, 5). The women who attended the conference responded by picketing the station and blocking traffic. *El Nuevo Diario*, a newspaper sympathetic to the Sandinistas, published an article about the 52 Percent Majority subtitled: "They Are Trying to Divide the [Women's] Movement." The reporter quoted an AMNLAE representative who called the 52 Percent Majority a group "coming out for free love and a ferocious defense of lesbianism. . . . The first thing that it advises a couple with problems to do is get a divorce."

When the same reporter then asked what AMNLAE's stance on lesbianism was, the AMNLAE representative replied, "What lesbianism? Why, we love men!" The article also said that the women who belonged to the 52 Percent Majority group were elitist, professional intellectuals with a high standard of living, unlike AMNLAE, which spoke for working-class women, for *el puro pueblo* (Randall 1992, 63–64).

It was a rough birth for a new movement, made rougher by the lack of a formulated platform of the new autonomous groups. The only decision of any import that came from the 52 Percent Majority Conference was to have another conference in which issues such as the organization of the movement would be discussed. In addition, lesbians were, in fact, coming out of the closet, and the Lesbian Collective Group did indeed attend the 52 Percent Majority, which every autonomous women's group supported (Criquillon 1995, 229).[5]

The *El Nuevo Diario* article was followed by a series of letters from the new women's groups, pointing out that there was no group called 52 Percent Majority; rather, it was a conference. They also asserted that the people who attended were not solely elitists from society's upper echelons but working-class women as well, and that the conference was a new means of approaching women's problems (Randall 1992, 64–66).

Individuals and collectives protested the negative coverage through letters and demonstrations. They protested by simply refusing to rejoin AMNLAE. They protested for the right to exist. Autonomous, self-defined existence was the message. The movement was the message.

The media midwifed the new movement, the new message. Even more so, the media helped to create the very movement itself. The media performs three mobilizing functions for social movements: First, it mobilizes participation by informing, motivating, and keeping in contact people who are otherwise inaccessible to the social movement. Second, media creates political facts by validating the movement's position as valuable. Finally, it broadens the scope of the conflict from the dispute to the society at large (Gamson and Wolfsfeld 1993, 114–17). By broadening the conflict to include the concept of autonomy from the FSLN, by articulating the issue of autonomy and women's rights coherently, and by helping to mobilize resources around an issue, the media itself played a role in the creation of the new autonomous identity.

According to Tarrow (1994, 191), the ability of a social movement organization to access media and use it for a group's own ends is essential for success. Because the media ultimately supported the new small women's collectives, it became a critical player in the development of the autonomous women's movement. The women's movement skillfully used the media to present its case, in effect, to help create a political movement from the disparate protest groups.

Control of the media was split between the FSLN and the Chamorro government. In 1990, *La Prensa* became the voice of the government. *Barricada* became critically independent from the FSLN. And in 1994, the right wing opened its first newspaper, *La Tribuna*. *El Nuevo Diario*, sympathetic to the FSLN, became a salacious tabloid. *El Nuevo Diario* published much of the conflict between AMNLAE and the autonomous women's groups and later the conflict with the *Casas de Mujeres*. In comparison, *La Gente*, the cultural supplement to *Barricada*, was edited by the intellectual, feminist, and critical Sandinista Sofia Montenegro. *La Gente* was obviously a women's magazine and by far the most sophisticated supporter of the autonomous women's movement. Long a supporter of eroticism, Montenegro edited a supplement that managed to out-titillate *El Nuevo Diario* while supplying critical information to the public about sexuality and the women's movement. In addition to print media, independent radio stations mushroomed. Cable television was brought in, opening up a plethora of viewing options to those who could afford it.

Leaders from both sides of the issue (AMNLAE and the new autonomous groups) were sufficiently experienced to make sure that the media was well informed about their actions. Although the first articles and radio reports about the new women's groups were negative, the autonomous women's groups rapidly presented their point of view to the media as persuasively as possible. The extent of media interest turned the battles between AMNLAE and the autonomous women's groups into political facts, political realities comprehensible and accessible to all. By granting the autonomous women's groups this status, their issues became "effective symbols around which people could mobilize; they [the issues] were attached to new value codes that often compete with previously existing codes. The substitution of these value codes involves personal, cultural and political change. In this case, it is not social mobilization per se that transforms [this] issue into a new political fact but its diffusion through the mass media" (Garcia-Guadilla 1995, 217).

The autonomy of some *Casas de Mujeres* is an example of the changing media presentation of the autonomous women's groups from lesbian man-haters to political activists in pursuit of freedom. AMNLAE created the *Casas de Mujeres* in 1988 as individual women's centers for medical, legal, and emotional help. Leaders of individual centers announced their independence after AMNLAE, under Baez, cracked down on them, firing the "feminists" because they were performing work outside AMNLAE's guidelines (*Barricada*, November 20, 1991, 5). However, the fired activists offered a more ideological reason for their dismissal. In a letter to a newspaper, signed by three leaders of *Casas de Mujeres*, they wrote that they were fired "because they were critical of the organization's top-down style of operation and its emphasis on work that reproduces women's subordinate role in the family, daily life, and the political arena" (Randall 1992, 64). These three leaders unilaterally declared their centers autonomous.

The separation of *Casas de Mujeres* from AMNLAE provoked another conflict between AMNLAE, the FSLN, and the women's movement. AMNLAE, backed by the FSLN, insisted that the material goods within the centers belonged to them and not to the new collective. The collectives insisted that the items belonged to the center and the neighborhood women who utilized it (Randall 1992, 65). Given that the houses were never supplied with expensive or extensive furniture or equipment, one might have thought that the question was moot. But tensions were running too high. There were physical tugs of war over such items as chairs and desks. Each tussle was recorded in the pages of the daily newspaper for everyone to read about. Eventually, AMNLAE gave up. Either it realized that the fights were ludicrous and were causing them to lose legitimacy, or it finally reacquired its full complement of chairs.

The squabbles between the two kinds of organization became a political argument about freedom versus control. The media elevated and transformed a trivial and internal disagreement into a symbol, the kind of symbol that would encourage the participation of more women in the autonomous women's movement (Gamson and Wolfsfeld 1993, 116). The symbolic value of the battle cannot be overestimated in a Nicaragua undergoing recreation. "Some issues are associated with emerging value codes that, in turn, constitute a new political culture. These issues are likely to be appropriated by societies through the mass media and to be imbued with political power" (Garcia-Guadilla 1995, 216). The *Casas de Mujeres* demonstrated how the mobilization of resources (material goods) and the creation of an autonomous identity work through the utilization of signs (media).

As more identities became autonomous and articulated during this period, the connection between identity, freedom, and autonomy became clearer. This precipitated the women's secretariats of the ATC and CST to also declare themselves fully autonomous from the Party and AMNLAE, citing the FSLN's rigidity and its lack of recognition of different interests, experiences, and leadership roles (Blandón 1994, 100).

It may seem peculiar that the women's secretariats waited so long to formally announce their de facto autonomy, given that their criticisms of the Party had been public for years. Their delay highlights the power of the preexisting Sandinista identity among not just the women leaders but also the movement at large. Few people could formally split from the Party and announce their independence without reluctance, regret, and doubt. So the formal separation was late in coming. In fact, it came after the new identity had already crystallized and the old Sandinista identity was no longer tenable.

Evers (1985, 55) writes that we have not one identity, a single complete subjectivity, but rather a mix of identities—some of which are activated. However, as Verónica Schild (1994, 74) points out, beneath this theory lies painful conflicts between contradictory identities: "To refer to lived subjectivities as contradictory is to speak of an intricate negotiation that often involves pain and anguish." The Sandinista identity of the semiautonomous women's groups was too powerful an identity and a commitment to break without pain and anguish. Therefore, the women's secretariats resolved the problem by waiting for that identity to become "deactivated." Only then did they declare themselves autonomous.

Mixed organizations, meaning those with both male and female members, such as the ATC and the CST, kept open spaces for women to organize. In fact, UNAG, the most traditional of these organizations, increased the size of its women's secretariat in 1994, frankly acknowledging the necessity to improve women's lives (interview Navarro). In the 1990s, mixed organizations in the rural areas organizing women to increase productivity continued to be more successful than autonomous women's groups or AMNLAE. Of all the women active in women's groups in Nicaragua, 19.7 percent belonged to mixed organizations, of which 72.7 percent had a bond or a tie to the women's movement (versus 92 percent of women-only groups) (Montenegro 1997, 376, 383). However, it was the women-only groups that engaged in the vast majority (78.6 percent of women's groups versus 35.7 percent of mixed groups) of the political lobbying and in performing political actions in the public sphere. Finally, only 14.3 percent of mixed groups espoused an explicit gender perspective (ibid., 391). Despite being the women's movement's catalyst for change in the 1980s, in the 1990s the women's secretariats of unions and other mixed organizations retreated into the background of the women's movement, ceding the role of catalyst to autonomous women's groups.

The women's secretariats performed one last critically important function for the autonomous women's movement. They assisted the disparate women's collectives in organizing the January 1992 conference, First National Encounter "Unity in Diversity," which would structure the women's movement for the remainder of the decade. AMNLAE did not help organize or attend the conference, and later the women's secretariats refused to attend, claiming that the conference did not present class as primary to understanding women's subordination. The autonomous women's groups accused the women's secretariats of subordination to their male leadership (Rusmore 1994, 15). Clearly, the women's movement still lacked unity at this point. Nonetheless, more than eight hundred women attended the conference, five hundred more than the organizers expected.

The January 1992 conference was critical to understanding the future organization of the women's movement because it was then that the structure was chosen. The choice of a movement's organizational structure is critical to the successful and sustainable development of a social movement and is a key resource to be mobilized. The issue of structuring the women's movement crystallized around the centralization versus decentralization of the women's movement debate.

One group of longtime activists felt that the women's movement needed its own autonomous yet centralized power structure to effectively counteract the government's policies, guarantee democratic participation, and efficiently unify the diverse elements of the movement. "The movement's lack of cohesion must be addressed if we hope to participate effectively in social transformation because for this you need collective strength" (*Barricada International*, November/December 1993, 21).

The group favoring decentralization wanted a movement based on horizontal networks for two reasons. The first reason was strategic. This group suggested that given the conflict with AMNLAE and the recent withdrawal of the women's secretariats, a highly centralized organization would further alienate other sectors of the women's movement. They suggested that what was needed was a flexible and diverse movement that allowed the easy inclusion of mixed organizations. In such a way, the whole of society could be included in and exposed to the women's movement and its ethos (Thayer 1994, 10). The second reason was based on women's own experience with the Sandinista women's movement, which led many of them to be suspicious of a central and hierarchical organization with power over smaller groups and individuals (*Barricada International*, November/December 1993, 21).

There is a further reason in favor of decentralization. An emphasis on identity and subjectivity as the motivating principles of participation meant that collectives would lean toward networks as an organizing principle. The women's movement via AMNLAE since 1987 and the 52 Percent Conference had strongly emphasized the subjective voice as both a moral and political statement. That nascent identity made networks the most reasonable option.

Networks have long been recognized as an essential element of social movements (Tilly 1978). Networks can be buried in the rhythm of daily life as information and participants circulate and convene around only one issue; membership can wax or wane, participation may be limited or temporary; and a network may be active only part-time (Melucci 1989, 60). Conversely, a network may be structured and formal and highly active politically, with a permanent membership that includes not just collectives and individuals but also NGOs and state workers, university and think-tank researchers, the Church, and political parties (Alvarez, Dagnino, and Escobar 1998, 15–16).

Despite the range of social and political interaction and internal makeup, networks are organized to achieve a single, focused goal, although that goal could be as tenuous as continuing to organize (Tarrow 1991, 3). A network's emphasis on goal attainment and thus on mobilizing resources means that it leaves identity formation predominantly to the collectives. In order to achieve its goal, a network generally divides among the collectives and other membership groups the tasks of organizing, fund-raising, writing, media communication, and so on. Whereas this could be seen as a hierarchy, it might more accurately be understood as a division of labor, as each woman's identity would be formed in her own collective. Identity formation outside the network constrains its own development, options, and resources according to the identity formed. Thus, networks are bounded yet loose units (Tilly 1984, 305).

The networks that the Nicaraguan women organized were flexible with little hierarchy, with multiple leadership positions, and with a collective orientation (Vargas 1994, 3). As a Nicaraguan women's activist explained, networks are a way "to coordinate, act together, discuss, and define strategies and positions to take with respect to the state and other women. At the same time, we all address [women's] problems in an autonomous way through our own institutions or organizations" (*Barricada International* 362, no. 6 [June 1993]: 23).

To protect its subjective voice found through sharing experiences in small groups, collectives at the January 1992 conference opted for networks as a mechanism to organize the movement. And indeed, the group favoring a decentralized movement won the vote. "The outcome of the [1992 conference] was a victory for the group which advocated networking" (Thayer 1994, 10). By the end of the conference, five networks and one study group were formed.[6]

With identity politics renowned for its lack of compromise, networks must somehow integrate harmoniously the various identities formed within the collectives. Respect for difference and diversity allows participants in networks to concentrate on the commonalty they share. Unabridgeable difference is assumed. As long as there is a common goal, praxis can reveal the world that is shared among people (Arendt 1958, 180–82). Difference, and respect for that difference, means that participants could separate and accept, as a strategy, what they held in common and what they did not. The revelation of the shared world created a common understanding, a consensus regarding priorities and approaches— in other words, a praxis for continued growth (Disch 1995, 151).

At the January 1992 conference "Unity in Diversity," the opening statement highlighted the autonomous women's movement's respect for difference: "To recognize difference as a fundamental fact of our existence is to incorporate politically the reality that we women live multiple dimensions of subordination and exploitation through the mere fact of being women. We are daughters, mothers, wives, or grandmothers, with a class, an ethnicity, a culture, a political option, a religious belief or a sexual option. And all of these have a concrete expression of discrimination" (quoted in Thayer 1994, 11).

The ubiquity of the discrimination against women promoted accepting difference as fundamental. To combat discrimination while accepting difference, networks became the form of joint action between groups and individuals.

By the end of the January 1992 conference, the autonomous women's movement had an organizational structure of identity-based collectives uniting into ad hoc networks that operated through public spaces to achieve social and political ends. Not all resources were as well chosen. During this two-year period of extreme chaos and confusion for the Nicaraguan women's movement, those resources wisely mobilized included the use of media and public spaces to attract and unify new participants in an autonomous women's movement. Examples of poorly mobilized resources included the failure of leadership to choose appropriate goals and means and the failure of the FSLN and AMNLAE to respond to the political opportunity to restructure the women's movement. The inability of AMNLAE, the FSLN, and even the women's secretariats of the unions to appropriately reposition their organizations for the changed circumstances of the 1990s meant that the new fulcrum of power would be outside these traditional institutions.

The shift in power from the traditional institutions to the autonomous women's movement was not evident between 1990 and 1992 because the autonomous women's movement was in the process of creating its own identity. As I have argued, an identity is decisive to the organizational structure of a social movement and its goal. Therefore, it is necessary to consider the identity under creation.

All identities have an ethical component that spurs individual awareness of, and resistance to, the dominant societal norms through group action to change the situation and through an articulation of an alternative to the status quo. This ethic is valued more highly than the tangible gains that the social movement attempts to make.

Because the ethic creates a world of meaning and transcendent values, its more strategic aspects can be missed. An ethos integrates the participants into the movement through the adoption of unifying and consistent norms and values, rituals, and language usage. An altered ethos can increase the margins within which the movement operates, thereby increasing its potential to achieve its ends. Conversely, an altered ethos can increase the base of participants in which the social movement operates, which also increases its potential to achieve its ends (Melucci 1996, 352). Certainly, the ethos that the autonomous women's movement created performed as both an identity and a mobilizing tool.

It is important to keep conceptually clear the reality of identity formation and articulation. An identity is under constant flux; it is under permanent negotiation and construction through a process of consciously engaged political action and self and group reflection. Participants in a social movement may present their identity as something delineated, unified, and static. This is, however, more the result of human nature imposing order, permanence, and continuity on an ever-shifting field than an intentional inaccuracy (Melucci 1996, 76). To appreciate identity formation, it is important to chronicle its dynamic within social movement organizations and the overarching ethos that offers the possibility of alliances and unity. Although the women's movement's new identity was not fully created in those two years of 1990–1992, the process for doing so had been initiated, and the direction in which the identity would move was also clear.

The new identity was based on an ethos of care organized around the body. Melucci refers to this ethic as the social movement's Utopia (1980, 221). It is the evocation of a Utopia that facilitates the women's movement from prepolitical to political action, because a Utopia offers women a critique of the status quo and a vision of a new system.

Throughout Nicaraguan women's literature and speech, there is an explicit evocation of Utopia. For example, the first sentence of the second paragraph of a recruitment pamphlet ("Venancia") of one of the sophisticated grass-roots women's groups is *"Tenemos una utopia"* (We have [or hold up] a Utopia). When *8 marzo,* another grass-roots group, received complaints that it was "utopianist," it countered that it had to be to change the present situation (*La Feminista* 2 [1993]: 15). Even Josefina Ramos, the acting director of the Center for Constitutional Rights "Carlos Nuñez" (CDC), a woman who is more a lawyer than anything else, worked the word *Utopia* into an otherwise dry discussion of gender versus class, equality versus equity. She explained why *Utopia* is used to discuss sociopolitical issues. *"Utopia* is the moral reservoir of humanity. Humanity lives within a utopia" (interview). Utopia is profoundly personal, and yet a society lives in a shared one; utopia is both a dream and a duty, an idea and a motivator. This is the deep moral well within which all are already living; it fuels the push to alter reality so that the personal and the collective Utopia become a political option.

Nicaraguan women had already experienced the connection between a justice-based, Utopia-driven movement and political change based on that Utopia. "This remains a powerful legacy in Nicaragua" (Klein 1995, 48). However, the Sandinista revolutionary Utopia had not sufficiently included women's reality. By enlarging the Utopia to include an ethic of care, women found a means to include women's reality in the collective Utopia.

Gioconda Belli, a Nicaraguan activist and writer, suggested that if a movement is based on an ethic of care, then resistance will inevitably become political action. If a movement is based on an ethos of care as a means to comprehend truth, then a protest has concrete means to become a successful political action, because an ethic of care will inevitably lead to social justice action. She suggested that the new women's movement should be based on an individual's and a group's understanding of the self, because how one understands one's self is affected and mediated by others. "If you operate from the principle of care, based on real needs that must be met and not on some notion of patriotism or Party loyalty, you'll be in a much better position to start solving the problem of misery, hunger, and underdevelopment" (quoted in Randall 1994, 189).

The ethos of care and the individual are enmeshed, because care has to begin with the self. AMNLAE's director of operations suggested that self-esteem is the first discovery a woman has to make. In order to accept oneself, a process of questioning and self-reflection is needed (interview Dávila 1994). Battling guilt and shame for *autoestima* became one of the ongoing themes of the women's movement, reflected in articles in *La Gente*, *La Boletina*, and finally heard in conversation.

After encouraging self-esteem, the women's movement then had to nurture collective subjectivity. AMNLAE was not interested in doing so, and the new groups that were fighting AMNLAE were too small and new to be effectual. And some of them did not last very long. Identity theory suggests that participants in identity-based collectives reorganize themselves frequently and almost spontaneously, because the guiding principle of identity is to have meaning-based action and an ethically or-ganized group. As a result, groups come and go in the movement while it surges and recedes in strength. The springing up of new groups is not a problem but rather an indication of a healthy, identity-based movement.

Nonetheless, some new groups did forge collective subjectivity and perform political actions. After the 52 Percent Majority Conference, women's collectives sprang up to discuss women's lives. Although there were exceptions, the collectives tended to be locally organized and the women generally knew one another in advance. As a result, women's collectives were often small and personal, articulating individual subjec-tivities. The collectives were initiated to discuss an issue or resolve a problem. Buried in the issue or problem was the kernel of the paradox or contradiction, which a critical and judging stance could determine. This approach helped to produce an identity. Through the collectives' organiz-ing themselves around that issue and articulating a critical stance and its alternative (that is, the Utopia), the group identity and the collectives grew. (For an example of this process, see *8 marzo* community center later in this chapter.)

It still was not evident how the identity-based groups would act as a political power without the Sandinista government's corporatism and without AMNLAE's organizing role. Criquillon (1995, 237) wrote at the end of 1992: "Political action as an organized and cohesive force with new ways of working that are acceptable to all the groups—something which is an aspiration of many women and would be very helpful in developing the strength to confront the government's backwards policies on women's issues—is the challenge before us." The challenge was met when AMNLAE and rest of the Nicaraguan women's groups were able to act in concert.

The need for the Nicaraguan women's movement to have some unity was obvious to all.[7] There was no way that the women's movement could be politically influential unless basic agreements could be reached between AMNLAE and the nascent autonomous groups. The autonomous women's movement could not ignore a group so powerful that it could call out six hundred women to vote for a foregone conclusion, that had access to mainstream sources of information, and that had contacts with influential political actors. This need for unity is a contention of the resource mobilization school, which sees unity as critical to building strength. At one level, this contention is true.

At the time of AMNLAE's 1991 conference, members of both AMNLAE and the autonomous women's groups called for unity (*Envío* 10:119 June 1991, 40). Unity, however, was elusive, because of AMNLAE's machinations and because of the strong emphasis on identity among autonomous women's groups. Because identity and the mobilization of resources mutually shape each other, a group that has a fundamentally different organization will also have a fundamentally different identity. And that identity/organization is nonnegotiable.

The unifying principle that all the women's groups, including AMNLAE, eventually embraced was the ethos of care. This gave the women's groups the ability to create strategic alliances and to integrate disparate groups into a movement. The primary conflicts around which the women's movement eventually organized were issues related to the body. Caring for the physical self was a natural extension of self-esteem.

Furthermore, because an identity is forged through subjectivity, through sharing the lived experience of being a woman, identity-based women's movements also place an emphasis on the body (Melucci 1989, 46).

Control over the female body became the locus of the fight between the women's movement and the Chamorro government. The politicization of the body was assisted by the development of women's health and law clinics. Although the topic of health care received little attention from either the women's movement or the mass media during 1990 and 1991, it emerged during 1992 as the most controversial and confrontational face of the women's movement. In order to explain how health care clinics became the basis for the women's movement, it is first necessary to explain their formation and emergence in the early 1990s.

Health and law clinics responded to the crisis in women's health (see Chapter 6), becoming a visible and pragmatic alternative to the government's structural adjustment policy and ideology. In the early 1990s, the health and law clinics were undoubtedly the most successful arm of the Nicaraguan women's movement, because the clinics integrated women's identity understanding based on the body; the mobilization of resources, including existing community groups, skills, and leaders; and then focused on resolving women's daily problems—including health concerns. Because of this integration of identity, resource mobilization, and conflict, clinics were effective in attracting new participants, achieving their goals, and growing politically influential.

Health clinics were able to mobilize four critically important resources that helped them to become the backbone of the women's movement in the 1990s. First, health clinics were initially promulgated and organized by AMNLAE and then by the women's legal rights and health semiautonomous Sandinista group, *Ixchen*. This change in leadership led to the creation of smaller clinics. Before 1990, there were AMNLAE's *Casas de Mujeres*, two dozen of which offered health care. There were two women's collectives that offered health care services, one in Masaya and one in Matagalpa. *Ixchen* opened its doors in 1988. By 1992, there were sixteen organizations bringing services to fifty-two centers in all the departments (provinces), including the autonomous states on the Atlantic coast, the Southern Atlantic Autonomous Region (RAAS) and the Northern Atlantic Autonomous Region (RAAN) (Ocón 1992, 3). Of these centers, 61.6 percent offered reproductive health care; 29.9 percent offered education (training through theater and workshops); 4.7 percent offered psychological support; 3.9 percent offered legal advice, mostly dealing with domestic violence (ibid., 7).

The second important resource available to health clinics was their ability to obtain money and attention from international organizations for health care and community education (Ewig 1999, 86 n. 21). Development agencies have increasingly directed attention and monies at women's health because it has become obvious over the decades that the key to economic, community, and sustainable development lies with women. For example, the continued high birthrate in Nicaragua will produce the following effects: by 2025, the population of Nicaragua will jump from 4 million in 2000 to 14.1 million, with the population of Managua (today 1 million) as high as 4.9 million. If drastic measures are taken, the population of Nicaragua could level at 8.7 million, meaning that Managua will have only 3 million inhabitants. The cholera implications alone are terrifying, given that at the moment only 29 percent of Managua residents have sewage disposal (Pizarro 1993). Presented with this potential impact of the government's policies on the future of Managua and Nicaragua, the women's health clinics received funding and support from NGOs, and even tacit support from urban planners, representatives of the City of Managua, agronomists, and journalists. Despite foreign funding, most clinics also required a token fee for service, reducing access for the poorest of the poor (Ocón 1992, 5).

Because of the reliance on external funding to support the clinics, there was the impression among some women activists that the women's movement was owned by the international development agencies. This impression was sufficiently strong that one of the women's collectives spearheaded a discussion of the issue at a conference. This collective claimed that the autonomous women's movement could not be autonomous unless it was financially independent.[8] When the director of a collective, María Theresa Blandón, was asked what she had in mind to replace the foreign aid, she replied that women's groups could open a bakery cafe (interview Blandón). Beside the fact that this suggestion would hardly liberate women from their stereotypical role in society, the idea was simply impractical. There was already a woman or a child selling sweets on every street corner. Perhaps Blandón's answer was poorly thought out, but it nicely demonstrates the difficulty of replacing foreign aid.

Foreign aid did not appear to overtly affect the women's movement. When women were asked if the funding source affected what they said or did, they replied that it did not.[9] However, it is true that clinics or collectives that could write a good proposal tended to receive more money. For example, the neighborhood women's collective *8 marzo* had a reputation of attracting foreign aid because foreigners (that is, Western-educated women) wrote their funding proposals, but the received aid was not necessarily used in the manner proposed.

The importance of money to fund the women's movement's pamphlets, magazines, materials, meetings, photocopies, and salaries is obvious. Foreign aid is a steady if not a generous supply.[10] It would be difficult for foreign aid, however, to direct the operations of the grass-roots groups, because those groups are identity-based. It would be equally difficult for foreign aid to direct the happenings and decisions made at a public space, because there are too many variables involved in creating a shared world. A women's movement made up of small groups and networks with occasional public spaces may not be able to attract large sums, but by its very organizational structure it is able to avoid being subordinated to the wishes of the funding agency.

Nonetheless, foreign funding does inherently contain certain limitations. First, there was always more demand than supply. Thus, the spread of women's health clinics and public health programs was dictated by the availability of capital rather than by women's needs. Second, financial dependence left some clinics vulnerable to external influences. For example, in 1995, Nicaragua's largest and most prestigious women's health and law clinic, *Ixchen,* was temporarily shut down after losing a funding source. U.S. senator Jesse Helms insisted that *Ixchen*'s American funding be stopped due to persistent rumors that *Ixchen* was performing therapeutic abortions. The director of *Ixchen,* María Lourdes Bolaños, vigorously denied those rumors. Nonetheless, the center could not continue without foreign funding. Not only were women denied access to quality maternal health care, but also there was a "chill" factor of offering controversial health care treatments that spread to other clinics.

Finally, a more hidden impact of international funding on the women's movement is that it creates professional activists. Matilda Lindo (interview) said that she would like to leave activism, but she was the only one in her family with a job and she was supporting her children and her grandchildren. The economy was so bad that NGOs were one of the few means of economic survival. Some suggest that professional activists are detrimental to a social movement because they can keep alive issues that lack grass-roots support (McAdam, McCarthy, and Zald 1988, 702). However, an identity-based movement mitigates that possibility, because the grass roots drive the collectives, networks, and public spaces. A more reasonable concern is that professional activists reduce the leadership turnover, which ultimately makes the movement stale. Again, however, a decentralized movement will mitigate that factor.

The third reason why health care became the backbone of the women's movement is because clinic workers, operating from previously established networks, were already trained and experienced in mobilizing grass-roots support. The Chamorro government refused to hire health clinic workers who had a known political loyalty. Given that the Sandinista government trained and then hired the health care workers during the 1980s, it was difficult to find any health care workers who were not partisan. These workers were trained in the Sandinista system of integrating health into neighborhood organizations, popular education, and legal reform.

The UNO government also refused to train new people to fill the old positions. The number of trained health care *brigadistas* fell to 1,500 in 1990 from 12,000 in 1989. No new *brigadistas* were trained in 1991. The government's reluctance to communicate and coordinate action with the NGOs that offered health care was evident during the 1992 national conference on health attended by twenty-nine different popular organizations and MINSA. The explicit purpose of the conference was to strengthen the coordination between groups and to improve relations between MINSA and the popular organizations. Yet only one official from MINSA attended. The twenty-nine groups utilized the time to improve coordination among themselves and to share information (Morgan 1995, chap. 2). Having been laid off by the government and with no hope of being rehired, these workers established autonomous health clinics.

An example of the evolution of women's activism from AMNLAE to autonomous health clinics is the health and law clinic *8 marzo* (the eighth of March, i.e., International Women's Day). Rogalia Sevilla Ramos, a community leader in a poor shantytown, started it. She lost four of her six children during the Insurrection and civil war, including one daughter who was tortured to death by Somoza's National Guard. She was the president of the mothers' support group, Madres H-M, during the war. In the 1980s, she worked in education and health brigades and in the neighborhood community group. She started *8 marzo* in 1987 as one of AMNLAE's *Casas de Mujeres*. It started in a humble home as a collective of women talking about their reality and how they could mutually help one another. Women's ethic of care and practical needs were woven together right from the beginning. The impetus for these meetings and the base of the collective were the neighborhood groups, that is, cells of micromobilization. In 1990, *8 marzo* became autonomous and began to offer health care, education, and legal help appropriate to its neighborhood. Today it has a staff of twelve, including two international volunteers, a full-time doctor, two nurses, and a well-equipped medical clinic. One of its goals is to train more women to act as leaders in order to expand the base of experience. Rogalia Sevilla sees the community and women's problems as integrated, and identity, the body, and practical needs as one and the same (interview Sevilla; Klein 1995, 51, 60). She has the experience to mobilize resources appropriate to her community. Sevilla's story exemplifies the successful mobilization of resources to form a neighborhood health clinic.

Sevilla's attitude also points to the final and most critical reason for why the community clinics became the backbone of the women's movement: the body was the ground upon which identity was built. The health care movement operated within the women's movement and included neighborhood movements or autonomous groups from all other movements. It did not operate within the government's health care structure. It was so well accepted that women's health was the cornerstone of the women's movement that the leaders of the health clinics are as well known today and quoted as widely as the leaders of AMNLAE were in the 1980s.[11] There is no pretense that health is seen as anything other than a woman's issue. For example, in 1991, *¡Sí Mujer!*, a women's clinic, opened its door with a statement of its intent: "Our center, integrated into the feminist movement, is demonstrating the solidarity power of women together in the fight to the end for the defense of all our rights that permit us to advance along the path to the conquest of our primary vindication of gender" (*Sí Mujer* 1994, 1).

Reflecting the new ethos of care, the clinics made a conscious effort to cultivate an egalitarian structure (doctor-nurse and practitioner-patient). The women attending the clinic were encouraged to become informed and active about their health, intending to "transform the passive object to an active subject with her own identity" (Ocón 1992, 5). The transformation from passive object to active subject was a critical precondition for women's participation in the Nicaraguan women's movement.

Initially, the clinics were not particularly concerned with the organization of AMNLAE or whether Dora María Téllez was elected to the National Directorate of the FSLN; political issues did not interest them. Although these issues were attracting attention and energy from other women activists, the health clinics were quietly solidifying their connections, organization, and stances.

Although the women's health movement lacked coherence, the health clinics had already mobilized their resources and already had a statement of identity. What they were lacking in 1990 and 1991 was the organizational structure integral to a social movement, one that created an intermediate space between the formal political realm and the private world of the body. In addition, the health clinics had no specific conflict with the government. Without a focused conflict, without an overarching organizational structure, the health care clinics would be limited as a social movement. This situation changed as the decade progressed.

Health and law clinics as centers of organizing were supplemented by the rise of NGOs to a position of influence in civil society. Throughout the 1980s, NGOs, like many other institutions, were not critical of Sandinista policies but rather supported the Sandinista vision of societal development. After the fall of the FSLN in 1990, several hundred new NGOs mushroomed up with a more critical and autonomous stance toward all political parties (MacDonald 1997, 103–8). These newer NGOs interacted with the more established centers for research and organizing, such as AMNLAE or UNICEF, sharing information and cooperating on achieving goals. Particularly influential on the women's movement were the NGOs that combined political organizing, educational courses, and research.

These include Cezontle, the Center for Constitutional Rights (CDC), the Center for Documentation and Information about Women (CEDIM), and Meeting Points.

Before the Nicaraguan women's movement could reinvent itself to deal with the Chamorro government, it had to take the unfortunate but necessary step of fragmenting under the weight of its own history. Despite the FSLN's repeated efforts to control the movement, the space for women to hear their own voice had been offered too many times and had had too many resources mobilized around it to stop the creation of their own identity. As a result, women's groups split from AMNLAE to pursue an autonomous creation of identity.

Because of the fragmentation, membership declined and the political influence of the women's movement in 1990 and 1991 decreased (Criquillon 1995, 236). The women's movement went through a painful, public, and sometimes ludicrous battle over its identity/organization. The fight pushed the FSLN into finally abdicating control over the women's movement. The semiautonomous groups disappeared or were severely constrained. The completely autonomous women's groups in Nicaragua remained politically uninvolved, having no umbrella organization, networks, or alliances. This weakness of the movement in 1990 and 1991 was recognized as such (Criquillon 1995, 235). Without an organizational structure, the groups could not act within the political arena. The organizational structure of the autonomous women's movement was not decided until 1992, and even that issue was divisive, pitting the forces of centralization against decentralization and excluding AMNLAE and mixed organizations.

The issue of identity and autonomy was the most salient during this restructuring, whether the women involved knew it or not. Women boycotted the AMNLAE conference based on its refusal to engage in identity formation. That some of AMNLAE's *Casas de Mujeres* were prepared to announce their autonomy from AMNLAE and suffer the consequences demonstrates the noncompromising nature of identity. It also demonstrates why autonomy is the manifestation of identity. Evers (1985, 55) puts autonomy, identity, and freedom on the same continuum. As one increases, it drags the others with it. Regardless of whether *Casas de Mujeres* performed the same services as AMNLAE, regardless of whether the women who ran the *Casas de Mujeres* remained Sandinista, it was intolerable that anyone would dictate their issues, priorities, and ways of understanding. Autonomy and identity are symbiotic.

At a loss without the dictates of the Party, the new autonomous women's groups were uncertain how to organize themselves, and so they decided to ask the grass roots, as happened at the 52 Percent Majority Conference. The participants had no issues to discuss except what the issues should be. The only means to decide what the issues should be was through listening to women's experiences and their understandings of that experience. Together, women created a collective understanding, or an ethos. The formation of this identity was achieved through a means that was complementary to its mobilization of resources—the grass roots. This allowed for the rise of new groups, organized in new ways. The collectives and, as much as possible, the health and law clinics were horizontally organized.

The period of restructuring the women's movement also demonstrated the pivotal importance of mobilizing certain resources, specifically leadership and media, during a time of confusion and uncertainty. Effective leadership of the women's movement shifted from the women's secretariats to the new groups: autonomous *Casas de Mujeres*, women's collectives, and health care clinics. Ineffectual leadership precipitated the decline of otherwise viable organizations, such as CONAPRO H-M women's secretariat. The rise of new leaders shifted the power balance in favor of the autonomous women's groups. The media was instrumental in recognizing that there was an ongoing shift in the women's movement and was helpful in explaining and defining that shift. While neither of these two components of social movements was absent from other time periods, they were given greater importance by the profundity of the restructuring of the Nicaraguan women's movement in 1990–1992.

The years 1990–1992 did not show the Nicaraguan women's movement at its best. In fact, since the beginnings of the movement in 1977, these two years were its nadir. The women's movement lost its political influence, many of its participants, and the resources necessary to respond to women's needs. However, as a result of this fragmentation and alienation, the women's movement acquired the elements necessary for a successful social movement: autonomous identity based on a Utopian ethos, control over resources, and a locus of conflict on the body.

CHAPTER 8

The Autonomous Women's Movement, 1992–1996

IN THE LAST YEARS OF THE CHAMORRO GOVERNMENT, the Nicaraguan women's movement had become so influential that most forgot that it had been in shambles at the beginning of the decade. However, the women's movement had not forgotten the lessons it had learned. It had spent the 1980s learning strategies to mobilize its resources, and it had learned the importance of an autonomous identity. It had spent the first two years of the decade breaking the last vestiges of central control over itself and formulating its own identity based on the subjective and articulated through the collective. Beginning in 1992, the women's movement restructured itself into grass-roots groups horizontally organized through loose networks operating in public spaces, using the government's insouciance about maternal mortality and women's status as a foil. This structure and criticism supported the identity being created so that the women's movement was able to maximize the strength of each component.

The sheer size and diversity of the women's movement in the 1990s, however, makes it difficult to package it into neat and comprehensible categories. Gone was the era when AMNLAE was the only game in town. Instead, there was the full flowering of an identity-based social movement, replete with almost two hundred women's groups operating through locally based collectives, public spaces, and networks (Pasos 1995). A 1994 study estimated that there were 150 (a conservative estimate) women's organizations (including mixed organizations) to promote women's issues, 100 groups, centers or collectives specializing in women's issues, 31 organizations or national institutions that had programs directed at women, 20 foundations or institutions of women, and 12 media spaces for communicating with women, including television and radio (Montenegro 1997, 375). The goals, ranging from increasing self-awareness to changing government policies, were as diverse as the groups. A primacy was placed on identity formation, and resources were mobilized appropriate to that identity.

This chapter will chronicle the emergence of four of the most powerful and influential networks in Nicaragua. These four networks attracted substantial domestic attention, influenced public policy, changed social norms, and even negotiated internationally with the Nicaraguan state. Nonetheless, these four case studies incompletely reflect the range of activities and interests of Nicaraguan women. It is hoped, however, that through examining the prominent networks of the movement, issues of fundamental concern to the majority of Nicaraguan women will be evident.

Three of these four networks became powerful because they correctly combined the elements necessary to become influential: identity formation, the mobilization of resources appropriate to that identity, and a goal around which to organize. Each case study of a successful social movement organization will not only explain a pertinent area of the Nicaraguan women's movement but will also highlight a key element of a successful identity-based social movement. Included in the analysis is a fourth example, of a failed network, because it too highlights aspects of social movement organizing.

The first network details the building of identity through sharing experiences in small collectives until a new understanding was achieved. With this new ethos, the network was able to organize at a national level, culminating in the passing of legislative reforms.

The second case study is an example of a failed attempt at organizing. This second network received a lot of publicity and, for a short period, was extremely active. It failed for the simple reason that it did not acknowledge or incorporate the components necessary for creating a self-sustaining, growing, and influential network. It did not ground itself in an identity, and its internal organization was flawed. The somewhat spectacular failure of this network demonstrates a second lesson about a successful social movement: the absolute necessity of integrating identity formation, appropriate structure, and goals, which was not evident to the activists. All were groping for a system around which to organize themselves, and sometimes even the best and the brightest of them made fundamental mistakes.

The third network studied was also successful. It had a well-understood identity and a high degree of political skill and other resources. Through the articulation of specific goals in public spaces, this network was able to influence contemporary political issues that affected women. The fourth case study is an example of the critical role of structuring women's groups into a sophisticated web of networks and of using other resources strategically in order to be sustainable and effective within the smallest community group and up to international forums. These three successful networks should further understanding of the reasons why the movement organized itself in the manner it did, the goals that it chose, and the resources that it mobilized. They also present the increasing complexity of state–civil society relations negotiated at the international, national, and community levels.

This analysis of the present-day Nicaraguan women's movement not only offers an understanding of the scope of activity of the movement but also demonstrates the validity of the argument made in the historical analysis: to be successful—that is, to continue to attract new members and to influence civil society and the state, a social movement organization must have three mutually reinforcing components—identity, resources, and a goal. The lack of any one of these components weakens the organization, mitigating its efficacy and sustainability.

Case Study 1: Women Against Violence Network
An Identity of Human Rights

Ten days before the national election in 1996, a bill protecting women and children from domestic violence came into effect. The Women Against Violence Network wrote and proposed the bill and, without the backing of any major party, indeed with "few real supporters within the National Assembly" (Ellsberg, Liljestrand, and Winkvist 1997, 89), got it unanimously passed. This accomplishment is even more impressive given that the network proposed the bill a mere year earlier after discussing it at the network's first conference. It appeared as if the Women Against Violence Network emerged from nowhere and yet was able to sustain a prolonged campaign against the government, make alliances with professionals such as judges, police, and forensic specialists, and create massive public support for its reforms.

The secret to the success of the Women Against Violence Network lay in its creation of an identity, an identity based on the body. With that identity came a novel critique of society and a new Utopia expressed in the language of human rights. Because this identity was new and not based in Sandinismo, it took years for the ethos to develop. As a result, it took a long time for the Women Against Violence Network to emerge into the public realm. But once it did, its identity was so articulate and persuasive to the vast majority of women that it was able to organize rapidly.

The Women Against Violence Network was born after the men returned from war and peace allegedly reigned. The economy was in dire straits, and unemployment and underemployment were high (see Chapter 6). The number of women abused by men rose markedly. The Nicaraguan Institute for Women (INIM) estimated that between 1990 and 1994, while all forms of reported violence increased by 12.6 percent, the number of reported rapes increased by 21 percent and the number of reported attempted rapes increased by 27 percent (*Nicanet*, October 9, 1995). According to one activist in a poor neighborhood in Managua, approximately 80 percent of families were affected by domestic violence (Klein 1995, 24). According to another study, one of two women had been physically abused by her partner, although only 2 percent reported the abuse to the police (*La Boletina* 26 [1996]: 86).

Before the studies were released, women were well aware of the problem. At the March 1991 autonomous women's conference, women began discussing this problem and decided that a network of collectives was needed to deal specifically with domestic violence. It then took more than a year for the network to become activated. It began in 1992 with representatives from twelve groups plus individuals who were not representing collectives for a total membership of twenty.

The women rejected common explanations for men's violence against women: men were inured to it after the war, they were frustrated with the economy, or they did not realize that it was wrong. The women instead defined gender inequality as the root of violence against women. Women's oppression is experienced at the fundamental level, through men's discipline and control over the female body.

Women arrived at these conclusions through sharing their experiences in small groups, reflecting on their feelings and attitudes. In so doing, awareness was created not merely within the individual but also within the group. This process must result in a recognizable emotional commitment to the group, or the creation of an identity will be stalled. Basing their discussion on the shared experience of being female and of experiencing domination at a bodily level bonded women to their common reality and radicalized the discussion, resulting in the rejection of the usual explanations for the male violence against women. The solution, therefore, required that men respect women's needs and bodies. This demand evolved to include women's reproductive control, women's right to paid labor, and women's right not to be treated as a financially dependent when not performing paid labor.

All identity-based groups then defined their future goals, which for the first few years of the Women Against Violence Network was to continue to reflect and discuss.[1] This slowly evolved into initiating relationships with political actors already active in the field in order to share the new understanding, which in turn sparked more discussion of the network's ethos.

The Women Against Violence Network was significantly assisted by the coordinating role of an NGO, Meeting Points. Meeting Points not only offered a place to convene but also supplied experienced, nonintrusive leadership to organize meetings, facilitate discussion, and publish, with increasing regularity, the new ideas in its magazine, La Boletina. A second NGO, this one Swedish, helped by collecting data and testimonies of women who had suffered from domestic abuse. These powerful life stories were pivotal in persuading legislators to include the psychological effect of violence as an injury when passing sentence (Ellsberg, Liljestrand, and Winkvist 1997, 89).

The Women Against Violence Network was also assisted, albeit unwittingly, by the Chamorro government's 1994 Reforms to the Penal Code, which publicly opened the discussion of violence against women. The 1994 Reforms criminalized rape for the first time but left domestic violence a private crime subject only to civil suits. This outraged women, politicizing the issue.

Finally, there was help through the development of a persuasive legal language. In preparation for the three international conferences sponsored by the United Nations, the 1994 Cairo Conference on Population and Development, the 1995 Copenhagen Conference on Social Development, and the 1995 Beijing Conference on Women, the Nicaraguan women's movement participated in a series of national and regional (both Central American and Latin American) preparatory meetings. The participants agreed upon a common vocabulary embodying their beliefs. This language was one of human rights and became the legal framework with which to express themselves. Although their underlying ethos may have been one of care for the self and others, women needed something more persuasive in the public realm, something comprehensible within the existing political language. Just as the women during the constitutional negotiations of 1985 abandoned the language of Sandinismo social justice in favor of the more effective language of civil liberties, so too did the women's movement in the 1990s abandon civil liberties for the more effective language of international human rights.

Human rights, as a fundamental legal principle, was enshrined in the Nicaraguan constitution, thereby including the civil liberties that women had already fought for and received—although human rights had not been extended to include women's right to live without violence. Human rights was also the language of international NGOs, legitimating and strengthening its usage. With human rights as a framework, women could explain their demands not only to legislators but also to society at large. The sophisticated language of human rights permeates the relevant documents, although it was also used more simply as a slogan to mobilize support: "For democracy in the country, the house, and the bed. No to violence against women and children" (La Boletina [1996]: 21).

By March 1995, three years after its first meeting and four years after it was first formed, the network's identity was sufficiently developed to extend beyond Meeting Points and to hold its first national conference. Five hundred women from professional groups, government agencies, the police, and grass-roots communities attended. At the conference, some of the 60,000 booklets analyzing laws and social mores that left violence against women unchecked were distributed. This publication also listed supportive collectives and agencies that dealt with the issue. Also, the conference attracted considerable media interest, which helped to publicize and legitimate the network's demands. As a result of the conference, a number of new collectives were spawned, strengthening the network. By the end of 1995, there were 150 collectives and ninety-two centers offering services to battered women in fifty-four towns. Combined, they would be able to call on between sixty and one hundred women for organizing meetings held in Managua (Ellsberg, Liljestrand, and Winkvist 1997, 84). Finally, the conference initiated the political action to rewrite the recently reformed penal code to criminalize domestic violence.

The Bill to Reform the Penal Code to Prevent and Sanction Intrafamily Violence was more commonly known as Law 230. It had three important components. The first was the introduction of eleven different means for women to obtain protection and support. The second was the legal recognition of psychological injury. Finally, it gave heavier sentences to violence between family members, up to a maximum sentence of six years in jail, a reversal of existing social and legal norms (*La Boletina* [1996]: 17–24).

Without the support of any major political party, the network had to muster widespread and sustained support from the average Nicaraguan. To do this, the network organized two commissions: the Media Commission, which informed the media of the network's criticisms, activities, and alternatives and produced stickers, buttons, and pamphlets; and the Church Commission, which had Law 230 endorsed by ninety Protestant and Catholic congregations. The network also revisited AMNLAE and the constitutional negotiations' successful technique of innumerable town hall meetings to discuss Law 230 and to mobilize support. By 1995, 57.1 percent of women's groups included human rights and combating violence as part of their work (Montenegro 1997, 391).[2]

The National Assembly, however, did not feel the need to present or read the bill. With the 1996 national election only a few months away, the network was worried that the bill would be delayed until the next legislative session and momentum of public support would be lost. New action was required simply to get it read during the Chamorro mandate. The network presented a petition with 40,000 signatures to the National Assembly demanding that it read the bill (*La Boletina* 1996, 64; Ellsberg, Liljestrand, and Winkvist 1997, 85); members of the network sat outside the National Assembly on a daily basis with leaflets and banners; they took out an advertising campaign in the newspapers and on the television and radio; and, finally, they began a letter-writing campaign, which accumulated 21,000 letters. Once the National Assembly agreed to read a watered-down version of Law 230, the next strategy was the preparation of briefing packages, direct lobbying of legislators in the hallways by well-known lawyers and psychologists, and the reintroduction of the original version. In August 1996, the vote was unanimously in favor of the original version of the bill. The legislators had to either vote for it or be accused of endorsing domestic violence, impolitic just before the election (Ellsberg, Liljestrand, and Winkvist 1997, 89).[3]

While clearly the Women Against Violence Network skillfully managed its lobbying, it attracted public attention only in March 1995 and yet achieved all its political goals by August 1996. This was not a long, drawn-out public battle. Such a campaign was unnecessary. Through forging an identity based on the body and articulating it through a language of human rights, women were able to make alliances with a broad spectrum of professionals and could consolidate support within the rest of the women's movement before finally persuading Nicaraguan society at large to endorse its actions. As the Network crowed after winning the vote, perhaps with some justification, "[The campaign] is a good example of what the women's movement can achieve when we unite our strengths and make the government respond to our interests" (*La Boletina* 1996, 21). Women were able to unite their strengths because they shared a common identity and language with which to express it.

Case Study 2: The National Feminist Committee
A Failure of Identity

The utter necessity to ground all political actions and strategies in a well-forged identity was not evident to every activist in the women's movement. The National Feminist Committee (CNF), the largest network of women's collectives, did not base its identity on personal experiences shared in small groups, but rather tried to be abstract, even impersonal, in its identity formation. Consequently, the network could not negotiate or resolve differing understandings of the role of women in society or agree on a Utopian alternative. Without this primary organizing ethos that set priorities and goals, the network could not strategize or use resources, and it rapidly dissolved.

The CNF was formed in May 1992. The organizing collective, called *La Malinche*, was composed of intellectually oriented ex-Sandinista activists. These women had been close to the Sandinista upper echelon during the 1980s because of the opportunities offered by the FSLN. By 1990, they had the sophistication of fifteen years of politics to hone the crafts of communicating, organizing, and leading. They used these skills to rapidly organize the CNF, and it became, for a short period, the most widely consulted and quoted network in Nicaragua.

La Malinche was deliberate in its use of abstraction, feeling that understandings and strategies built solely on identity limited that identity to the familiar: "In effect, the political has come to be reduced to the personal, instead of being distilled from the personal towards a critical understanding of how structures of power construct difference. . . . In the end, no politically useful understanding of how difference is constructed emerges" (Goetz 1991, 145).

Therefore, *La Malinche* believed that a social movement that wished to become highly political or engage in economic development—both issues of primary concern to it—had to be augmented by a more abstract approach. One of Nicaragua's leading Sandinista intellectual-activists and a member of *La Malinche* recognized this need and felt that she was uniquely positioned to respond: "I feel like I need some sort of methodology with which I can theorize about what I've experienced and move to a higher level of consciousness. As an intellectual, I think my role is to try to achieve a synthesis with which we can renovate our practice. . . . [I] need to find a way out of the dead end that the Left has brought us to, the dead end of the revolution, even feminism's dead end" (quoted in Randall 1994, 304).

To meet this need for a new methodology, she and half a dozen women of similar sensibilities founded *La Malinche*. It wanted to forge a new theoretical framework with which to move the rest of the women's movement from a personal and historically concrete identity based on the body to a more abstract understanding. The new abstraction would allow the identification of problems and solutions outside the well-explored precepts of social justice Sandinismo. Ideally, this new perspective, this higher level of consciousness, would generate new forms of political practice and effective responses to the economic crisis.

La Malinche initiated the CNF, a network of women's collectives, to participate in developing the new methodology. The collectives that belonged to CNF spanned economic and ethnic backgrounds. Starting with sixteen women's collectives, expanding to thirty in 1993 before shrinking to twenty-five in 1994, the network consisted of Costeña (English, Protestant, and black) women from the Atlantic Coast, peasants from the northern mountains of Matagalpa, and artisans from the "developed" area of Masaya. Not all of these areas were Sandinista during the war: the Atlantic Coast was hostile to the FSLN during the counterrevolutionary war of the 1980s and only slightly less so in the 1990s; Matagalpa was emphatically nonpartisan; and Masaya was Sandinista. Each of these collectives had distinct areas in which they already worked, such as health, economy, or law. They worked together within the CNF to create a shared understanding of women's role in society. For example, the monthly meetings of the CNF analyzed the women's movement, the construction of leadership, alliances, spaces, feminist power, racism, maternity, legislation, and sexuality (interview Blandón; *La Feminista*, August 3, 1993; December 4, 1993). The participants then took that understanding back to their own collectives or groups, spreading ideas and approaches. Despite the differences in interests and activities, the CNF was united in its desire to respond to the economic crisis (interview Blandón 1994). A response to women's economic hardship was the focused goal of the network.

But the network's Utopian alternative, which offered an overarching and organizing ethos, was confused. Partially the confusion was due to the radical rethinking of women's status in society. For example, the names of both the organizing collective, *La Malinche,* and the network itself were based on a profoundly different understanding from the rest of Nicaraguan society. Malinche was the female translator for Spanish conquistador Hernán Cortés. Her skills enabled him to splice together an alliance among the Indians colonized by the ruling Aztec nation and thereby defeat it. Today, *malinche* means traitor. The collective, *La Malinche,* wanted to counter that interpretation of history and instead see her as a survivor and a linguist in an unimaginably difficult period.

The network's name, the National Feminist Committee, was equally problematic. Although the word *feminism* was not new to Nicaragua—there had been too many international conferences and international activists in Nicaragua for the word not to have some resonance—the popularization of the word was a relatively new phenomenon. And like most new concepts, its meaning was initially debated. Likely reflecting its point of origin, the word *feminism* meant not only the pursuit of gender equality but also connoted foreign, white, and privileged. Thus, any

163

group that called itself "feminist" aligned itself with this broader context. The CNF fought a losing battle over the image this word evoked, giving long explanations of its meaning in the newspapers (*Barricada International*, September 1993, 21).

The confusion was not resolved by the First National Feminist Meeting in October 1993.[4] One purpose of the conference was to determine the meaning of the word *feminism*. A clear definition of the word was needed "to further the theoretical feminist understanding of our reality ... [which would be] a huge step towards solving the ideological and political confusion in the country and the women's movement" (*Barricada International*, November/December 1993, 18). Although twelve strategies detailed how to achieve equality, the actual concept was never defined.[5] Instead, the concept was considered to be in the process of emerging, and feminists were "women in transition" (ibid., 21), although it was unclear from what and into what these feminists were transmuting. By the tail end of 1993, a women's rights broadsheet was still putting the symbol of a Western, well-educated woman beside the word *feminist* (*La Gente dic* 29, 1993).

Another reason why the Utopian alternative failed to emerge was that identity formation was hampered by *La Malinche*'s top-down approach. *La Malinche*'s primary task within the network was ideological training through seminars directing the ideas and interests of the other collectives. Thus, identity was not created as much as an education was given. The CNF, then, acted as educators for the rest of the Nicaraguan women's movement. The network organized two conferences to discuss its new ideas of feminism and political action, and published a bimonthly magazine, *La Feminista*, to debate feminist concepts. Its print run of 1,000 copies was distributed through the network and to the interested public.

Although its work was primarily educative, *La Malinche* was not hostile to identity formation. Quite the contrary. *La Malinche* was frank about its desire to create a new identity, a new philosophy of life divorced from the revolutionary socialism of the FSLN. To do so, CNF sponsored a conference called "Aquelarre" (interview Blandón; *Barricada International*, November/December 1993, 23). Conferences can be used to consolidate identities around specific goals. Rarely, however, are they used to create identity, because of the emphasis that identity formation places on reflection. With the Aquelarre Conference, the CNF tried to create a new identity, but through education, thereby sidestepping reflection.

The education, or rather reeducation, was about witches. According to the conference, instead of being scary and malicious harridans, these women and their knowledge represented women's traditional power before it was supplanted by medical science. An aquelarre is a witch's cabal; the CNF, led by *La Malinche*, attempted to use the aquelarre as a new locus of power, freedom, and knowledge. Consequently, the Aquelarre was convened with a ritual-type dance and a drink from a witch's brew while the spectators wore pointed black hats. The opening speech described women's ancient and now lost power. The document the CNF presented for discussion summarized the history of the Nicaraguan women's movement. The document emphasized the failure of the Sandinista ideology to respond to women's demands and of women's struggle to express their needs outside the language of Sandinismo. The conference embodied a well-planned strategy for escaping Nicaraguan history and for creating a new common understanding.

It was unlikely, however, that using a witch motif could create a new identity, because the conference shifted identity formation from a grassroots reality to a concept both European and medieval. Identity is born of subjectivity and reflection, not of a history lesson of a foreign culture. Nicaraguan women could not even easily pronounce the foreign-sounding word *aquelarre*, but instead chose to refer to it as "Aka," the same slang used for an AK-47, the weapon of choice during the counterrevolutionary war. In addition, the document that *La Malinche* produced for discussion at the conference was too esoteric for most of the women to read aloud without stumbling over unfamiliar polysyllabic words. On the whole, the dominant response of the conference's participants was to ignore the attempt to create a new collective identity.[6]

The inability of *La Malinche* in 1994 to effectively communicate its ideas to the grass roots did not appear to perturb the collective. When asked about the complex language used during Aquelarre and its appropriateness, Blandón agreed that it was indeed complex, but she indicated that if women couldn't understand then they'd have to learn. She recommended that women pick up a dictionary. As intellectual-activists, the members of *La Malinche* expected themselves to be ahead of the masses, leading the way. They were willing to be patient (interview Blandón 1994).

Although *La Malinche* may have had patience, the network it was leading was strained by the new ideas. The network had lost the old identity it once possessed of articulating the economy and other concerns from a shared and grounded perspective. Yet the new identity of witches' power was not generally embraced. One longtime grass-roots organizer no longer understood why she and her collective should be members of the CNF, what the CNF's purpose was, and what her role should be. When she raised this at a meeting, one of the members of *La Malinche* snapped back, "We all know why we are here. Why don't you?" (interview Lindo). What was confused and uncertain at the grass roots was clear and self-evident to the members of *La Malinche*.

Several months after the Aquelarre Conference, the tension between the conflicting identities led to an internal revolt. In an effort to mitigate the top-down direction of the network, *La Malinche* was replaced by a new executive committee made up of a number of women from different collectives. Blandón called the reshuffling "tyranny of the passive majority against the active members" (interview Blandón). The reshuffling, however, did not stem the discontent. In the beginning of July, a member of the CNF not from *La Malinche* correctly predicted that the CNF would crumble because no new identity was emerging from the reorganization to give again an ethos for the network (interview Lindo).[7] By Christmas 1994, the CNF was officially disbanded.

The career of the CNF is a cautionary tale for those interested in identity-based social movements. Most obvious is the critical importance of forging an identity before pursuing political action. Just as AMNLAE in the late 1980s suffered from a lack of a clear identity and its confusion over that issue became its field of conflict, so too was the CNF's field of conflict over its basic beliefs rather than its focused goal (which was to ameliorate economic hardship). As a consequence of the confusion over their identities, both AMNLAE and the CNF had limited political influence despite ample resources.

The CNF also demonstrated the limitations of an identity-based social movement. First, a network is healthier if the executive is drawn from a number of collectives rather than from just one. Thus, leadership positions should be dispersed and rotate throughout the network rather than concentrated in one group. Rotation diminishes the possibility of one group leading the rest and thereby imposing an identity, and instead grants a structural preference to the locally formed collectives' identities. Second, a network's identity and goal must be grounded in reality. That is, a collective identity is formulated by a shared subjectivity emerging from reflective grass-roots collectives, not enacted through lectures about foreign symbols. The CNF was not based on a local knowledge and did not build upon women's self-definition. Building on both local knowledge and self-definition would of course entail building on the Nicaraguan history from which *La Malinche* was attempting to escape. Regardless of the need for a more abstract identity to propel the Nicaraguan women's movement into the political arena, the structural limitations of the formation of identity leave little room for pure abstraction.

The CNF may have been dissolved, but *La Malinche* carried on, joining the Honduran-based network of Central American intellectually oriented activists, *La Corriente*.[8] While participating in it, these ex-Sandinista intellectual-activists changed their theoretical approach to women's issues in Nicaragua, appreciating the necessity to theorize from the concrete Nicaraguan reality rather than from an international and abstract perspective. They perceived themselves as the women's movement's gramscian organic intellectuals working to unite the women's movement, to consolidate a strong feminist leadership, to link Nicaraguan women's specific problems with globalization, and to develop Nicaraguan women's own concept of feminism (Montenegro 1997, 400, 405).[9] Using this approach, *La Corriente* has been able to disseminate a broader and clearer vision of feminism more in keeping with the rest of Nicaraguan society; it ultimately deemed all in the women's movement to have a feminist essence because their motivation was to eliminate subordination and discrimination (ibid., 402). These intellectual-activists remain a vital part of the Nicaraguan women's movement, speaking publicly, publishing extensively, and persuading 79 percent of the women's groups and 62 percent of mixed organizations to identify themselves as having a feminist character (ibid., 401).

Case Study 3: Democratizing Politics
A Focused Goal

Although the classic example of organizing an identity-based network begins with building identity through small collectives, it is not in fact the only way for an identity-based network to become powerful and influential. With a clearly understood identity and skilled usage of resources, a network organizing primarily through public spaces can make an impressive political impact. To be effective, however, the network choosing to organize in this fashion requires a highly focused goal.

At approximately the same time that the CNF was organizing its conferences, another network of politically active women was also achieving recognition. At first blush, it appeared to share traits with the CNF. Like the CNF, it had few identity statements and dissolved itself in a year. That, however, is where the similarities ended. Unlike the CNF, this network had a well-understood identity, albeit unspoken and unpublished, and achieved many of its clear and focused goals. Unlike the CNF, this network was small, making a larger impact than its numbers warranted. This network did not dissolve as much as it submerged itself in the fabric of daily living, reemerging under a different name as the need arose. Although the name changed with each reinvention, the identity, the goals, and the participants remained mostly the same. The networks that they convened were successful because the identity of genderized Sandinismo had already been well worked out during the 1980s and early 1990s, and resources were relatively abundant and accessible due to the positions and skills of the participants. When the opportunity arose to democratize political structures and parties, these women coalesced rapidly, organizing and lobbying primarily through public spaces.

The necessity to democratize politics to make it more amenable to women became the goal of a number of Sandinista female activists. After the Sandinista loss at the 1990 election and with AMNLAE's declining support among Nicaraguan women, these activists decided that the organizational structure of the FSLN had to be democratized to attract women's support and participation. Later, women spread the democratizing impetus to society-wide political structures. It was hoped that with increased numbers of women being politically active at more levels and functioning in more horizontally organized and accountable political structures, the rollback of women's rights would cease.

Sandinista women did not organize themselves through small collectives but rather strictly through networks that operated only through public spaces. Networks that emerge and then submerge themselves need public spaces to persuade the state and civil society (Cohen 1983, 111), to strategize around achieving a specific goal, and to expand political rights through the definition of the movement's boundary of acceptance of new ideas (Cohen 1982, 38–40). "Public spaces become the arena for the contended definition of what is political, that is, of what belongs to the polis" (Melucci 1997, 221). Public spaces are the political arm of an identity-based social movement.

Although public spaces are free from external control and thereby leave the identity nonpartisan, they straddle the public and the private spheres, mediating demands between one and the other. As a result, public spaces can incorporate resources and actors from the state, even hostile ones. With the networks of politically active women, the participants in the public spaces included some elected representatives and bureaucrats, as well as professionals and workers from NGOs (both foreign and domestic). Thus, the division between civil society and the state, still unclear in corporatist Nicaragua despite Chamorro's neoliberal efforts, remained blurred in public spaces.

In order to democratize the party structure of the FSLN, Sandinista women wanted to have a greater number of women involved at all levels in the FSLN. The Sandinista female superstars were well represented and respected, but at a lower level women were either invisible or had joined autonomous groups (not just women's groups but also neighborhood committees, disabled people's organizations, and environmental groups, among others). The role of women at the intermediary level had been progressively diminished since the revolution in 1979 (interview Herrera). After the uproar caused by the failure to include Dora María Téllez on the National Directorate at the First Congress 1991, Ortega had to promise to include a woman the next time around. But Sandinista women wanted more than just the appointment of another superstar. They wanted a structural change in the system so that women would be incorporated at all levels.

New tactics were called for, and Sandinista women were too experienced not to realize it. They had an opportunity to increase women's participation and democratize the structure of the FSLN at the 1994 Extraordinary Congress. Earlier that year, AMNLAE had suggested a structural change, proposing that 50 percent of all Sandinista nominees going into the 1996 general election be women. But there was such an uproar from both the men and the women at this radical stance that AMNLAE dropped it. AMNLAE was told that it could reasonably expect 20 percent (interview Dávila). In order for this structural change in the organization of the party to occur, it had to be approved as policy in the FSLN's 1994 Congress. This Congress held the FSLN's first election for individual leadership positions rather than for a slate of candidates. It decided who would run the Party: the Daniel Ortega/Tomás Borge orthodoxists or the Sergio Ramirez/Doris Tijerino renewalists. It was sufficiently difficult to predict who would win the vote that both sides needed to court the women's vote, although neither side wanted to alienate the mainstream.

AMNLAE's acceptance of the realistic option of a 20 percent quota for female nominees did not satisfy a number of Sandinista women. The relationship between the autonomous women's movement and AMNLAE was slowly improving. After the departure of Gladys Baez, the FSLN appointed Dora Zeledón as coordinator of AMNLAE. Zeledón, unlike previous appointees, was not one of the Sandinista superstars but rather a lower-ranking Sandinista. She initiated a process of reflection and examination on AMNLAE's role with the FSLN, its relationship with the rest of the women's movement, and its new identity and goals. This process took almost a year, ending in 1993. Although it maintained its emphasis on class liberation, AMNLAE shifted its basic training to include self-esteem, health issues, and violence against women. In addition to maintaining women's centers, in 1994 AMNLAE began a rotating bank. To receive a loan, women had to attend accounting classes and gender training. Demand for the loans far outstripped the supply of money. Although AMNLAE had declared its autonomy from the FSLN and strongly pursued alliances with the autonomous women's movement (Quandt 1997, 86), AMNLAE was still conservative and too much of a negotiator between the FSLN and the autonomous women's movement.

Instead, María Dolores Ocón, a member of the hitherto quiet Professional Women's Network, organized a conference for all Sandinista women, active or not, to discuss AMNLAE's proposal and what women should demand at the Extraordinary Congress. At the conference, the women called themselves *Las Mujeres Autoconvocadas* (Self-Convoked

Women), meaning that they belonged to neither political division and therefore answered to no one but themselves. This identity allowed them to avoid the fissures within the Party. Sandinista women had already grappled publicly and privately with their identity in relation to the FSLN and Sandinismo. With the creation of the autonomous women's movement, there seems to have emerged a quiet consensus that activists who kept their affiliation with the FSLN could be highly critical of the Sandinistas but nonetheless work within the system, changing it from within. As the saying went, "Before I was a feminist, I was a Sandinista." As a longtime Sandinista activist said, "Sandinismo was like a glorious love affair that soured. But now we are friends" (interview Barahona). Milú Vargas explained that one could be an activist for women's rights outside the FSLN and yet work within it as well, because the FSLN was the political arm of a social justice movement. She was working toward social justice within the most logical political organization, which allowed her the option to criticize the Party even though she was an alternate representative of the FSLN in the National Assembly (interview).[10] This well-articulated and well-known identity allowed Sandinista women activists to bypass AMNLAE and to embed themselves in the autonomous women's movement (Quandt 1997, 86).

All the women's secretariats showed up for the conference of *Las Mujeres Autoconvocadas*, as did AMNLAE and a number of individuals from the lowest and the highest rank within the FSLN who normally did not attend conferences. The conference was one day long, with the goal of consensus that 50 percent of the FSLN nominees in the 1996 elections would be women. There were obviously a number of differences between the women at the conference arising from internal affiliation with the FSLN, the nature of daily work, the range of commitment to the FSLN, and personal understandings of the specifics of Sandinismo or social justice. Like the January 1992 First National Meeting "Unity in Diversity," which organized the women's movement, the public space absorbed these differences because of the well-established, overarching identity of Sandinismo and the immediate and focused goal of 50 percent. Thus, the women shared and enhanced their common world.

After the conference, AMNLAE, the unions, and the rest of the Sandinista women's groups organized around the demand for 50 percent representation. This demand was included as an issue for discussion in all of the regional and local meetings before sending a representative to vote at the 1994 Extraordinary Congress.

The discussion of the 50 percent quota was spirited throughout the nation. The national discussion about women, politics, and rights demonstrates how a social movement organization through the use of public space influences the debates in society, broadening its understanding of democracy. The CNF feminists found themselves with strange bedfellows when their claim coincided with that of conservatives who stated that there were not enough competent women to hold so many positions of power. The debate brought to light questions of power and how to differentiate "good" power from "bad" power (interview Blandón), the role of ethics and power (Zeledón 1993, 2), and the functioning of democracy within the constraints of inequality (Vargas 1994).

At the Congress, the final agreed-upon quota of all party positions to be allocated to women was 30 percent. Later, other political parties, not wanting to appear sexist, also promised women a 30 percent quota for representation within their party positions and nominees (Pasos 1995), although none of them later fulfilled that promise. *Las Mujeres Autoconvocadas* had attained its explicit goal of increasing women's political participation through the use of a public space.

Given the tension surrounding the definition of the functioning of a democracy, and given that the newly elected Ortega stripped his competitors and their supporters of their Sandinista affiliation and positions within the party, it is remarkable that *Las Mujeres Autoconvocadas* was not also brought down by its far more radical demands. The high profile and positions that many of the women of *Las Mujeres Autoconvocadas* enjoyed may have helped in attaining the goal of increasing women's representation within political parties because it allowed them access to political leaders and sources of political power. Also, *Las Mujeres Autoconvocadas* was not targeting just the Party in an effort to broaden the sphere of freedom against an incursionary state. Rather, it was targeting both civil society and the Party with the hope of persuading both of the value of women's political participation. Finally, the demand for the quota had strong and unified support from AMNLAE and indeed from all of the Sandinista women's organizations, leaving little room for a splintering.[11] The very source and organization of *Las Mujeres Autoconvocadas* straddled public and private, civil and political spheres. This protected *Las Mujeres Autoconvocadas* from the fallout over the control of the Party.

After winning the battle, *Las Mujeres Autoconvocadas* disappeared. Because a Sandinista identity was already well established, there was no need to create one through collectives and sustain it through a network. As a result, *Las Mujeres Autoconvocadas* could exist only in public spaces.

Las Mujeres Autoconvocadas resurfaced four months later to formulate a platform for the 1996 election. Again, the discussion was focused, practical, and strategic. Again, there was no explicit creation of identity. The value of their critical Sandinismo was self-evident to them and did not merit debate. At the meeting, *Las Mujeres Autoconvocadas* also distributed a document that reflected on the relationship between women's collective identity, the FSLN, and democracy.

Entitled "A Democratic Society As Understood and Aspired to by Women" with its theme of "democracy according to women," the document dealt with democracy, ideology, economy, the social realm (subdivided into two parts, education and health), law, and politics. It then inserted this discussion into a wider context of social movements and the Sandinista Party. It analyzed the women's movement as "multiple expressions of women organized around concrete objections and actions." Decentralization, networks, and an autonomous identity based on an ethos of care were strongly encouraged, as were individual virtues such as self-esteem and self-expression. *Las Mujeres Autoconvocadas* presented a vision of society, democracy, and rights as an extension of the ethos of care. The ethos of care, as argued earlier, is the reflection of the women's movement's identity and the organizing principle behind the mobilization of resources.

This document provided the blueprint for the Nicaraguan women's movement to organize social movements, to respond to concrete concerns, and to affect the national political sphere. Sandinista women envisioned political parties, a women's movement, and a society based on a profound penetration of equality, participation, and empowerment, widening the understanding of democracy and politics to every sphere and group in the nation. The vision was grounded in individual expression and collective identity and was further grounded in the political sphere emulating the grass roots rather than vice versa.

In 1995, the FSLN accepted the document as a foundational under-standing of women and democracy. It was accepted by most of the women's groups and NGOs, and then by all the countries of Central America (Pasos 1995). "The Democratic Society As Seen and Aspired to by Women" was the transcendent political framework that the CNF failed to create through the Aquelarre Conference.

After the successful promulgation of their document, *Las Mujeres Autoconvocadas* once again disappeared, this time permanently. However, in 1995, politically active women came together again at the First National Convention of Women and Politics. With the threat of an electoral sweep by the far-right Liberal Alliance, even non-Sandinista women shared the concern that the next government would continue to roll back the gains that women had achieved during the Sandinista era. The First National Convention of Women and Politics was not merely an attempt to safe-guard women's rights but also a defense against the increasing political polarization precipitating the rise of ever-more right-wing governments (Montenegro 1997, 368–69, 389).

Ironically, INIM initiated the Convention of Women and Politics (in-terview Matus 1998), which then spawned a series of seminars so that women could share their understandings and experiences. Again, the public space served to create a common world among women of differ-ing political leanings and resulted in the creation of a new network, the National Coalition of Women, for which the women's movement took credit (interview Blandón 1998). In turn, this network wrote and lobbied for a Minimum Agenda that all political parties should endorse. The Min-imum Agenda bore a remarkable similarity to the document produced by *Las Mujures Autoconvocadas,* "The Democratic Society As Seen and As-pired to by Women." Despite its clarion calls for virtues such as respect, dignity, and tolerance; human rights understood as civil, political, social, economic, and cultural rights; and development in the areas of education, economy, and law; the Minimum Agenda did not include reproductive rights per se but rather the weaker right to reproductive health services (National Coalition of Women 1996, 10).

The Minimum Agenda was well publicized through the women's me-dia outlets and more mainstream press. On March 8, 1996, the National Coalition of Women marched with the autonomous women's movement in support of women's rights. With six months remaining before the general election, the National Coalition had the time to lobby political parties for their endorsement of the Minimum Agenda. Thanks to Scandinavian governments and NGOs, it also had the financial resources to continue organizing and lobbying the establishment. By the time of the election, the National Coalition of Women managed to get the FSLN, the National Resistance, and the UNO to commit to implementing the Minimum Agenda if elected. The Liberal Alliance of Alemán refused to sign the Minimum Agenda (Luciak 1997, 6).

The networks that these highly political women created were only to achieve a short-term and highly focused influence on the political sphere. Their goals were to expand women's political participation and rights and to redefine the functioning of a democracy. These ideas were expressed, publicized, and lobbied for in public spaces because they are the arena in which the political actions of a social movement take place. The networks further used public spaces to adroitly strategize and organize themselves before persuading both the state and civil society. In so doing, public spaces exposed the limits of the boundary of the acceptance of new ideas, both within the women's movement and within society at large.

The drive to democratize politics was successful in as much as the demand for women's political rights deepened the discussion of women's democratic needs and rights, outlined the boundary of the acceptance of what women perceived as necessary to participate fully and freely in the public sphere, and starkly cast the shortcomings of both the status quo and the incoming Alemán government. More concretely, women's demands were integrated into the 1996 federal election.

The election was controversial due to electoral irregularities. These irregularities were uncorrected, so the official election results had the Liberal Alliance with forty-four seats, or 52 percent, and the FSLN with thirty-seven seats, or 38 percent of the popular vote. Arnoldo Alemán headed the Liberals, the party that represented the dictator during the sham elections of the 1930s to 1970s. The Alemán family had been staunch supporters of the dictatorship. After the revolution, his property, like that of all who had been closely affiliated with the dictator, was seized by the FSLN, and Alemán himself was jailed and released in 1979. Nonetheless, he remained in Nicaragua throughout the 1980s, increasing his land holdings. In 1990, he was elected the mayor of Managua, a position he held until becoming president in 1996. While mayor, he beautified the city, installing fountains and traffic roundabouts, planting trees, and knocking down crumbling buildings. These programs were remarkably popular, even among the poor, and made a visible if superficial difference to the city. Throughout his tenure, Alemán publicized how much he was getting done versus the stalemated National Assembly. During his election campaign, he promised to similarly modernize the country. Funded by the domestic elite of Nicaragua and American expatriates, including the rich expatriate Cuban community, Alemán won the election, although probably not by the extent suggested by the official results.

During the election, the FSLN fulfilled its promise of a 30 percent quota of women's participation. From a total of ninety Sandinista candidates, thirty-two (or 35.6 percent) were female versus 18.9 percent in the 1990 election. However, the female candidates were mostly running in ridings where the FSLN was unlikely to win. The men were given preferential access to the safe seats. Sandinista women were outraged at the FSLN's placement of women in no-win seats. Weakened by the split with the MRS and worried about the powerful showings of the Liberal Alliance at the polls, the National Directorate agreed to "braid" (i.e., alternate) male and female positions in the establishment of the national list (Luciak 1997, 10, 11). This resulted in four women running in safe ridings being elected to the National Assembly. At the 1996 election, more female Sandinistas were elected than in either of the previous two elections. Including alternates, women held a total of twenty-three seats, or 31.9 percent, of the Sandinista total. However, there were only eight (22 percent) female members elected to the National Assembly, with the majority of women elected as alternates (fifteen, or 41.7 percent). Despite the braiding, the number of women holding seats in the National Assembly actually dropped from 23.1 percent in 1990 to 22 percent in 1996 (Luciak 1997, 13).

Nonetheless, what the Sandinistas accomplished looks impressive when compared to the record of the winning party's female participation. The Liberal Alliance had only eight female candidates running with fourteen alternates, none of whom was in prominent positions or safe seats. Not a single Liberal Alliance woman won a seat in the National Assembly.[12] Although several of the smaller parties ran women, some of them won not a single seat, male or female, and others won seats only for the men. Only the Conservative Party (with two seats) and the Independent

Liberal Party (with one seat) each had one female legislator (Luciak 1997, 13). This meant that female representatives were essentially a Sandinista bloc, weakening the ability of a network like the National Coalition of Women to continue to democratize politics through focused but nonpartisan public discussions. Furthermore, the contrast between the number of seats that women held in the National Assembly versus the quantity of alternates calls into question the value of braiding and the usefulness of quotas as a method of increasing female participation and of democratizing politics.

If the value of the goals that women in politics pursued proved questionable, the issues raised and the debates provoked were beneficial not merely to the women's movement but to all who cherished an active citizenship and democracy. Any of the women's groups could have initiated these discussions; however, the women interested in democratizing politics did it in a particularly efficient manner. They had a well-established, thoroughly debated identity, plenty of resources, and a highly focused short-term goal of influencing the immediate political agenda. With these components, women could organize themselves, lobby society and political parties, and redefine democracy and the role of women within it, almost exclusively through public spaces.

Case Study 4: Women's Health Network
Mobilized Resources

The most sustained and effective critique of the Chamorro government's policies about women came from the Women's Health Network. The network, which included all sizes of groups, from the smallest collective in the most rural parts of Nicaragua to international NGOs, had an identity and a locus of conflict based on the body. But this identity had a number of modes of articulation, including international conventions on women's issues, human rights, and an ethos of care. Different subnetworks expressed various aspects of the identity depending on the forum, the participants, and the immediate goal. Given the sheer range of its participants, the network, not surprisingly, undertook a number of strategies and approaches. More unusually, it also had more than one focused short-term goal. It wanted to change the government's health care policies affecting women, replace the state's health care services, and change the symbolic content of motherhood. While it was able to achieve the last of its goals, it was only partially successful in replacing the state's health care, and was wholly unable to force the government to change its policies, although it did encourage the government to open a space for negotiation. The different forms of identity with different goals operating through different subnetworks, collectives, NGOs, and health clinics should have created an ineffectual mess. However, the resources, especially the structure of the internal organization, were superbly mobilized, and thus the network became powerful and influential in Nicaragua.

The scope of activity of the Women's Health Network reflects the number of collectives involved, and therefore the potential power that the network can call upon. In the first six months of the Women's Health Network, there were 216 activities (*La Gente,* July 12, 1992, 11).[13] This may seem like a great many, but given the number of collectives in the Women's Health Network the number becomes more understandable. The Women's Health Network included neighborhood women's collectives from all the major urban centers. As well, it included all the women's health/legal clinics, AMNLAE's *Casas de Mujeres,* independent *Casas de Mujeres,* and the regional health organizations funded by the Ministry of Health, which operated with a high degree of autonomy. In addition, there were other networks that intersected with the Women's Health Network: The Professional Women for Development Network, the Women's Health Network "María Cavallieri," the NGOs that worked in health, and the think tanks, the Fight Against Maternal Mortality Commission, Meeting Points, and CEDIM. The Women's Health Network intersected through its member NGOs, the government's health organizations, and the international community in support of women and health, such as the New York Women's Environment and Development Organization (WEDO).

The Women's Health Network integrated all the collectives and clinics at a departmental (provincial), national, and international level. It allowed each unit to mobilize, organize, and publicize around the issue of health as each unit saw fit. For example, the health clinic ¡*Sí Mujer!* operated autonomously from the network, collecting its own information, producing its own pamphlets, and mobilizing its own constituents. The Women's Health Network "María Cavallieri" also operated autonomously. In comparison, five of the Managua neighborhood collectives banded together to organize joint marches and to utilize the same pamphlets. Each group highlighted issues that it thought were the most relevant.

Although highly decentralized with differing mandates, these groups were able to come together in subnetworks to pursue common goals. The collectives chose their own priorities for social and political change, and then participated to the extent desired in the appropriate subnetwork. Although the subnetworks communicated with one another on special occasions, there was sufficient overlapping of participants, interests, and joint activities, as well as extensive media coverage from both the women's as well as the mainstream media, that the network as a whole remained integrated and mutually supportive. In effect, the subnetworks formed a web of activities, modes of consciousness and commitments, and identities.[14]

The health and law clinics, with the support of international and domestic NGOs, attempted to replace the state's health care services. Although data are sketchy, it is indicative of the growth of NGO health care funding that between 1988 and 1992 it increased 48 percent (Centro de Información y Servicios de Asesoría 1997, 89) with the major growth occurring after 1992. The health and law clinics informed women about their bodies and empowered them to be active participants in their health care. The clinics were also able to mobilize neighborhood women for political events, women who might otherwise not be politically active.

Regardless of the spread of health care clinics and of the type of health care that they offered, women's health continued to suffer. It was affected by too many factors such as poverty, family needs, violence, and stress to be wholly ameliorated. Replicating some health care at the neighborhood level could not completely replace the withdrawal of the state from social services.

In order to inform and influence the rest of civil society of the crisis in women's health, a subnetwork began and then organized around Maternal Mortality Day. Thus began a deeply symbolic battle over the meaning of motherhood. Motherhood was one of the most powerful symbols in Nicaragua and had previously been used successfully for political purposes: by AMPRONAC in 1977–1978, by the Sandinistas during the war, and by Chamorro to win the 1990 election. Now the women's movement began to use it. As Tarrow has pointed out, networks unite around commonly understood symbols to achieve goals. The organizers of Maternal Mortality Day fought to change the glorification of the mother as an ever-sacrificing, passive nurturer into an awareness of maternity as jeopardized by an unfair and inadequate health care system, occasionally leading to death.

Maternal Mortality Day is May 28, a day originally chosen by Costa Rica, which shows the cross-national diffusion of strategic ideas (McAdam and Rucht 1993). More to the point, it is also Mother's Day, a day marked by an excess of sentiment, even by Nicaraguan standards. Using the established Mother's Day to discuss maternal mortality shows the strategic canniness of the Women's Health Network. Maternal Mortality Day has increasingly dominated Mother's Day. The growing impact and success of the Women's Health Network in changing the symbol were reflected in the change between 1991 and 1994 in the media coverage of the Women's Health Network.

In 1991, the Mother's Day editorial in *Barricada*, the newspaper most sympathetic to women's rights, could only envision motherhood within a Marxist framework: "The problem with mothers is not a simple topic but rather an economic and political problem. In our society, divided into bourgeois landowners and high dignitaries of the Church on one side and on the opposite the proletarians and the *campesinos* who sell their labor to the exploiter, the mother as well is enslaved by invisible threads that tie her to the capitalist engine of exploitation" (May 29, 1991, 4). By the following May, the Maternal Mortality Day Subnetwork began to make an impact on *La Barricada's* coverage of Mother's Day. For the following two years, the confused reporting on the role of motherhood reflected the battle over control of the symbol. By 1994, articles on maternal mortality dominated the coverage.[15] Mother's Day was not merely a day to celebrate motherhood but a day of gratitude for having survived the experience. In comparison to *La Barricada's* changing presentation of Mother's Day, *La Prensa,* the government newspaper, continued with its saccharine presentation of the joys of motherhood.

The Maternal Mortality Day Subnetwork was adroit at using mass media to communicate its ideas to civil society. In order to change the symbol of motherhood, the Subnetwork engaged in eye-catching demonstrations publicized by the media. Beginning on Mother's Day 1992, mothers whose daughters had died in childbirth carried signs with their daughters' names and their ages at death. The women paraded up and down in front of the National Assembly and marched up the street. It was a stunning display of pain initiating action. Many of the female deputies, including Azucena Ferrey (conservative and head of the reactionary Women and Family Coalition), came out to talk to the women. This event was covered by the local media, granting the demonstration legitimacy and helping in the transformation of Mother's Day into a political issue.

The ability of the women's movement to shift the symbolic value of Mother's Day reflected its ability to mobilize resources strategically. The Women's Health Network was able to change the symbol of motherhood because it pointed out its inconsistencies: the paradox of worshipping motherhood in a society that denies maternal health care. The network also offered an alternative: changed laws, abolished patriarchy, and altered democratic practices.

These alternatives, clearly political in orientation, were the focus of different subnetworks of the Women's Health Network. One subnetwork directly petitioned the government, demanding courageously if pointlessly that it counteract the statements by the Catholic Church and various government ministries that maternal mortality was a natural occurrence and that there was little anyone could do about it except place one's faith in God. So the first statement in the petition was that maternal mortality was not an act of God but rather a response to declining social services, unwanted pregnancies, and complications arising from illegal abortions. Although the Women's Health Network had been active for just one and a half years at this point, it had no difficulty expanding from the grass-roots experience to making the connection between the social, political, and economic relationships of power; it had no compunction about directly confronting the highest political and social powers in the nation.

Another group of subnetworks organized for international conferences, positioning itself as the nexus between the international community, the state, and domestic political organizations.[16] All of these international conferences had preparatory meetings at the national, then Central American, and finally Latin American levels. The three years of continuous planning for international conferences spread and consolidated ideas and approaches through sharing documents and research, through consulting the grass roots and NGOs, and through cooperating with professionals, technicians, and, finally, government-appointed bureaucrats. In much the same way that the internal structure of a social movement is a resource to be correctly mobilized, so too is a series of conferences, or public spaces, a useful tool to assist in the development of a successful social movement.

One cannot say that these meetings created an identity, but they did reflect the network's overarching and unifying ethos of care. In addition to formulating a Nicaraguan perspective on the overlapping topics of the international summits, the cycle of domestic conferences was aimed at changing government policies affecting women by levering support through the international community. As seen in Chapter 6, the Nicaraguan state proved equally adroit at using the international community to bolster its own position.

The mistake the women's movement made was in underestimating the government. If the FSLN in the 1980s was continuously surprised by the articulate and uncompromising nature of the women's demands, then the women's movement in the 1990s was equally surprised by the articulate and uncompromising nature of the Chamorro government's position. The assumption that the women's movement made was that the Nicaraguan government would crumble under the combined onslaught of the Women's Health Network and international pressure. But the state had the strength, the cunning, and the ability to negotiate or stand firm, depending on the situation.

Perhaps as well, the government's stance was a result of the nature of the relationship between social movements, states, and conflicts. If conflict is an impetus needed to create a social movement, then one might say that the reverse is also true: the demands of a social movement contributed to the crystallization and hardening of the government's position. As the women's movement became stronger and more focused in its criticisms of the government, the government too became increasingly adept at offsetting and undermining the women's movement both domestically and internationally. They learned from each other in a mutually creative dynamic.

The increasing sophistication of the government's response to the women's movement highlights an incorrect assumption of social movement literature. The explicit assumption of both the resource mobilization and identity thinkers is that with an effective and powerful social movement, the state can be reformed either through lobbying (resource mobilization), changed cultural discourse (Alvarez, Dagnino, and Escobar 1998), or a mixture of the two (Cohen and Arato 1992). The tacit assumption is that the state will change in the direction encouraged by the social movement. As the Chamorro government demonstrated, however, the impact of a social movement on its surrounding environment and on the government is uncontrollable and thus unpredictable.

The benefits from the international conferences and from direct government lobbying were further publicity throughout the nation around the issue of women's reproductive rights and maternal mortality, a sustained and focused locus of conflict around which the women's movement could organize, and the opening of more public spaces in which the women's movement could organize, including the insistence that the government open one for negotiations. Combined with the Maternal Mortality Day Subnetwork, the Women's Health Network changed dominant symbolic norms, informed civil society and the state, and replaced some government services.

The Women's Health Network clearly demonstrates the difference between the Sandinista women's movement in the 1980s and the women's movement under state-imposed neoliberalism and Catholicism. The FSLN enacted a health care program, choosing goals and then implementing them through government-trained health care specialists. To deal specifically with women's health, the FSLN funded AMNLAE's women's centers and a women's hospital. Despite the participation of AMNLAE, a mass organization, women's health care was not a political issue per se but rather part of the FSLN's social justice agenda. With health care, the Sandinista women's movement and the FSLN shared the same general goal and thus were able to act cooperatively and effectively to improve women's health. However, women created no identity around the body, had limited and controlled opportunity to petition the government for different services, and had few resources of their own.

In comparison, women's health care became the paramount political issue under neoliberal economic policies and conservative Catholicism and exemplified the hostility between the women's movement and the Chamorro government. Because women were forced back into the home with fewer possibilities of leaving it and fewer resources to expend on organizing, the women's movement had to decentralize extensively, dealing with local needs at the local level. In effect, the women's movement went to where the women were. Networks were horizontally organized, with each group granted a high degree of autonomy from the others. Leadership was democratically chosen, as was the extent and form of involvement. Organizing itself through networks allowed the Women's Health Network to operate throughout the nation, from the most rural of areas to the international arena. Although highly decentralized, the network was also highly integrated, uniting women's health and law clinics, NGOs, women's collectives, and women's research groups. It focused on issues surrounding the body yet included women's human rights, demographics, sexuality, economics, and empowerment. It operated in public spaces, created its own spaces, and insisted that the government open a space for negotiation. Again through networks, it joined the international movement for women and health as a development and rights issue, yet it based itself on Nicaraguan reality. The Women's Health Network is not just an excellent example of how the women's movement under the Chamorro government reorganized itself to emphasize identity and autonomy. It is also an example of superb mobilization of resources to achieve goals, specifically the internal structure of the social movement itself.

The autonomous women's movement has been a power unto itself since 1992. The women's movement and the government conflicted predominantly over policies and symbols written on the body. Finally, in the 1990s, it was possible to see the women's movement organized against the state. According to Tilly (1978) and Tarrow (1994, 191), a state provides a focused target for social movements, facilitating their growth. AMPRONAC united women against the state. However, AMNLAE and the semiautonomous women's groups could not provide such a target due to the corporatist nature of the Sandinista government. Thus, AMNLAE and the semiautonomous women's groups had to find their source of conflict outside the government. This proved possible but was nonetheless difficult. However, the overt hostility of the Chamorro government to women's rights, specifically women's right based on the body, promoted the development of women's identity and politics on this issue.

While the women's movement was able to replace services through its own health and law clinics, to open new spaces for the articulation of political rights, to transgress the symbolic boundaries of society, and to reform the penal code to criminalize domestic violence, on average, the government's public policies held firm. The women's movement was able to achieve so much against a sophisticated and ideologically driven government because of the movement's ability to mobilize resources, articulate an identity, and focus on clear short-term goals.

The resources that the women's movement had available to it in the 1990s were international sources for funding, a vast repertoire of political skills from fifteen years of organizing, the support and interest of the mainstream media and the creation of its own media, and its own internal structure, including the use of public spaces. The autonomous women's movement in the 1990s organized itself on collectives and neighborhood groups, uniting through ad hoc networks and public spaces to achieve political and social change. Networks and public spaces served to organize diverse and isolated collectives in order to influence civil society and the state, discover the limits of the acceptance of the women's movement, and forge the movement's overarching guiding ethos. Networks and public spaces allowed identity to move from shared personal testimonies to political action, and to combat the government's policies by attracting media attention, articulating a persuasive critique and alternative, and creating social consciousness about an issue. In addition, networks and public spaces worked their political influence more subtly through disseminating documents and information, organizing courses and meetings, and involving women's sections from unions and other mixed institutions.

None of this is to suggest that there was agreement on all issues. On something as fundamental as structuring the movement, not all activists agreed with the need to decentralize through networks and identity formation. The mode of organization that was so clear with hindsight was something that the women's movement had to grope toward, a truth about mobilization that had to be discovered.

Despite the eventual consensus that emerged about how to organize the movement, differing approaches, priorities, and identities still existed. Organizing a movement through networks assumes differences and similarities among the movement's members but allows them to create common goals and strategies while respecting different identities. Despite the efforts of the women's movement to centralize organization and understandings, it became obvious that the women's movement was, and will be, based on diversity. Public spaces were able to overcome differences by focusing on the similarities, goals, symbols, and strategies that unite women. In comparison, difference within a network, as the CNF demonstrated, was more difficult to transcend due to the necessity of a network to have its own identity. Nonetheless, if the goal is focused, then different approaches, emphases, and understandings can be absorbed, as the Women's Health Network demonstrated.

If the identity and goal were already well established, then a public space could be immediately convened and networks and collectives bypassed, as *Las Mujeres Autoconvocadas* demonstrated. However, if the identity was new, then it would have to grow to be familiar enough that it could create a successful public space, as the identity of the Women Against Violence Network did. If the identity was unfamiliar, then the public space would only produce confusion or quiet dismissal, as the efforts by the CNF showed. The downfall of the CNF suggests that even if the identity was well established, its root must be indigenous and not imported.

A social movement with its identity rooted in the body yet a holistic enough ethos to encompass all aspects of sociopolitical change, with the ability to skillfully mobilize all resources available to it, and with its focus on achieving specific goals, can become powerful and influential, regardless of the lack of political opportunity to change the status quo—as the Nicaraguan women's movement in the 1990s has proven. Furthermore, with its structure and identity, the Nicaraguan women's movement would be flexible enough to respond to the incoming president, Arnoldo Alemán, ensuring its success under another government hostile to women's rights.

Plus Ça Change

AN ANALYSIS OF THE CHANGES within the Nicaraguan women's movement from 1977 to 1996 demonstrates the salience of three organizing components of a social movement: autonomous identity, strategic mobilization of resources, and focused goals. For a social movement to be sustainable and successful, it is also necessary that these three components be mutually reinforcing, or else the movement will not be strong enough to attain its goals, continue to attract participants, and influence the political sphere. The absence of any one of these components undermines the viability of the social movement. This conclusion holds true whether the Nicaraguan women's movement was organizing under a repressive dictatorship, revolutionary socialism, or neoliberalism. This analytical approach to the study of a social movement also explains the reasons for the direction that the Nicaraguan women's movement took, its successes and failures, and its ability to reorganize itself quickly in response to the profound and rapid sociopolitical and economic changes that Nicaragua was experiencing.

The analytical framework that I have developed is grounded in social movement theory. Social movement theory is generally composed of two schools of thought: resource mobilization, which concerns the strategic organizing of a movement, and identity, which concerns the transformative ethic underlying a movement's mobilization. In an effort to be comprehensive, however, both schools of thought have recently begun to include each other in a complementary fashion. While I used an amalgam of thinkers as the most reasonable means of utilizing both schools, I found it necessary to augment and redefine some of the core concepts.

First is the concept of grievance as a fundamental element of a successfully organized social movement. I suggest that conflict must be focused and become the social movement's goal in order for the social movement to be successful in mobilizing resources and influencing the public sphere. Without a focused conflict, it is difficult for a social movement's networks and public spaces to transcend differences and formulate effective political action, or even to mobilize resources and participants.

In addition to suggesting that conflict must be focused into a goal, a historical analysis of the Nicaraguan women's movement suggests that the internal structure of the organization and the movement is critical to achieving its goals and articulating identities. Internal structure becomes a resource to be mobilized like any other resource, such as money, skills, and communication.

The most effective means through which the women's movement organized itself was through networks. Networks are organized around common goals with a division of labor within the network to perpetuate itself. Networks can be extraordinarily complex, stretching from the grass roots, through departmental (provincial) levels, to become national networks, and finally operating in the international sphere. Because networks offer participants the opportunity through their small and supportive collectives to define their own identity, goals, and commitment while nonetheless allowing them to act in a larger and better-organized political process, networks are one of the few means by which identity-based groups can organize themselves while still granting primacy to identity formation. Networks are organized by like-minded collectives or through convening in public spaces.

Public spaces, which are intermediate and mediating ad hoc instances that lie between the public and private spheres, the state and civil society, do more than articulate a social movement's conflict. Public spaces are the political arm of a social movement. They outline the movement's boundary of acceptance of new ideas, influence civil society and the state, and organize concrete political action. Public spaces assist a social movement's development by forging and solidifying the movement's overarching identity. By bringing people together to discuss a specific issue, through focusing on commonalty, differences can be bridged and a common understanding, a "common sense," can be created. Public spaces can be the product of both the growth of collectives and networks and the creator of both collectives and networks. Thus, the utilization of public spaces is a critical and complex aspect of social movement growth and maintenance.

The complexity of what constitutes resources and how best to utilize them suggests that resources are not objective and concrete tools but rather a highly subjective interpretation of what constitutes a tool. This diminishes for social scientists the quantitative aspect of social movement analysis and instead posits the analyst in the realm of interpretation. Like activists trying to gauge the best means to develop and strengthen their movement, social scientists must grope toward appreciating the uniqueness of each social movement's resource mobilization.

While it is critical to mobilize resources and then direct them to achieve a specific goal, the bedrock of a social movement is identity formation. The importance of identity cannot be overstated. Identity is a personal understanding of one's life shared and shaped through a group. This ethic must also include an alternative understanding of how society might work and a commitment to implementing that vision. Identity draws people into the group and motivates them to act. As the collective grows, it has a tendency to splinter, because the highly personal approach to creating this identity lends itself to fragmentation. Within a network and a public space, this is not a problem, as collectives can still unite around a common goal while maintaining their own identity. Diversity, then, must be one of the guiding principles of the social movement so that differences can be sustained.

Identity formation presupposes a number of factors. First, the collective must have autonomy from outside influence in order to create its own subjectivity without the fear that "incorrect" ideas will arise. Such autonomy did not fully occur within the Nicaraguan women's movement until 1991. Second, identity formation presupposes that humanity has within itself the capacity to critically analyze its own history, judge it, and then learn from it in order to present new ideas and approaches based on the failings of the past. Therefore, identity must be grounded in and yet transcend its own history. If identity formation cannot perform this feat, then no identity-based group or social movement can grow or operate successfully.

The successful growth of a social movement involves more than just identity formation. The interaction of the three components of a social movement must be complementary. A social movement cannot withstand the tension of an identity that is at odds with its mobilization of resources. For example, during the 1980s the Sandinista identity was one of equality, justice, and freedom, yet the organization of AMNLAE was hierarchical, dictatorial, and sexist.

The components are not merely complementary but are also mutually creative. Thus, they are neither discrete units nor independent operations. The ethos affects the very means by which a group arrives at a decision, as well as the decision itself. The implementation of the decision narrows the locus of conflict into a focused goal, which in turn gives a greater understanding of the nature of the barriers facing the participants. This affects the participants' understanding of their world and the shaping of their alternative to that world. As the goal and the identity become clearer, the means of attaining that goal, that is, the strategies and resources, become clearer, including what constitutes a resource and what does not. Thus, a social movement, like its constituent components of identity, resources, and conflict, is a socially constructed and changing human artifact.

The analytical framework above has provided a persuasive model for explaining the Nicaraguan women's movement. The theory explains why AMPRONAC was able to be so successful in such a short period of time. Its effective autonomy from the FSLN allowed AMPRONAC's decisions and voice to be driven by the grass roots. Women listened to one another in public spaces and formulated their own understanding of what constituted social justice or Sandinismo. AMPRONAC had a focused conflict with the dictatorship and a decentralized organization with a high degree of alliance-building through networks, and sophisticated communication skills. Thus, it was able to achieve its goals of attracting more women, empowering them to change their understanding of women's role in society, and undermining the dictatorship's legitimacy and support.

The theoretical framework also explains why women, having made such impressive breakthroughs as female military leaders, were unable to maintain their newfound status. With discussion, understandings of reality are shaped and realized at a sociopolitical level. It is not merely the act of doing that transforms reality but also the acts of naming, recalling, and analyzing that transformation within a group that gel transformation into the rhythm of daily life. Female guerrilla fighters may have shattered a stereotype, but without the opportunity to discuss their act, the stereotype was able to reimpose itself, eroding the normalcy of the new equality. In less than five years, female guerrilla fighters became a historical anomaly rather than a herald of a new beginning.

Discussion of women's new role and what Sandinismo meant for women was performed by AMNLAE during the early years of the Sandinista government. Social movement theory effectively explains AMNLAE's early successes, which were a result of its Sandinista identity; its access to sufficient resources to organize, including selective alliances; and the nature of the goals that it had to attain. Due to the coincidence of interests between the revolution and women in the early years of the revolutionary government, AMNLAE was able to be successful, and the status of and opportunity for women in Nicaragua rose. After the FSLN won the 1984 election, the revolutionary government's need to consolidate its power through granting of goods and services to previously marginalized people diminished, and the need to fight the counterrevolution took precedence. As a result, the ability of the women's movement to fulfill the demands of its constituents diminished.

Social movement theory is also persuasive in explaining AMNLAE's failure to maintain its momentum. Its hierarchical structure and lack of control over its other resources, its inability to create its own autonomous identity, and its lack of focus on specific gender inequalities and rights inevitably resulted in its slow decline. With the constitutional negotiations, AMNLAE's control over the women's movement was broken when women at large began to engage in a public critique of patriarchy. This process of independent criticism was preceded by rural women workers criticizing their lack of access to goods and services and their restricted options and freedoms as women. AMNLAE then attempted to engage in similar practices with its constituents. The rise of women's secretariats within gender-mixed unions provided the means by which these criticisms could be heard. More horizontally organized than AMNLAE, with distinct goals of material or symbolic gain and a semiautonomous identity mostly driven by the grass roots, women's secretariats were able to organize in public spaces, express new ideas, and achieve their goals. Nonetheless, they lacked complete autonomy to define themselves as they wished.

The years of revolutionary government were essential to the women's movement because the events of this time period taught women how to organize a movement. It also taught women the value of autonomy and identity as organizing principles of the women's movement. If the Nicaraguan women's movement has an impressive scope of activities and influence in the 1990s, at least partial credit must be given to the support of the FSLN and the opportunities that it offered women in the 1970s and 1980s.

The analytical framework developed to explain the Sandinista years of the women's movement is equally effective in explaining the Nicaraguan women's movement in the 1990s. It was able to organize itself so well so quickly because it had experienced leadership, a steady supply of external funding, extensive communication, and skillful horizontal organization via networks, ad hoc public action, and public spaces. Its identity was personally and locally created through small groups with a transformative ethic of care, beginning with the self. This new ethos could be expressed in a number of ways, including care as a human right, care as adequate health care, and care as the ability to democratically participate and influence society. The government provided the field of conflict with its conservative understanding of women's societal role and its neoliberal structural adjustment that together reduced women's status in society, restricted their options, and threatened their very lives.

Because the Nicaraguan women's movement in the 1990s was composed of the three essential elements of identity, resources, and goals, and because these elements interacted in a positive and mutually supportive fashion, the women's movement was able to have considerable impact. Participation in the movement increased dramatically. In 1990, there were eight women's groups. In 1991, there were approximately a dozen, with no networks but two visible public spaces convened. In 1993, there were close to one hundred women's groups and half a dozen networks. By the end of 1995 there were two hundred groups with a dozen networks and a continuous cycle of conferences. New public spaces opened at universities through women's programs. Even mixed institutions, which had a reputation for being cautious in their approach to new ideas, were creating their own spaces for developing gender awareness.

With so many participants in so many different organizations and institutions, it was possible for branches of the women's movement to mobilize a high level of support for social change. This can most clearly be seen in the range and number of participants active in the Women Against Violence Network and the Women's Health Network. As a result of successful mobilizing, the penal code was extensively revised to criminalize domestic violence for the first time. The new laws had supporting infrastructure from the Women and Children's Police Stations, increasingly politicized by the women's movement. The Women's Health Network was able to replicate some essential health services through neighborhood health and law clinics, and through NGOs.

Less obvious but no less important, the women's movement was able to engage the government in dialog, forcing it to acknowledge the value of women's demands. Both the FSLN in 1987 with *La Proclama* and the Chamorro government with its international support for women's rights made normative statements supporting gender equality and criticizing entrenched patriarchy. Although little of consequence came from these statements, they nonetheless embodied a criticism of the societal roles that each government had worked so hard to create, thereby undermining its own ideology and strengthening the women's movement's alternative.

Similarly, the women's movement was able to engage Nicaragua at large in a dialog on women's rights and civil liberties, the definition of power in a democracy, and the best method to deepen and expand democratic participation. The women's movement from AMPRONAC onward attempted to redefine citizenship and to strengthen democracy. This dialog was constitutionally codified, became the operating standard for some political parties, and deepened Nicaraguans' awareness. Given how radically democratic the women's movement was, one might also say that the movement normalized democratic practices in a nation with little experience with them.

The symbolic values of society were also transgressed through the lengthy debate over motherhood. Although political parties had used the symbolic content of motherhood to shore up support, it was not until the 1990s that the women's movement reappropriated the symbol and defined it as women themselves chose. The changed public discourse, from the constitutional debates to international agreements, from the definition of motherhood to the definition of care, permanently affected the nature of the Nicaraguan society.

As individuals within the Nicaraguan society, women themselves were probably the most affected. From AMPRONAC until today, women frequently refer to the transformation in their understanding of themselves and their capabilities. Slowly, a conception of justice for women and a sense of entitlement emerged. In the 1990s, the women's movement concentrated on increasing women's self-esteem as fundamental to all other changes. Before women can shift from passivity to action, they have to become subjects of their own lives, makers of decisions that affect their day-to-day living. With self-esteem and an understanding of the forces allied against women, women can fight to improve their options and rights both within the intimate sphere and within society.

The ability of the women's movement to influence society is to some extent affected by the state. The undeniable reality of a social movement's relationship with the state is that the state ultimately wields more power and influence over the lives of women than does the social movement—regardless of the number of neighborhood health and legal clinics and community networks. Thus, the scope of influence of a social movement is always shaped by the ideological and material opportunities offered by the state. This reality could not be more starkly exemplified than by comparing the women's movement and the status of women in Nicaragua under the FSLN in the 1980s, and under the Chamorro government in the 1990s. Under the tutelage of the FSLN, the women's movement may not have had an autonomous identity, control over its resources, a focused goal, or even a growing and sustainable movement, but nonetheless Nicaraguan women were considerably freer from externally imposed legal, economic, and social constraints than they were under the Chamorro government, when the women were able to construct a powerful and autonomous movement for itself. Ironically, the state more supportive of women's needs produced a less able women's movement; the state more hostile to women's needs produced a more capable women's movement.

Because of the critical role played by the state, it is important to analyze the relationship between it and the women's movement. That relationship, with the exception of the Somoza dictatorship, was surprisingly complex. Even under Chamorro, the women's movement and the state extensively negotiated with each other to maximize their respective positions and achieve their goals.

Every Nicaraguan government had an ideology about women's role in society, which it implemented through public policies and buttressed through the actions of state and affiliated institutions. It was the FSLN, however, that made the politicization of women part of its ideology, promising women's rights in its guerrilla platform of 1967, initiating AMPRONAC to help overthrow the dictator before the triumph in 1979, and then using AMNLAE and NGOs to achieve social justice goals, to assist in the 1984 election, and to support the civil war. Depending on the goal to be attained, the Sandinista definition of what constituted the female ideal shifted from guerrilla fighter to mother before becoming confused in the late 1980s. The FSLN's creation of this new politicized role for women and the tensions between the Sandinistas' and women's conceptualization over what that role should be produced uncertainty about gender roles in society.

Because a government, rather than women, defined women's activism, women's political role was vulnerable to appropriation by a different power. Chamorro used both the Sandinista definition of the politically involved, self-sacrificing mother and the confusion over an alternative role for women to legitimate her own election and her ideology about women. The same political role that the FSLN developed and which was initially beneficial to women's position in society was used as a tool against women. Thus, a political conceptualization of a role can work both for and against the group conceptualized. This is why the Nicaraguan women's movement battles over the symbol of the mother: not only is it attempting to change the content of the symbol for strategic reasons, but it is also attempting to reappropriate from the powerful the meaning of women's own actions. Although the battle certainly is not over, this is the first time that the Nicaraguan women's movement has controlled to this extent the meanings of women's public roles.

Although all the states attempted to control the content of women's activism, ultimately they failed. Once the government organized women, it could not control the demand for self-definition, in other words, identity formation. Short of criminalizing all independent speaking, publicizing, and organizing, the governments were unable to halt the women's movement's march toward autonomy and freedom.

A government could affect the development of the women's movement, however, depending on the spaces that government offered for the movement to organize; for example, the grass-roots meetings of the ATC women's secretariat precipitated a profound change in the women's movement. A government could also affect a social movement through the extent of its involvement in and control over those same spaces; for example, the government's control over the Women and Children's Police Stations coopted and confused many women activists. Of course, the government, through choosing to be corporatist in structure or hostile in approach, affects the response of the women's movement. At a more subtle level, state issues outside the purview of the women's movement also affected it deeply.

In addition to foreign aid and structural adjustment policy, Chamorro's insertion of Nicaragua into the global economy resulted in increased access to international conferences. Thus, as the political economy went global, so too did political spaces. From international conferences, Nicaraguan women gained new ideas and strategies in what McAdam and Rucht (1993) call the "cross-national diffusion of ideas." Although the Sandinista women's movement attended the 1987 Latin American Women's Meeting and CONAPRO H-M organized an international conference on Women and Law in Latin America in 1989, Sandinista women did not as a whole integrate themselves into the Latin American women's movement.

Yet in the 1990s, the autonomous women's movement attended international meetings regularly. Each conference was preceded by extensive meetings to formulate a Nicaraguan position. These meetings were steered by a network struck specifically to organize for that international conference. International women's magazines, such as *FemPress* from Chile, became available. In 1995, one of the women's networks joined *La Corriente*, a regional and radical women's network, enmeshing the Nicaraguan reality into a wider framework and institutionalizing the introduction of foreign ideas into Nicaragua. Thus, international public spaces became an established part of the Nicaraguan women's movement, offering it new strategies and ideas for achieving goals.

The government may have been able to influence the movement through public spaces, but that was practically the only arena in which the social movement met the state. With a highly decentralized movement, there was no one central authority with which the state could negotiate or control. As a result, many small groups flagrantly violated the government's interdiction on birth control or possibly even abortion. Only the largest, oldest, and most prestigious of the health clinics, *Ixchen*, was disciplined over rumors that it offered therapeutic abortions. But even it did not stay closed for long. The state was unable to confront the mushrooming myriad of local groups, which were capable of coalescing in public spaces to confront the government. This was an unexpected advantage of decentralizing the women's movement.

Another unanticipated aspect of successful mobilization was the impact that it had on state–social movement relations. The assumption is that the stronger the social movement, the better able it is to lobby the government and society in favor of the social movement's stance. Yet in the first four years of the Chamorro mandate, the exact opposite happened. The state actually became increasingly hostile to the women's movement, both domestically and internationally, hardening its stance, polarizing domestic opinion, and making subsequent state–social movement negotiations more difficult. It can be concluded from these events that the surrounding environment is difficult to predict, much less control. The optimism in the literature about the potential of social movements in the developing world to improve the status of women must be ameliorated to recognize this reality.

Likewise, the potential for civil society to adequately replace government services is sadly overstated. Some services, such as health care, education, and social infrastructure, are still best supplied by a government rather than by a quilt of clinics. The women's health and law clinics may have been able to offset the worst of the impact of Chamorro's expenditure reductions, but the level of women's health was nonetheless lower under Chamorro than under the FSLN. The need for a supportive state is equally true for laws protecting and promoting women's labor and political rights, and women's equality and freedom. Not only can civil society organizations incompletely replace the state, they should not be expected to. Just as an autonomous women's movement is necessary to safeguard women's equality, so too is a supportive state irreplaceable.

Even without a supportive state, even within a context of poverty and sociopolitical restrictions, Nicaraguan women have still been able to fight back, defining themselves, their needs, and the obstacles against them.

Then women organized to implement their understandings. This perseverance has typified the women's movement from its inception in 1977 to battle the dictatorship, through the Sandinista years in power, to the Chamorro government. Nicaraguan women's fight for equality and freedom is far from over; the incoming Alemán government has already attempted to reduce the spaces for women's organizing and has stopped all state negotiations with the women's movement. Certainly, the women's movement will continue its fight.

Nicaragua, 1996–2000

BY THE TIME OF THE MILLENNIUM, Arnoldo Alemán was mostly through his political term in office and was eyeing his prospects for the future. His popularity had flagged during his time in office. His government had been plagued by accusations of rampant corruption, the economy had been heavily damaged by a hurricane, and the concentration of power in the executive had elicited criticisms from even his own party members. The FSLN was not doing much better. It was shaken to its core by accusations of child sexual abuse leveled against its party leader, Daniel Ortega, and was divided by its cooperation with the Alemán government. For women, their economic, social, and political status between 1996 and 2000 was even more threatened than it had been under Chamorro.

Alemán encountered some unanticipated obstacles during his governing. One of them was the comptroller general. Corruption had been a tiresome reality of life under the dictator, Somoza, but the lack of accountability and financial transparency meant that the extent of it was obscured. The Sandinistas may have bungled the economy, but there is little evidence to support accusations of widespread and profound corruption.[1] Although the Sandinistas accused the Chamorro government of corruption, there was again little evidence of it, and many discounted the Sandinista accusation as political white noise. Then Alemán came to power and appointed Agustín Jarquín to the position of comptroller general (also known in English as the national auditor).

Jarquín had run as a Christian Socialist during the 1996 presidential campaign. He was offered and he accepted the sinecure of the comptroller's office and turned it into a vehicle to fight corruption. His first target was the outgoing Chamorro government. He discovered financial irregularities in the Central Bank which resulted in $500 million going missing. During further investigations into state services and individuals during Alemán's time in power, the comptroller disclosed corruption among high-level officials of the state-owned telecommunications (TELCOR), collusion between the presidents of the Nicaraguan Investment Fund and the National Development Bank (BANADES) over the award of unauthorized loans and overdrafts, corruption of 108 public servants resulting in disciplinary actions, and criminal liability within twenty-seven public services resulting in fines totaling $4 million (*Central America Report* 17 July 1998, 4–5).

These actions alone would have garnered him praise and controversy, but then in 1998 Jarquín moved against Alemán himself. The president voluntarily admitted that his personal assets had increased in value 900 percent between 1990 and 1996 while he had been the mayor of Managua. However, he refused to submit his finances for public record, despite its being a legal requirement. In 1999, Jarquín accused Alemán of skimming money from state services and facilities and with that money buying property from farmers impoverished by Hurricane Mitch and by the government's economic policies. Jarquín also criticized the 1999 annual budget, because approximately $130 million, or 20 percent, of the budget was given to the president and the Central Bank for discretionary usage. The comptroller insisted that this money be itemized. The budget, like all previous budgets during the Alemán government, was larger than the budgets during Chamorro's time in power. This was mostly due to this 20 percent spent on confidential expenses, as Alemán called the money (*Central America Report*, September 4, 1997, 3). The budget, long delayed, finally received approval from the Liberal-dominated National Assembly, with only a few minor changes.

Of all the eight charges that Jarquín made against Alemán in 1999, one of the most serious, because it involved international banking actors and not just Nicaraguans, was the sale in January 1999 of the state-owned Nicaraguan Bank of Industry and Commerce (BANIC). Jarquín disclosed irregularities in the sale of 51 percent of BANIC's shares to a Florida-based bank. This American bank was owned by existing BANIC executives using "borrowed" names. Alemán and his family received "favors" for government approval of the sale. To the embarrassment of the World Bank, the sale was assisted by one of their own financial consultants. To the fury of BANIC executives and Alemán, the sale was annulled by Jarquín (*Central America Report,* September 10, 1999, 1).

Alemán accused Jarquín of turning corruption into a personal vendetta against the president because Jarquín had lost the presidential election, although their political rivalry preceded the presidential election. Alemán attempted unsuccessfully to change laws so that the presidential office was free to use any state or public good without financial oversight. Jarquín's life was threatened, and he was under security protection (*Central America Report,* March 5, 1999, 4). From November to December 1999, Jarquín was jailed for fraud because he had hired a journalist to investigate corruption and, with Jarquín's knowledge, the journalist used a pseudonym to do so.[2] The journalist was also jailed. Jarquín's popularity jumped from 29 percent to 45 percent, while Alemán's sunk to 10 percent (*Envío,* December 1999, 4).

Although neither man was successful in bending the other to his will, Jarquín's perseverance and Alemán's response have politicized the issue of corruption. The U.S. government has supported Jarquín in an increasingly hostile and polarized political environment. Some European bilateral aid has been frozen, and the possibility of Nicaragua's debt being forgiven has been jeopardized. This politicization has led to public showdowns, the chanting of slogans, and mass demonstrations.[3] A demonstration in March 1999 against government corruption and to support Jarquín brought out 1,500 people. A CID-Gallup poll conducted in April 1999 found that 77 percent of Nicaraguans had doubts about Alemán's honesty (*Central America Report,* May 14, 1999, 2) while a University of Central America (UCA) poll showed that 45 percent felt that Alemán's government was the most corrupt government versus 17 percent for the FSLN's time in government, and 2 percent for Chamorro's. The same poll also found a high level of support for Jarquín personally and his crusade against corruption (*Envío,* April 1999, 43–50).

Tracking corruption and suggesting the extent of the largesse enjoyed by the elite must have been particularly galling for those impoverished by the ongoing structural adjustment policies and by Hurricane Mitch. Alemán's continued structural adjustment policies of reducing government expenditures resulted in 4,800 laid-off state workers; tax system reform; increased costs of public utilities; telecommunication and pension privatization; and a reduction in the size and role of the National Development Bank, which made small loans to farmers and business people. Unable to attain loans and driven by mounting debt, small farmers and agricultural cooperatives were forced to sell their land for a fraction of its real value. New latifundios began to emerge on the best land owned by Alemán and his friends, foreigners, and government officials from the last three governments (*Central America Report*, January 22, 1999, 3). Of the 3,800 agricultural cooperatives that existed in 1990, only 400 were existence in 1999 (*Envío*, July 1999, 10). The state had shrunk to the point that its ministries were incapable of functioning. The Ministry of Health during 1998 was able to execute only 9 percent of its investments because it lacked the capacity to implement its own policies and programs (*Envío*, October 1999, 9).

Despite these reforms, the debt still stood at $6.1 billion and servicing it absorbed 50 percent of export earnings. This sum was two and half times what the government was spending on health care and education combined (Nicaraguan Solidarity Campaign 2000). Because of the size of the debt, Nicaragua qualified as one of the highly indebted poor countries, and thus was potentially able to have some of its debt forgiven. The IMF, World Bank, and the Paris Club were sufficiently pleased with the state of the economy that Nicaragua received partial debt relief of $200 million from the Paris Club.[4] Although the lower debt meant lower interest payments, of the newly available money only 27 percent was spent on social programs, with the remaining going to finance and economic infrastructure. In January 1998, a new enhanced structural adjustment fund (ESAF II) was signed, with the IMF and the World Bank locking Nicaragua into this spending pattern.

The ESAF II proved to be controversial not only in Nicaragua but also internationally. The United National Development Program (UNDP) publicly criticized the signing of the ESAF II because of the severe poverty in Nicaragua. The UNDP expected that poverty would remain or even increase under the new structural adjustment program. According to the 1999 UNDP Human Development Report, 46 percent of Nicaraguan children will not get past grade four, and the income for 43 percent of the populace is limited to one dollar a day. A study by the University of Central America (UCA) and Nitlapán Institute showed that only 18 percent of the Nicaraguan populace had all its basic and nonbasic needs met, while 48 percent suffered from chronic poverty, a further 15 percent lived at poverty level, and 19 percent had seen their standard of living go down markedly in the previous few years (*Envío*, October 1997, 15). Unemployment remained high at 60 percent, with lack of credit for small farmers producing for the domestic market. Illiteracy and malnutrition were rising, and cholera and leptospirosis epidemics were ongoing (NSC and CIT, *Special Report*). In addition to these policy-induced crises, Nicaragua was also suffering from a drought caused by El Niño. Up to 60 percent of staple food production was lost in thirty municipalities, precipitating a state of emergency in those areas (*Central America Report*, March 12, 1998, 5).

The impact of the ongoing structural adjustment galvanized political action for debt relief at a global level. At a G7 summit in Cologne in 1999, member countries, supported by the World Bank and the IMF, agreed to speed up the process of debt forgiveness for highly indebted poor countries if the state explained how it would redirect the newly available money to reduce poverty and provide evidence of its stability and governability, which included stopping corruption and giving greater independence to its institutions. Alemán failed to provide the World Bank and the IMF with a satisfactory report on either issue. His report on poverty reduction was sufficiently absurd to be described by one Nicaraguan sociologist as a "letter to Santa Claus" (*Central America Report*, spring 2000, 7). Alemán refused to submit a more reasonable report, complaining that it would infringe on national sovereignty. As a result, Nicaragua has not had more of its debt forgiven.

There were, nonetheless, bright lights in the otherwise dismal economic picture. Before the hurricane, the economy was averaging 4 percent growth rate per annum, inflation had dropped into the single digits, the fiscal deficit was kept to 10 percent of gross domestic product, and internal reserves were increasing. However, any optimism about the economy was eliminated in October 1998. Hurricane Mitch sat over the northern regions of Nicaragua for five days. The wind and rain were incessant and devastating. Some areas received one and half times their annual rainfall during those days. Lake Managua rose four meters. Twenty-one rivers overflowed, eighty bridges, including thirty-five main ones, were destroyed, and 1,800 kilometers of road were destroyed or severely damaged. Ninety health centers were demolished, with another 417 health posts affected, and 343 schools were also ruined. Materially, it was estimated that $100 million was lost in agriculture, with reconstruction and rehabilitation costing a further $1.4 billion.

The loss of life was high, numbering almost 4,000, with whole villages being swept away or buried in mud slides. Those who survived may have lost their homes, as 25,000 houses were destroyed, with 145,000 made uninhabitable and 800,000 people left homeless. Drinking wells were spoiled from the flooding. Up to 30 percent of the Nicaraguan populace was affected.

The hurricane struck a week before a major harvest. Immediately after Hurricane Mitch, the dry season began making resowing without irrigation impossible. Of the second-cycle bean crop, 71 percent was lost and of the corn crop, 51 percent was lost, with 3 percent of cattle, 7 percent of horses, 8 percent of pigs, and 150,000 chickens also lost. For small farmers, their next crop would not be for another seven or eight months, consigning them to certain destitution. Of the coffee crop meant for export, 30 percent was lost. The crops that did survive had to be guarded day and night from the local starving people. People were not the only ones going hungry. Because so much of the local food supply, local habitat, and, presumably, also cats had been wiped out in the flooding, rats started invading the towns and villages looking for food. In Río San Juan, some 75,000 rats were killed in a single day. The health implications of this burgeoning plague remain as yet unaddressed.

Alemán refused to declare a state of emergency because he was worried that such an announcement might scare off foreign investment. He also refused the medical relief offered by the Cuban government because it was socialist. The outcry on the latter decision was so great that two weeks later, he reversed his position and Cuban doctors were allowed to enter the country and treat the people. Alemán continued to lose popularity over the organization of the disaster relief. Those areas that favored Alemán in the last election received aid, while those that were Sandinista did not, regardless of the level of damage suffered. A study done by the autonomous civil society organization, the Emergency and Reconstruction Civil Committee (CCER), found that four months after the hurricane, 30 percent of its victims had received no aid whatsoever. In comparison, 62 percent of those who said that they suffered no material or human losses received government aid. In one area with 94 percent unaffected, those people admitted to receiving aid (*Envío*, April 1999, 6). The Catholic Church was also implicated in the accusations of favoritism because it channeled much of the state aid.

Due to the level of destruction and the cost of reconstruction, the Paris Club and the Inter-American Development Bank (IDB) agreed to a three-year moratorium on debt repayments. They did not agree, however, to waive the interest for those three years, so the debt has continued to accumulate. The IMF agreed to a five-year interest-free loan of $1 billion. The IMF and USAID money went for major infrastructure support, leaving the rural areas isolated.

The amount of money flowing into Nicaragua for reconstruction purposes was too tempting for the sticky-fingered government. According to the government's newly formed Secretariat of External Cooperation, run by Alemán's daughter, the Nicaraguan people were given almost $60 million in aid from private sources in the weeks and months after the hurricane. Of that, approximately $40 million was channeled through the government and $20 million through NGOs. According to economists, of every dollar in aid funneled through the government, seventy cents was spent on bureaucracy or lost to inefficiency or corruption (*Envío*, December 1999, 23). Given the level of corruption, aid organizations and governments have hesitated to fulfull their promised aid. The government of Alemán announced that according to its calculations only 18 percent of a promised $406 million has been paid out (*Central America Report*, February 4, 2000, 4).

The economy grew by 3.6 percent after Hurricane Mitch, fueled by a 7 percent growth in construction. The construction boom, however, did not lower the unemployment level because of the high number of young people entering the job market. Inflation rose to 18 percent, with a decline in exports of 13 percent and a 1.4 percent increase in imports. The trade deficit rose to its highest level ever of 38 percent of gross domestic product, which normally would not be sustainable. However, supported by foreign aid and by $800 million in remittances from the 20 percent of the Nicaraguan populace that had emigrated over the previous decade, the Nicaraguan economy was still able to stagger along.

The FSLN was also staggering under the weight of accusations of sexual abuse and of selling out to Alemán. On March 2, 1998, Zoilamérica

Narváez, stepdaughter of Daniel Ortega through his marriage to Rosario Murillo, accused him of having sexually abused her since she was eleven years old until the recent past. In the initial conference, she claimed that she forgave her stepfather and her mother and would not be pressing charges. Ortega made no public comment, although Narváez's mother did, accusing her of being mentally disturbed and having a hidden political agenda to divide the FSLN just before its May 1998 conference. The women's committee of the FSLN refused to grant her a hearing. Leaders of other political parties refused to support her, comment on the issue of child abuse, or make any political points from Narváez's accusations, saying that it was a private matter. The Women Against Violence Network publicly supported her but agreed that the biggest impact from Narváez's accusations was bringing the topic into the public domain.

As it turned out, no one stood against Ortega at the May Congress, and he, Tomás Borge, and many other members of the old guard were re-elected to their party positions unanimously. The Congress did not deal with the critical issues facing it. These included not only the allegations of sexual abuse facing Ortega but also the Party's need to modernize and transform itself to maintain popular support and its need for financial transparency, specifically regarding the origins of the party's funds and the number of businesses it owned. The marginalization of dissent was enhanced by the well-sourced rumors that anyone who called for a public forum on these issues—especially on Narváez's allegations—would have their Party membership suspended or would be disciplined in other ways.

Narváez responded by calling for Ortega to be stripped of his parliamentary immunity and to be charged criminally. When Ortega refused to face criminal proceedings, she attempted to have the court deprive him of his immunity. When the court refused, Narváez filed suit with a higher court. On October 27, 1999, Zoilamérica Narváez with Vilma Nuñez, the president of the Nicaraguan Human Rights Center (CENIDH), as copetitioner presented a denunciation of Nicaragua to the Inter-American Human Rights Commission in Washington. Nicaragua was charged with violating two treaties that it had ratified, the American Human Rights Convention and the Belem do Pará Convention, in which Nicaragua pledged to prevent, eradicate, and sanction violence against women. Consequently, the petition charged Nicaragua with obstructing and denying justice, and violating human rights by not responding to the lawsuit that Narváez had previously filed in March 1998 against Ortega for prolonged sexual abuse and sexual harassment. Although 68 percent of Managuans surveyed in a CID-Gallup poll conducted six months after the accusations were made supported stripping a public official of immunity when facing serious criminal charges, the same poll showed that Ortega's popularity increased slightly. This was taken as a public endorsement of Ortega's innocence (*Envío*, September 1998, 10). Even Sandinistas who willingly admit that the FSLN needs to be modernized do not think that the allegations of sexual abuse of a minor is one of the more important issues the Party is facing (Central American Women's Network, winter 1999, 2).

In such a climate of disregard about domestic violence and abuse, it was possible for the FSLN to remain a viable political force. Although the FSLN and the Liberal government of Alemán had been negotiating over issues such as property and the labor law since Alemán had been elected, no interparty alliance immediately emerged. The FSLN staged and participated in street demonstrations protesting the government's refusal to recognize agreements about property ownership reached between the FSLN and the government of Violeta Chamorro. After continued public negotiations with groups from civil society and secret meetings with the FSLN, the new Liberal government recognized some of the agreements reached while Chamorro was in power. The new law, the Urban and Agrarian Reformed Property Law, came into effect in January 1998. It allowed the Somoza family to reclaim the title to their land. Although all the members of the FSLN voted for it, not all the Liberals did. Only 75 percent of Alemán's party voted for it; the rest criticized it for favoring Sandinista land holdings. The United States also criticized it for denying some naturalized American citizens their previous land holdings.

The process of negotiating agreements proved fragile. When Alemán stacked the executive and the committees with his own people and did not include members from other parties contravening the constitution, the FSLN boycotted the National Assembly. Regardless, the Liberals proceeded with the legislative process because they had a quorum. Alemán continued to concentrate power in his own hands. Attempts by the National Assembly to propose legislation for debate were frustrated by executive pressure. The president proposed eight out of every ten laws. By late 1998, even other Liberals were criticizing Alemán for fusing the party and the state, for consolidating an autocracy, and for *caudillismo* (*Central America Report*, September 11, 1998, 2).[5]

In order to legally consolidate power in his own hands, Alemán needed to reform the constitution. In order to pass constitutional changes, the Liberals and the FSLN had to negotiate an agreement. Constitutional negotiations dominated the political agenda of both parties from August 1998 until the new constitution was announced in August 1999. "El Pacto," as it is has been dubbed, further divided the FSLN both for its process of closed-door meetings and for its end result of creating two-party *caudillismo*.

One of the key reforms was to the Electoral Law. Written in 1984 and reformed in 1995, the Electoral Law did need to be reformed again. According to legal experts, there were some sixty irregularities and/or ambiguous articles, of which a quarter were fundamental. In El Pacto, 86 of 208 articles were eliminated and 70 were rewritten. The end product, however, skewed the electoral system in favor of a two-party state. The presidents of the electoral councils at both the departmental (provincial) and municipal levels can be only Liberal or FSLN and will alternate between the two. Independent mayoral candidates can be eliminated from running through popular petition. It is so difficult for smaller parties to even register, much less run in an election, municipal or national, that socialist politician Domingo Sánchez said of the new law, "It is forbidden to spit and forbidden to swallow the saliva" (*Envío*, March 2000, 13).

The percent that a presidential candidate needs to win in the first ballot and thereby avoid a run-off vote was reduced from 45 percent to 40 percent and to 35 percent where the party leads its closest rival by at least 5 percent. The FSLN hopes that, as the party with the single largest block of votes, it might regain power with a lower percentage needed to secure the presidency. The ability of the FSLN to call up the single greatest block of votes, however, was undermined by another electoral reform that allowed absentee votes, that is, votes from those who have emigrated, as those voters tend to be hostile to the FSLN.

Another constitutional reform of El Pacto was the reorganization of the office of the comptroller general so that the comptroller and his deputy are appointed by and answer to a committee of five members who are appointed by both parties. This dilutes the autonomy and the influence of the comptroller to investigate, publicize, and pursue governmental corruption. Immunity and impunity are assured, because after the president loses power, he would automatically be given a seat in the National Assembly, thereby maintaining his immunity. That immunity could only be removed by a vote of two thirds of the National Assembly. Furthermore, the ex-president could manipulate the National Assembly and the government from his titular seat in government.

El Pacto also reformed the role of the superintendent of the banks and other financial institutions. Formerly elected by and answering to the National Assembly, now the superintendent is appointed by and answers to the president. The superintendent at the time El Pacto was announced was summarily fired and given seventy-two hours notice. A loyal Liberal replaced him. The office of the comptroller general was not allowed in to make an inventory of holdings during the exchange of power. Through monitoring the country's, businesses', and individuals' finances, the superintendent is now in the position to tell the president important inside information about banking transactions, business statements, and the organization of an individual's finances. Corruption is institutionalized through this reform and protected by the reorganization of the office of the comptroller general.

The FSLN also benefited financially from El Pacto. According to Vilma Nuñez, president of the Nicaraguan Center for Human Rights (CENIDH) and ex-Sandinista, "More important than all of this [El Pacto's electoral reforms] is the 'under the table' pact, all the unannounced deals aimed at guaranteeing economic power for the Ortega brothers and their allies. This is not just speculation; the real motivation behind the pact is to guarantee the party leadership, among other things, certain very valuable properties that are currently in the hands of the cooperatives or that form part of the Area of Workers' Property (APT)" (*Envío*, January/February 2000, 17). The APTs, granted worker-ownership by the 1990 Transition Protocol negotiated by the FSLN and the Chamorro government, had run up massive debts and been driven into bankruptcy, apparently intentionally. Shares in these companies, especially the best properties, are owned predominantly by the elite of the FSLN, Sandinista economic groups, and labor union leaders. El Pacto forgave those debts, which have been estimated at $40 million. Consequently, the values of these shares have increased. Without financial transparency or accountability, however, there is no mechanism by which profit/loss or even ownership can be traced. It is even unclear exactly how many of these companies there still are.[6]

Despite the benefit to the FSLN and despite Ortega's insistence that 99.9 percent of Sandinistas supported El Pacto, the FSLN continued to split over the value of the constitutional reforms. When El Pacto was put to the vote in the National Assembly, one third of Sandinistas refused to vote in favor of it. The constitutional reforms are even less popular with the Nicaraguan populace. Beside the issue of institutionalized corruption, 79 percent of Nicaraguans surveyed rejected assigning posts on the basis of party and 63 percent rejected the bipartisan organization of the country's political system.

Since El Pacto was signed, Alemán has submitted a declaration of probity to the new office of the comptroller general's Supreme Council covering his mayoral years 1990 to 1996. It does not include the growth of his assets while president. The newly appointed superintendent of banks has closed down the Popular Credit Bank, which was the last bank to explicitly offer credit to small and medium producers. Without access to credit, these farms become vulnerable to bankruptcy and to being sold at a reduced price.

By negotiating El Pacto, the FSLN in effect admitted that it could not create and maintain the broad alliance with which it won the revolution and governed the country between 1979 and 1990. With El Pacto, any person or party that was left of center would have to operate under the control of the FSLN, an FSLN that marginalized dissent, concentrated power in fewer and fewer hands, and enjoyed ill-gotten profits. In turn, Alemán effectively admitted that he needed allies to run the country; one man was insufficient. He needed the façade of a democracy and an elite made acquiescent through the division of spoils. El Pacto created both that democratic façade and that elite.

The U.S. ambassador to Nicaragua has publicly supported the constitutional reforms because they offer stability. The ambassador might have mistaken stability for the consolidation of power and capital. Instead of stability, it appears that El Pacto is galvanizing new political actions. A new political coalition sprang up called the Democratic Movement. It was comprised of Sandinista splinter groups and six other political parties, the huge and influential Emergency Relief and Reconstruction Coalition, fifty other social organizations and economic guilds, and individuals. As an alliance, it spanned the political spectrum from left to right and has divergent goals. It was, however, an alliance large enough and with enough resources to be registered and to run in the next elections in 2002. The organizers hoped that the Democratic Movement could provide an alternative to the FSLN or Alemán's Liberals, and thus have a chance of governing.

Such optimism proved misplaced in the run-up to the November 2001 general election. The ability to fulfill the protocols of El Pacto were irrelevant. Of the seven parties who tried to register to vote, only the Liberal Party was able to do so officially, although the FSLN later was also allowed. Both the well-established party, the Yatama Party, which represents the Misquito Indians, and the newer National Unity Coalition were denied the right to register. There was no adequate reason given for this denial, as both groups fulfilled the requirements of El Pacto. After complaints about electoral procedures were made to the ombudsman's office and the ombudsman agreed with the aggrieved, the government cut its 2001 budget by 40 percent (*Economist*, December 16, 2000, 66).

The ex-comptroller Jarquín, noting the reality that even those who follow El Pacto's electoral procedures cannot register their parties, has entered into negotiations with the FSLN to run as its new leader. The values of Jarquín's Social Christian past and his actions during Alemán's time in office complement Sandinismo and could potentially prove popular. In order for Jarquín to run, Ortega would have to agree to step down and permit a changing of the guard. Previous attempts to loosen Ortega's grip on the party have failed. Now he might move, as he is both more protected politically and financially and more vulnerable due to the continuing controversy over Narváez's accusations. With Jarquín, the possibility exists for the FSLN to return to its original stance of opposition to oppression, and attain power.

Any society organized by and for the elite is inherently unequal. Women, already at a disadvantage economically, socially, and politically, will tend to suffer more than men under a system that does not recognize justice and equality as having any value. And indeed, Nicaraguan women have had to struggle harder to maintain what little they had under the Chamorro government. Just as AMNLAE in the late 1980s harkened back to the early years of the revolutionary government as a golden period of possibility and production, and then the women's movement under Chamorro harkened back to the Sandinista period as the golden period, so women under Alemán's government harkened back to the time when Chamorro was in power as a kinder, more open and progressive government toward women's issues. The refusal of Alemán or his ministers to recognize the value of the women's movement or to open any space for joint action or negotiation with it has proven frustrating to female activists.

The women's movement, however, did have assets going into Alemán's period of governing. The women's movement was well organized internally, knowledgeable about what it was facing, and experienced in dealing with an uncaring government. It has kept the organizational structure it developed in the early 1990s of identity-based groups at the local level intersecting through nationwide networks to agitate in public spaces for a specific social and political change. It appears as if the role of international NGOs assisting the women's movement has been enhanced as the Nicaraguan women's movement becomes more sophisticated, successful, and international. Hopefully, as a result, the women's movement has been able to mitigate some of the worst impacts on women of Alemán's policies.

Alemán made it clear throughout his campaign that he was not interested in moving forward as much as he was in turning the clock back. He consciously evoked the era of the Somoza dictatorship, including women's previous social status as wives and mothers. Soon after he was elected, he attempted to reorganize the Nicaraguan Institute for Women (INIM), the government organ that negotiated with the women's movement at the Beijing Conference, implemented the Women and Children's Police Stations, and supported the passing of the Law 230 to Prevent and Sanction Intrafamily Violence. The INIM recognized both gender-based inequality and the complexity of women's lives. Officially at least, the INIM was supposed to counteract that reality.

Alemán proposed replacing the INIM and the Institute of the Family with a "superministry," the Ministry of the Family. It was immediately apparent from the name that the ministry would relegate a woman's role to one held only within the family. The explicit mandate of the superministry was to restore the "traditional family," which it defined as a "a man, a woman, and their children" (Nicaraguan Solidarity Campaign 2000).

The outcry from foreign governments, NGOs, and the women's movement halted the government's attempt to replace the INIM and the Institute of the Family, but in 1998, two years later, the government was able to override objections and create the superministry. Humberto Bellí, still the minister of education and well-known conservative Catholic, was appointed to the new superministry. He resigned soon after because of the meager budget the superministry had been given and because his replacement at the Ministry of Education was dismantling his work (*Envío*, May 1999, 30). Alemán appointed another man, Luis González, to replace Bellí.

Because the superministry is so underfunded and because women in prerevolutionary times were little seen and less heard, there have been few if any policies dealing with women or women's issues. This policy direction was unlike that of Chamorro, who, as her mandate continued, negotiated an increasingly sophisticated space for women's actions and issues. On the one hand, ignoring women's groups has done them no harm and indeed has ceded the field of play to them. On the other hand, the state ultimately holds more power than does civil society, especially with a government increasingly centralizing power in its own hands. By refusing to acknowledge any structural discrimination against women, by refusing to engage in any dialog with women's groups, and by refusing to open a space for the women's movement and the state to act jointly, the women's movement is left with reduced opportunities to enact change within the structure of policy making, fewer options to strategize around, and less access to government resources.

The lack of recognition from the government has not impeded the women's movement from operating politically at a national level. Within a year of the 1996 election, the government and some civil society organizations completed their negotiations over the land-ownership issue. Left out were the FSLN, women's groups, peasant organizations, and unions. Simultaneous to the government-initiated negotiations, these groups organized a competing public negotiation over property. Women's groups were very dynamic at this dialog, gaining recognition that land title in both rural and urban areas should go to the couple, not just the man (*Central America Report*, October 9, 1997, 8). Neither series of negotiations amounted to much change in public policy. The two groups were hampering each other's efficacy. Both the Liberal government of Alemán and the FSLN must have realized this as secret negotiations between the two parties were also happening simultaneously. These secret negotiations culminated in the publicly known but closed-door negotiations over constitutional reform, that is, El Pacto.

The continued structural adjustment policy and Hurricane Mitch meant an increasingly harsh economic environment for women. As the poorer of the two genders and with less access to credit, means of ownership, and trade skills, women found economic viability more difficult. In addition, the government's cutbacks meant that the Women and Children's Police Stations, one of the success stories of the Chamorro government, had their funding reduced or eliminated. This has meant that the Women and Children's Police Stations have become dependent on foreign aid to survive or have closed their doors (*Central America Report*, spring 2000, 10–11).

The decline in legal support for women and children suffering from domestic violence was regrettable, given how active the Women Against Violence Network has been. Already high profile, the Women Against Violence Network was kept in the media spotlight by the accusations of child abuse against Ortega. The network took up Zoilamérica Narváez's case to raise public awareness of domestic abuse and of the relationship between positions of societal, political, and economic power and power within the home. The Women Against Violence Network supported stripping Ortega of his immunity because it perceived such an action not only as a means of attaining justice for Narváez, but also as a means of highlighting the relative impunity of those who commit violence against women and children. Frequently consulted and quoted, the network was able to continue attracting new members and persuading more members of the public to support its perspective.

The extent of the media coverage permitted wide publication of recent statistics from a 1998 study of domestic abuse by the Nicaraguan Statistics and Census Institute. According to the survey, three out of ten Nicaraguan women have experienced physical or sexual abuse from their partner, two of the ten in the past year. Of the women who had experienced domestic abuse, three of ten experienced it while pregnant (Nicaraguan Solidarity Campaign 2000). The Network was also able to quote a study in León which found that one of four girls and one of five boys were abused by a family member before they reached the age of eighteen, with 70 percent of the victims being under the age of eleven (*Central America Report*, March 12, 1998, 1). The Network used the opportunity to criticize the implementation of Law 230 to Prevent and Sanction Intrafamily Violence, which, due to the judges' and lawyers' differing definitions of violence, the lack of regulations, and the lack of sensitivity and awareness, was weaker than it should have been. The appalling statistics found in these studies were supported by another 1998 study of demographics and health, which showed that 46 percent of women eighteen years of age or under were pregnant or already mothers. Nonetheless, the absolute number of children that women had was dropping from 5.8 in 1995 to 3.9 in 1998. One third of women suffered from physical or sexual abuse, and of those only one third ever told anyone about it. Even if seriously hurt, only 50 percent of abused women sought medical attention (*Envío*, May 1999, 31).

When Hurricane Mitch hit, the network's women's centers acted as temporary shelters for the homeless. The natural disaster, however, increased the level of domestic violence against women (*La Boletina*, January 1999). The Women Against Violence Network initiated a mental health program to tackle the posttraumatic stress, combining the suffering from Mitch with the suffering from domestic abuse.

In June 1999, the Women Against Violence Network and NGOs working in the same area sponsored their second two-day national conference, called "Breaking the Silence." The topic was sexual abuse within the family and incest. It was preceded by six regional forums and followed by more regional forums. It was considered to be extremely successful because it attracted a high degree of attendance, including representatives from the police, the judiciary, and the Ministries of Health and Education; it also attracted a high degree of media attention. Some positive results were the promise from the Ministry of Education to maintain contact with the Women Against Violence Network to include education about violence in the school curriculum and the possibility to improve the application of Law 230. It must be pointed out, however, that without government support to regulate and enforce existing legislation, much less pass laws to alter the reality of domestic violence, the best that the network can hope for is heightened social awareness and improved societal norms of behavior.

While domestic violence may have been a high-profile issue, the women's movement has been active in other areas as well. In the wake of Hurricane Mitch, the women's movement, as one of the best organized social movements, was highly active and effective in putting its policies forward. Immediately after the hurricane, civil society organizations created a committee called the Emergency and Reconstruction Civil Committee (CCER). The committee was a broad-based association of unions, guilds, NGOs, social movements, territorial networks, and producers' associations. Women were worried that they were being left off and their needs and priorities would be forgotten as a result, so they got themselves put on the committee. Through them, a number of women's networks were included in the CCER, for example, AMNLAE, the Women Against Violence Network, and the Women's Health Network. Gender, as well as youth and children, race, and the environment were all considered to be themes that cut across and integrated all the proposals for reconstruction (Emergency and Reconstruction Civil Committee 1999).

An example of how women's involvement with the CCER helped women was the creation of a new group, the Women Builders of Condega. Through the CCER, a small English NGO volunteered to help women rebuild their houses. The CCER put them in contact with one of its member groups, the Women Against Violence Network, which helped to identify which women were left homeless by the hurricane. In turn, the network contacted one of its member groups, the Women's Collective in Condega, a remote northern town. In turn, the Women's Collective created a new group called Women Builders of Condega. This new group, with English help, built thirty new houses for female heads of households and their families. In the process of learning how to build their own homes, the Women Builders of Condega acquired marketable skills that were in high demand during the reconstruction. The demonstration effect of capable women in a nontraditional job also made an impact on the community at large, as well as the women themselves. In effect, the hurricane became an opportunity to empower and train women (Conference on Violence in Nicaragua 2000). The Women Builders of Condega is another example of women activists utilizing every resource, including one as destructive as a natural disaster, to improve women's lot.

The sheer efficacy of the women's movement was reflected in another high-profile action. The Minimum Agenda originally put forward during the 1996 electoral campaign was re-presented to the Nicaraguan people to remind them, in the post–Hurricane Mitch environment, of what the women's movement and many unions and social groups consider to be the bare minimum for sociopolitical and economic development. In the process of re-publicizing it, the women's movement was implicitly and unsubtly criticizing the government for its lack of development.

Although the ability of the women's movement to ameliorate the appalling levels of poverty, violence, and hopelessness is limited, it seems reasonable to assert that without the movement, the status of women and women's options to alter that status would be much worse. It is a saddening reality that as long as the Liberal government and the Sandinista opposition bolster the status quo, women must fight for their human rights and basic survival. Fortunately, Nicaraguan women have always fought and fought well for themselves, their children, and society. And they continue to fight.

Notes

1. Amparo's Story

1. The story of Amparo's life has been drawn from the unpublished manuscript by Vicki McVey, *My Beloved Revolution*. The role of women before, during, and after the Nicaraguan revolution has inspired a number of intellectuals to record the thoughts and deeds of the women. Those interested in more life stories of ordinary women doing the extraordinary are invited to read Margaret Randall's works; Daly Heyck 1990; Daniel 1998; Solá and Trayner 1988.

2. Likely, Somoza was trying to curry favor with American president Jimmy Carter, who was concerned about Somoza's record on human rights abuses.

3. For an analysis of Nicaragua's incipient chaos during the Chamorro coalition government, see Isbester 1996.

4. Civil society is "a sphere of social interaction between economy and the state, composed above all of the intimate sphere (especially the family), the sphere of associations (especially voluntary associations), social movements, and forms of public communications" (Cohen and Arato 1992, ix). Tarrow (1990, 1991, 1994) does not disassociate civil society and the state as profoundly as the rest of the school does. However, he is the exception.

5. Melucci has watered down the recognition of influence to the point of meaninglessness. Since "their mere existence is a reversal of the symbolic systems embodied in power relationships," social movements' success lies in the fact of their existence (1985, 813).

2. Overthrowing the Dictator, 1977–1979

1. La Oficina Central de Censo, Censo de 1920 (Managua) 1920.

2. La Oficina Central de Censo, Censo de 1950 (Managua) 1950.

3. This presentation was so convincing that one of the first books written after the revolution also described AMPRONAC this way. See Black 1981, 101.

4. It is interesting to note that Jaime Wheelock had been in Chile during Allende's term.

5. Ramirez-Horton (1982, 151) calls it "not an easy task."

6. As an example of the separation between women and their day of celebration, International Women's Day had previously been used to protest the nuclear bomb (Randall 1981, 15).

7. Sections V, VI, and VII.

8. See reprint of AMPRONAC's *Programa* in Maier 1980, 151–55.

9. Maier 1980, 69; Chinchilla 1983, 10; The Sandinista Historic Program section 7 re army in Marcus 1982, 16; Ramirez-Horton 1982, 152. The concept of the "new man" was best promulgated by Che Guevara as an individual who transcends the self (physical and mental) to achieve an elevated moral level. This could only be achieved through commitment and probably sacrifice to prolonged guerrilla warfare, preferably *foco* style. For more on Guevara's understanding see his essay, "Man and Socialism" (1967, 121–38). For an eloquent portrayal of this theory as it pertains to Nicaragua, see *Fire from the Mountain* (1985), the first book in the autobiography of Omar Cabezas, a Nicaraguan guerrilla fighter, especially pages 83–93. The Sandinista ideal was that this methodology would be applied to the Nicaraguan society as a whole. For an analysis of that ideal, see Judson 1987. Needless to say, it proved to be less successful in times of peace rather than warfare and less successful on a mass level, which left the ideologues of the FSLN open to charges of millenarian aspirations (Navarro-Génie 1993).

10. For a number of honest interviews with female guerrilla fighters and the level of pain that they experienced from causes ranging from genderized torture to abandoning their children, see Randall 1981; Daly Heyck 1990; McVey 1995.

11. The FAO included the Higher Council of Private Enterprise (COSEP), the employer's federation; the hierarchy of the Catholic Church; the opposition newspaper *La Prensa;* the trade union coalition UDEL; the conservative Nicaraguan Democratic Movement (MDN); *Los Doce;* and later the Agüerro Conservatives.

12. *Los Doce* formally split from the FAO in November 1978 to formally join the MPU, but the FSLN realized the nature of the FAO once negotiations with Somoza began in early 1978.

13. Chuchryk (1991, 144) writes that AMPRONAC was "reasonably successful in mobilizing women." This may be academic understatement or impossibly high standards.

14. There are numerous examples of this. For a theoretical explanation, see Schild 1990; Kirkwood 1985.

3. The Glory Years, 1979–1984

1. In particular, the entrenched machismo of Borge was a blow to gender equality because of all the commandantes he had the most credibility and was the most persuasive supporter of women's rights.

2. There is of course another means by which women have entered the political realm: the extension of unalienable rights. However, civil rights uses the concept of equality between the sexes, a concept that had no currency in Nicaragua before 1979 and only gained currency through women's military participation.

3. Lancaster (1992, 84) tells of contracting dengue while in Managua and as a result of his sickness having the women of the two neighboring houses where he had lived squabble over who was the worse housewife.

4. Other laws of importance to women decreed during this period were the elimination of the sale of children for adoption, the prohibition of the sale of breast milk substitute, and the promotion of breast-feeding.

5. Because there is no tradition of common law in Nicaragua, each and every legal change must be written and passed as a clear and distinct law. Judges cannot interpret previous rulings or expound on legislation such the Statute of Rights and Guarantees.

6. By the 1990s, this group would be augmented by workers from NGOs, technicians, and observers.

7. According to Walker (1985, 106), the proportionally equivalent size of an army interested in overthrowing the American government would number between 850,000 and 1,280,000 troops.

8. It is an interesting commentary on Nicaraguan society that the organization would never really include wives or sisters. Mothers' prime responsibility was always to their children, regardless of the age of the offspring. Therefore, a married man who is away at war was his mother's concern, not his wife's.

9. It is difficult to exactly determine AMNLAE's membership because AMNLAE included Madres H-M and may also have included women who used AMNLAE's *Casas de Mujeres* or any woman who participated in the women's secretariats of unions, because they sat on AMNLAE's executive, too. However, there was a significant reduction in the percentage of female members of the Sandinista Party between 1979 and 1987, from 38 percent to 24.3 percent (Chuchryk 1991, 158; Síu Bermúdez 1993, 1). AMNLAE stopped recruiting new members from unions and neighborhoods (Murguialday 1990, 120–21). In addition, the creation and growth of semiautonomous women's groups in the latter years of the Sandinista era would have siphoned off discontented women from AMNLAE. For example, only 4 percent of all employed women are professionals, and yet women are 40 percent of the professional (and highly critical) semiautonomous group CONAPRO H-M (Chuchryk 1991, 158).

10. It is hard to say why this is the case. They should have supported the FSLN more than the men, given how much access to goods and services the FSLN had given women. There are suggestions that this is because of the bloodshed of the war, about which women supposedly feel more strongly. I think it more reasonable that the women were never included in the Sandinista ideological morale boosting. Unless they were directly involved in a Sandinista organization, they were outside the loop. This conclusion can be drawn from Judson's work (1987) on Sandinista revolutionary morale.

11. The elections were held a year earlier than planned. In preparation for the first election, the government sent delegations around the world to study how other countries hold them. Ironically, the delegation to the United States was denied entry visas. Opposition parties were guaranteed a role as competitors of the government, although some chose not to participate. According to the *New York Times*, October 21, 1984, "the

[American] administration never contemplated letting [opposition candidate and leader of the Coordinadora Democratica (CD) Arturo] Cruz stay in the race, because then the Sandinistas could justifiably claim that the elections were legitimate." Emergency restrictions were suspended so that parties could organize and carry out active campaigns. Ninety-three percent of eligible voters registered, 75.4 percent of registered voters voted, 70.8 percent of registered voters cast valid ballots (Jonas and Stein 1990, 16).

4. The Confused Years, 1984–1987

1. Presentation in support of the thesis of falling productivity is extremely problematic, as no agency or ministry had accurate or complete information. Furthermore, farmers lie. For example, before the revolution, cotton farmers exaggerated the quantity of cotton produced in order to receive higher loans, which they had no intention of paying back. After the revolution, the cultural tendency toward verbal inflation expanded the crop production beyond credibility. All the analysts comment on this aspect of the data. As a result, analysts tend to pick and choose from various sources, depending on the credibility of the source and the ideological agenda of the writer. Data compilation tends to be a cocktail of sources. For more on the methodology of the writers see Colburn 1986, 6; Gilbert 1988, chapter 4, n. 45. Nonetheless, there is no consensus on whether productivity was indeed falling and, if so, by how much.

Ultimately, I went with the thesis on declining productivity because I could not understand why the government was making significant changes to its agrarian reform, not merely changing state farms to cooperatives and then to individual title, but also the extent of the latitude that it gave to the women's secretariat. The FSLN would not allow AMNLAE to use the word *feminist* until 1987, did not acknowledge that women would not achieve full emancipation through socialism until *La Proclama* and then ignored the implications of that for the rest of the decade, shot down the bid of Dora María Téllez in 1991 for the National Directorate, tried to shut down the growing feminism of AMNLAE in 1991, and refused to accept the feminist analysis of the CNF in 1994, even though it was the Bancada Sandinista that sought out the CNF's support and not vice versa. Yet in 1984 they allowed a public and continuous criticism of patriarchy from the women of the ATC. Placed within a context of the rest of the FSLN's actions, this only seems possible if productivity and popular support were significantly falling and the women were needed to boost it. The logical explanation is the following: Absolute amounts of harvest were increasing. However, the amount of unused land expropriated by the government and given to the peasants outweighed the absolute increase in crops. The amount of total acreage under production increased by 26 percent between 1979 and 1985 (Collins 1986, 272–73), even though average agricultural output for both domestic and export crops according to the most positive figures show average production increased by 22.28 percent (Collins 1986, 274–75). So, per acre, production was dropping. If the more reasonable position of the unions is taken (a slight increase in absolute amount), then the 26 percent increase in land had a negligible impact on exports.

Economist Stahler-Sholk has a different explanation for declining production. He suggests that the macroeconomic policies "delinked" the state from the producer, that is, the repression on nonessential consumer items acted as a disincentive to large producers; and supply constraints and price fixing led to a growing gap between what the government and the market were paying, which also acted as a disincentive (1990, 76–77).

2. It was relatively easy to find a market in western Europe for Nicaraguan bananas and coffee but considerably more difficult to find a market for its industrial products. This increased Nicaragua's dependence on the USSR and eastern Europe.

3. It was 850 acres in the densely populated and fertile region in the Pacific coastal area. The size of the farm that was vulnerable to these kinds of expropriation significantly increased in the less densely populated areas of eastern Nicaragua.

4. To offset spiraling inflation and low productivity, similar economic reforms were going on in the other sectors of the economy. Currency was devalued, tax collection improved, large-scale and unaffordable capital investments received less funding, a hiring freeze began, and social expenditure decreased (Hoyt 1997, 112).

5. Wives and daughters could also be the beneficiaries of land titles, which makes the Agrarian Reform Law the first agrarian reform in Latin America to benefit women in their own right and not through kinship ties or through their roles as mothers (Padilla, Murguialday, and Criquillon 1987, 128; Deere 1985, 176 also includes Cuba and Mexico on the list of countries that include women in agrarian reform).

6. There is another way to break down the kind of women's work that was being performed: by export versus domestic consumption crops. There are advantages to doing it this way, because more changes happened in the export agroindustry than in the domestic. As well, by breaking down the figures this way it is possible to see that women's labor in the agricultural field was not being represented by mass organizations. With the method that I use, it implies that all labor was covered by the ATC or the UNAG, and on a state farm or a cooperative. This is absolutely not the case. However, I have used this method because I am examining the political impact of the women's secretariat within the ATC. For more on the other methodology see Perez and Siú 1986; Murguialday 1990, 156–57.

7. Murguialday 1990, 156. On page 197, however, she uses the figure 8,000, which is more reasonable for a participatory study that lasted almost two years. One of the two is a typo.

8. Murguialday's more detailed figures put the construction of collective day-care centers and children's dining rooms in 1987 at twenty-seven and fifty-seven, respectively, in 1988 sixty-nine day-care centers, and in 1989, thirty-nine (1990, 174). However, these figures do not include state farms, which may be what drove up Collinson's figures.

9. Padilla (et al. 1987, 136) is skeptical of this figure or the relevance of women's attendance in the first place. Padilla, Murguialday, and Criquillon, the authors of the article, suggest that women did not attend the union meetings in anything like these percentages not only because were they held at the same time that the evening meal

had to be cooked or the children minded but also because they did not understand the technical issues raised. The authors do not present statistics to back up their case. However, they are some of the most experienced workers in the women's movement and helped to create the ATC women's secretariat. In a sense, they do not need statistics, because they have lived it. My own feeling is that 89 percent is too high an attendance at anything Nicaraguan except (a) a baseball game, (b) a special meeting like AGM, (c) a census-taking with a foreigner present. On the other hand, it is reasonable to assume that women's attendance rose as a result of the women's secretariat.

10. Moore (1978, 477) considers it critical that new ideas of social justice be presented to the people in order to give them a language and a framework to critically analyze the status quo and offer alternatives.

11. This is McAdam's (1982) cognitive shift. According to McAdam and Moore, recognition of injustice is necessary for a successful mobilization of resources. It also avoids the problem of the free-rider syndrome.

5. The Limits of Autonomy, 1987–1990

1. CONAPRO H-M women's secretariat was funded by the Swedish and Spanish governments and private donations from the United States.

2. By 1990, abortion was effectively available on demand in the women's hospital in Managua, a geographical restriction to be sure. Legalization would remove its stigma and extend its practice to hospitals throughout Nicaragua. When the FSLN tried to legalize abortion, it realized that it had seriously underestimated the extent of the political ire and the potential divisiveness the topic drew, and the government backed away from legalization but allowed the practice to continue openly.

3. If the Sandinistas had won the 1990 election, it is more than likely that AMNLAE would have been democratized and eventually autonomous while still operating within the context of the FSLN. Some academics think that AMNLAE's process from captured social movement to democratic autonomy was the result of not merely the emergence of a feminist voice but also the resolution of the tension between Marxism and feminism (Murguialday 1990, 190–94; Maier 1990; Chinchilla 1990, 373). For more on this discussion, see Sargent 1981. Amalia Chamorro thinks that the emergent feminism in the late 1980s marked the creation of the first truly feminist movement (Chuchryk 1990, 157).

4. These organizations were the National Union of Farmers and Ranchers (UNAG), the Association of Rural Workers (ATC), the Sandinista Workers' Committee (CST), the National Association of Teachers and Educators (ANDEN), Nicaraguan Confederation of Professionals—Heroes and Martyrs (CONAPRO H-M), Federation of Health Workers (FETSALUD), Union of Journalists and Writers (UPE), and Mothers of the Revolution—Heroes and Martyrs (Madres H-M).

5. In a machista culture, men are unable to negotiate or compromise without losing face, whereas compromise is considered to be the natural role for women. This is why some thought that the only person who could bring peace to Nicaragua was a woman.

6. In comparative per capita terms, the Nicaraguans lost in the Insurrection alone

(1977–1979) seventy-five times the number of lives that the Americans lost in the Vietnam War (Walker 1982, 20; 1991, 53).

7. Chamorro's conservatism guaranteed that the women activists, despite their frustration with the FSLN, would vote Sandinista. Thus, the FSLN concluded that it need not respond to women's demands.

8. The loss of lives during to the war and the economic crisis are the typical interpretation of the election from both Nicaraguan and foreign analysts (McCoy 1991, 117). There are, however, some exceptions. Arturo Cruz, vice president of UNO, in his article written jointly with Mark Falcoff (1990) insists that it is due to democratic demands of the Nicaraguan people, which would no longer tolerate a repressive communist regime. Giocanda Bellí puts the loss to political machismo, calling the FSLN comandantes "gorillas beating their breasts standing up to the USA, living the myth of the heroic guerrilla fighter. But that was not the reason why people supported or fought for the revolution; the people wanted a better life. They did not get it. So they switched their allegiance" (quoted in Randall 1994, 188). This is an interesting perspective, as most other Sandinistas have suggested that if more ideological work had been done to bind the people to Sandinismo, to make the new man out of every citizen, then sacrifice would not have mattered as much.

9. There were complaints that as soon as an AMNLAE worker became really competent, the FSLN transferred her to another ministry (Schultz 1980b). While this is undoubtedly true, in the long run, it assisted the development of the women's movement by training innumerable women in gender issues and then spreading them throughout the state.

6. Under Chamorro, 1990–1996

1. The women's movement itself lacked consensus. Activists were uncertain whether the law was good overall (because it criminalized rape) or bad overall (because it emphasized family and heterosexuality) (interview Gomez).

2. This is approximately one in every sixty-six women. In contrast, one in every 10,000 women dies in childbirth in wealthier nations.

3. The range of statistics about maternal mortality is unfortunately wide. United Nations Population Fund estimated that for every 10,000 live births there were three hundred maternal deaths (Fondo de Población de las Naciones Unidas 1993, 15).

4. The Ministry of Social Action (MAS), in its 1993 study found that the number of maternal deaths from abortion dropped from 1990 despite the decline in health care funding (Ministra de Acción Social 1997, 8). MAS drew no conclusions from this finding.

5. The Police Stations did respond to the women's movement's critiques and lobbying tactics (*Aquelarre: Latin American Women's Magazine* 16/17 [spring/summer 1995]: 43). This response prompted Aminta Granera to acknowledge that "the Police fear and respect the [Women's] Movement" (quoted in Montenegro 1997, 377). There are other, less sophisticated examples of how the Chamorro government responded to the women's movement. In 1995, the government announced a progressive new policy on maternal and child health care, a direct result of pressure from the women's

225

movement. The government, however, did not fund it adequately, invalidating its goal (Ewig 1998, 90).

6. For more on the politics of bracketing gender, see Franco 1998.

7. See for example, Alvarez 1998, 311: "The Beijing process suggests that the increasingly formalized linkages between Latin American feminists working in NGOs and those acting within male-dominated policy arenas, political parties, state institutions, and multilateral agencies have significantly improved the leverage of feminist rights advocates in recent years."

7. Nadir and Rebirth, 1990–1992

1. There may have been extenuating circumstances. Téllez was not in favor of unqualified worker rebellion and thus may have lost some support from the Nicaraguan Workers Front (FNT) over that (*Envío* 10, no. 22 [September 1991]: 8). However, Sergio Ramirez, who also did not fully support worker rebellion, was elected to the other open position. As well, Milú Vargas said that what kept Dora María Téllez out of power was sexism (interview). However, in another interview, she is quoted as saying that what kept Téllez out of power was sexism and the organization of the election (i.e., votes were yea or nay for a slate of nine rather than for individuals) (Randall 1994, 135).

2. This is drawn from my interviews with the leaders of the women's movement. Diversity and acceptance were a tenet of the women's movement. This was evident in the pamphlets that one could pick up in Nicaragua. The one exception to this stance is the creation of the Creole women's movement on the Atlantic Coast of Nicaragua. Feeling threatened by the Spanish incursion into the Atlantic Coast in the 1980s and 1990s, the black, Protestant, English, and Creole-speaking women are organizing themselves along ethnic/cultural lines in a highly exclusionary fashion (interviews Brown; Cunningham; Cruzes; Ingram; Lindo).

3. According to *La Barricada* (March 10, 1991, 12) up to four hundred women participated.

4. Like Tijerino, Baez had dealt with her share of sexism within the Party and found it galling. She was also fully prepared to fight it—but only within the boundaries of the Party. For a revealing portrait of Baez, see Randall 1981.

5. The extreme antagonism of AMNLAE to lesbianism is reflective of the Nicaraguan macho culture. Its appearance in the discussion in the early 1990s is interesting timing. The FSLN, initially unconcerned and even uninterested in homosexuality in its early years in power, became increasingly hostile to its existence, even though no one actually came out of the closet. This approach parallels that of the FSLN to the women's movement as well. As long as power needed to be consolidated, issues such as sexuality were at the very least on the back burner if not actively overturned. Once in power for a spell, machismo reasserted itself into the functioning of daily life. However, just as the women's movement proved impossible to control, so did the homosexual rights movement. For more on homosexuality in Nicaragua (both male and female) see Lancaster 1992, 235–78; Adam 1987; Randall 1992, 68–76; 1994, 265–85.

6. The networks were *La Red de Sexualidad* (Sexuality Network), *La Red de Mujer y*

Salud (Women and Health Network), *La Red de Mujeres por la Educación laica, gratuita, bilingüe para todas las etnías y no discriminatorias* (Women for Lay Free Bilingual Education for All Ethnics without Discriminations Network), *La Red de Comunicación y de Periodistas Mujeres* (Female Journalists and Communication Network), and *La Red de Mujeres Contra la Violencia* (Women Against Violence Network).

As well, a study group was formed. Called *la Comisión de economía y medio ambiente* (Economic and Environment Commision), it was made up of five subcommissions on political economy, agriculture, industry, environment, and social subjects. It made no pretense of planning an action. It was interested only in research and development of strategies.

7. There is a notable exception to this statement. Dora María Téllez said, "The organizational dispersion doesn't worry me, not in the women's movement. . . . I am not concerned about the lack of unity in the feminist movement, because with all its differences, it's essentially Sandinista in nature; its dynamic is Sandinista. And this is important. It doesn't matter that there are different philosophical tendencies if there's coordinated political action" (quoted in Randall 1994, 258, 260). Note that Téllez has pointed out the need for a basic unifying ethos and the organizational means to achieve distinct political goals. She is, as usual, correct in her analysis, although it will be several years from the date of this interview before the women's movement acts in a coordinated fashion.

8. Aquelarre Conference, Managua, March 1994.

9. Field notes. Nonetheless, Ewig (1999, 93) found that foreign-funded NGOs forfeited their democratizing potential through constant internal struggles over money. She further found that the better-funded NGOs had more clout and were in leadership positions vis-á-vis their poorer cousins. She concluded that financial inequality caused a structure inequality within the health care movement.

10. For example, both AMNLAE and the UNAG were given a one-time-only loan of $5,000 each to begin women's microbusinesses, which included training and salaries. I also followed from inception to fruition the Northern Women's Network. They used existing resources to build themselves, before applying to Oxfam-Quebec for funding for their first conference. The total cost of the conference was $1,000, which included media, material, a meal for the participants, rental of a center for a day, lodging and transportation for those from afar. The money was easily obtained. To the best of my knowledge, Oxfam-Quebec did not exert any control over the content or the style of the network or conference.

11. Field notes.

8. The Autonomous Women's Movement, 1992–1996

1. There was in attempt in 1992 to have sixteen days of political action, but the campaign did not attract many participants or much attention.

2. It is interesting to note that in the survey violence against women and children and human rights were collapsed into one program. This underscores how completely the Violence Against Women Network was able to absorb the language of human

rights. Dagnino (1998, 47) suggests that redefining human rights is a constitute element of social movements.

3. In August 1997, the first case of psychological injury was successfully prosecuted (Ellsberg, Liljestrand, and Winkvist 1997, 90).

4. This meeting was to prepare a national stance for the November 1993 Latin American and Caribbean Women's Meeting in Costa del Sol, El Salvador.

5. Unpublished document, First National Feminist Meeting, October 1993.

6. Field notes.

7. Lindo did not use this language. According to Blandón, the CNF disbanded because there had been unequal sharing of tasks (i.e., concentration of leadership in too few hands), failure to follow through on commitments, and personal tensions (which is frequently how identity conflicts are perceived by those involved) (Montenegro 1997, 399).

8. It has since switched its primary seat to Managua in the spacious headquarters of the old CNF.

9. Gramsci suggested that every class produces intellectuals who offer it awareness of itself in relation to the economy, society, and politics. Gramsci considered the function of the intellectual to be organic to that class, that is to say, their relationship to their class is not formal or mechanical but naturally evolving with the ideas and the analysis integral to the structure of the historical system (Gramsci 1971, 3–23, 351–57). Gramsci summarized the primary function of the intellectual as "educative" (ibid., 16).

If class is extended to include gender, then the role of feminist intellectuals becomes clear. These thinkers, newly grounded in the historical reality of Central America and Nicaragua, will transmit ideas appropriate to that reality to the wider women's movement. As educators, the intellectuals of the CNF will influence ideas and actions of the women's movement. In a sense then, these hard-working, well-intentioned, and well-educated women will still be educating from the vanguard of the movement.

10. This stance, as it specifically relates to women, was supported by Leticia Herrera (interview) as well as most of the interviewees of Sandinista women quoted at length in Randall 1994. They appear to be driven by social justice and consider the FSLN, despite its faults, to be the only reasonable option.

11. It might be tempting to suggest that AMNLAE and *Las Mujeres Autoconvocadas* operated as a good cop/bad cop team just as AMNLAE did with CONAPRO H-M in the late 1980s, i.e., AMNLAE was the conservative apologist and *Las Mujeres Autoconvocadas* the radical push for change. In fact, the meeting to gain the consensus of 50 percent quota that *Las Mujeres Autoconvocadas* organized and to which it invited all Sandinista women came as a surprise to AMNLAE. Dora Zeledón said that she felt betrayed and tricked because she felt that the agreement had already been reached to request a 30 percent quota and settle for 25 percent. The fact that AMNLAE was not included in the discussion to preempt the 30 percent request and instead demand 50 percent is a demonstration of the extent to which AMNLAE's allegiance to women over the FSLN hierarchy was still not trusted.

12. It should be noted that simultaneous to the federal election there were depart-mental (provincial) and municipal elections. At the local level, the Liberal Alliance en-joyed considerable success as well, and women were better represented.

13. An activity is anything that is formally organized for the public from a meeting to a demonstration.

14. I am grateful to Alvarez, Dagnino, and Escobar (1998, 14) for this analogy. Ac-cording to them, the word *web* better describes the frameworks of meanings that in-fuse new cultural meanings into political practices and collective actions because *web*, unlike the word *network*, suggests the inclusion of different modes of consciousness and practices of nature, neighborhood life, and identities.

15. They were on the editorial page, page 4, and letters to editor (*La Barricada*, May 19, 1994, 8; May 27, 1994, 4; May 28, 1994, 6).

16. *Voces de Mujeres* organized for the 1994 Cairo Conference on Population and Development, *La Inciativa de Mujeres hacia La Cumbre Social* organized for the 1995 Copenhagen Summit on Social Development, and *La Comité Nacional hacia Beijing* or-ganized for the 1995 Beijing Conference on Women.

Epilogue. Nicaragua, 1996–2000

1. There are many who accuse the Sandinistas of engaging in a corrupt and cynical money grab when, as a lame-duck government, they passed Laws 85 and 86 guaran-teeing ownership to the beneficiaries of the agrarian reform program. The reality of those laws is that they benefited many more poor people than wealthy, that they re-sulted in a public, contested, and later an accepted change of ownership, and that some individual titles held by the highest ranking Sandinistas were returned to their previous owners. This is not how corrupt governments operate. However, it must also be noted that the Sandinistas had no reason to loot the treasury, because they assumed that they would be in power indefinitely. For the best chronicle of corruption under the Somoza dictatorship, see Millett 1977.

2. It should be noted that the FSLN when it was in power jailed Jarquín half a dozen times.

3. My personal favorite slogan is "Each person an accountant!"

4. Before Hurricane Mitch and the campaign by the Jubilee 2000 to forgive the debt, Nicaragua owed 27 percent of its debt to multilateral agencies, 27 percent to Paris Club creditor countries, and 42 percent to non–Paris Club creditor countries. Re-cently, Britain, Canada, and Sweden have forgiven their debts to Nicaragua.

5. A *caudillo* is a strongman, a leader who operates above the law and without re-straint. Based in the nondemocratic, vertically organized traditional culture of Latin America, *caudillos* have occasionally been populist and progressive. More typically, they have been oppressive, violent, and corrupt.

6. Davis, Aguilar, and Speer (1999, 60) maintain that the FSLN, unlike other politi-cal parties, still mobilizes and organizes the marginalized for the democratization of civil society at large, rather than solely for its own purpose of being reelected.

References

Acosta-Belén, Edna, and Christine E. Bose. 1995. "Colonialism, Structural Subordination, and Empowerment: Women in the Development Process in Latin America and the Caribbean." Pp. 15–36 in *Women in the Latin American Development Process*, ed. Christine E. Bose and Edna Acosta-Belén. Philadelphia: Temple University Press.

Adam, Barry D. 1987. "Homosexuality without a Gay World: The Case of Nicaragua." ARGDH Newsletter, 9, no. 3: 6–10.

Agurto Vílchez, Sonia. 1992. *Analisis de la Situation Actual de la Población Nicaragüense: Un Analisis de Género*. Managua: Autoridad Sueca para el Desarrollo Internacional.

Alexander, M. Jacqui. 1991. "Redrafting Morality: The Post-Colonial State and the Sexual Offences Bill of Trinidad and Tobago." Pp. 133–52 in *Third World Women and the Politics of Feminism*, ed. Chandra Talpade Mohanty, Ann Russo, and Lourdes Torres. Bloomington and Indianapolis: Indiana University Press.

Altamirano, Hulda. Reseacher, Estelí. Interview by author. August 10, 1994.

Alvarez, Sonia E. 1990. *Engendering Development in Brazil: Women's Movements in Transition Politics*. Princeton: Princeton University Press.

———. 1998. "Latin American Feminisms 'Go Global': Trends of the 1990s and Challenges for the New Millennium." Pp. 293–324 in *Cultures of Politics, Politics of Culture: Revisioning Latin American Social Movements*, ed. Sonia E. Alvarez, Evelina Dagnino, and Arturo Escobar. Boulder: Westview Press.

Alvarez, Sonia E., Evelina Dagnino, and Arturo Escobar. 1998. "Introduction: The Cultural and the Political in Latin American Social Movements." Pp. 1–29 in *Cultures of Politics, Politics of Culture: Revisioning Latin American Social Movements*, ed. Sonia E. Alvarez, Evelina Dagnino, and Arturo Escobar. Boulder: Westview Press.

Alvarez, Sonia E., and Arturo Escobar. 1992. "Theoretical and Political Horizons of Change in Contemporary Latin American Social Movements." Pp. 317–30 in *The Making of Social Movements in Latin America: Identity, Strategy, and Democracy*, ed. Arturo Escobar and Sonia Alvarez. Boulder: Westview Press.

Americas Update. Monthly. Toronto.

Aquelarre: Latin American Women's Magazine.

Arana, Mario. 1997. "General Economic Policy." Pp. 81–96 in *Nicaragua without Illusions: Regime Transition and Structural Adjustment in the 1990s*, ed. Thomas W. Walker. Wilmington: Scholarly Resources Books.

Araújo, Ana María. 1985. "Hacia una Identidad Latinoamerica: Los Movimientos de Mujeres en Europa y América Latina." *Nueva Sociedad* 85 (July/August): 89–92.

Arendt, Hannah. 1958. *The Human Condition*. Chicago: University of Chicago Press.

————. 1961. *Between Past and Future: Six Exercises in Political Thought*. New York: Viking Press.

Assies, William, Gerrit Burgwal, and Ton Salmon. 1990. *Structures of Power, Movements of Resistance: An Introduction to the Theories of Urban Movements in Latin America*. Amsterdam: CEDLA.

Association of Nicaraguan Women "Luisa Amanda Espinoza" (AMNLAE). 1983. *Una Mujer Donde Esté Debe Hacer Revolución*. Translated by Latin America Working Group. Toronto: Latin America Working Group.

————. 1987. "I Was Born with the Revolution: Workshop on Women in Nicaragua, April 4, 1987." Managua: AMNLAE and the Oficina Gubernamentales de la Mujer.

————. 1989. Encuentro Nacional de Mujeres de la Fuerzes Fundamentals "Nora Astorga." "Logros, Compromisos, y Demandas." Managua: AMNLAE and the Oficina Gubernamental de la Mujer.

————. 1993. "Estrategia Nacional de AMNLAE." August 7.

Avendaño, Nestor. 1994. *La Economia de Nicaragua: El Año 2000 y las Posibilidades de Crecimiento*. Managua: Nitlapan and CRIES.

Babb, Florence. 1993. "Negociando Espacios Domesticos y Sociales: Genero y Poder en la Nicaragua Posterior a 1990." Tradicido por Consuela Guayara. Paper presented at "Luchas por Espacio Social: Género y Poder en América Latina." Mexico City: July 28–August 5.

————. 1996. "After the Revolution: Neo-Liberal Policy and Gender in Nicaragua." *Latin American Perspectives* 23, no. 1 (winter): 27–48.

Barahona, Milagro. NGO worker (NORAD?). Interview by author. July 1994.

Barricada (Spanish). Daily newspaper. Managua.

Barricada International (English). Bimonthly magazine. Managua.

Bayard de Volo, Lorraine. 1995. "Testing the Limits of Maternal Identity: The Mothers of Matagalpa, Nicaragua, Post 1990." Paper presented at the Latin American Studies Association Conference. Washington, D.C.: September 28–30.

Beaudoin, Denise. Lawyer, CST Women's Secretariat. Interview by author. August 1, 1994.

Bennet, Vivienne. 1995. "Gender, Class, and Water: Women and the Politics of Water Service in Monterrey, Mexico." *Latin American Perspectives* 22, no. 2 (spring): 76–99.

Bermúdez, Leydia. Administrative assistant, CONAPRO H-M. Interview by author. April 13, 1994.

Black, George. 1981. *Triumph of the People: The Sandinista Revolution in Nicaragua*. London: Zed Press.

Blandón, María Teresa. 1994. "The Impact of the Sandinista Defeat on Nicaraguan

Feminism." Pp. 97–101 in *Compañeras: Voices from the Latin American Women's Movement*, ed. Gary Küppers. London: Latin American Bureau.

———. Coordinator, CNF. Interview by author. January 6, 1994; March 7, 1994; June 20, 1994; January 15, 1995.

———. Coordinator, La Corriente. Interview and translation by Cathy Feingold. July 21, 1998.

Blandón, Mirna. Coordinator, CONAPI, Matagalpa. Interview by author. April 19, 1994.

Bolt, Mary. Sub-director, Xochiquetzal. Interview by author. February 23, 1994.

Booth, John A. 1985. *The End and the Beginning: The Nicaraguan Revolution*. 2nd edition. Boulder: Westview Press.

———. 1996. "Nicaragua: Revolution and Retrenchment." Pp. 421–38 in *Latin American Politics and Development*, 4th edition, ed. Howard J. Wiarda and Harvey F. Kline. Boulder: Westview Press.

Booth, John A., and Thomas W. Walker. 1993. *Understanding Central America*. 2nd edition. Boulder: Westview Press.

Bouchier, David. 1979. "The Deradicalisation of Feminism: Ideology and Utopia in Action." *Sociology* 13, no. 3: 387–402.

Boyle, Catherine M. 1993. "Touching the Air: The Cultural Force of Women in Chile." Pp. 156–72 in *Viva: Women and Popular Protest in Latin America*, ed. Sarah A. Radcliffe and Sallie Westwood. London and New York: Routledge.

Brenes, Ada Julia, et al., eds. 1991. *La mujer nicaragüense en los años 80*. Managua: Ediciones Nicarao.

Brockett, Charles D. 1988. *Land, Power, and Poverty: Agrarian Transformation and Political Conflict in Central America*. Boston: Unwin Hyman.

Brown, Angelica. FSLN Deputy of Regional Council, RAAS. Interview by author. July 8, 1994.

Brown, Doug. 1990. "Sandinismo and the Problem of Democratic Hegemony." *Latin American Perspectives* 17, no. 2 (spring): 39–61.

Buechler, Steven M. 1993. "Beyond Resource Mobilization? Emerging Trends in Social Movement Theory." *Sociological Quarterly* 34, no. 2 (spring): 217–35.

Bulmer-Thomas, Victor. 1983. "Economic Development over the Long-Run: Central America Since 1920." *Journal of Latin American Studies* 15 (November): 269–94.

———. 1988. "The Economics of Central America." *Latin American Research Review* 23, no. 3: 154–69.

Burbach, Roger, and Orlando Nuñez. 1987. *Fire in the Americas: Forging a Revolutionary Agenda*. London and New York: Verso.

Burns, E. Bradford. 1987. *At War in Nicaragua: The Reagan Doctrine and the Politics of Nostalgia*. New York: Harper and Row.

Bystydzienski, Jill M., ed. 1992. *Women Transforming Politics: Worldwide Strategies for Empowerment*. Bloomington and Indianapolis: Indiana University Press.

Cabezas, Omar. 1985. *Fire from the Mountain*. Translated by Kathleen Weaver. London: Cape.

Caldeira, Teresa Pires de Rio. 1990. "Women, Daily Life and Politics" Pp. 47–78 in *Women and Social Change in Latin America*, ed. Elizabeth Jelin. Translated by J. Ann Zammit and Marilyn Thomson. London: Zed Press.

Central America Report. Monthly. Guatemala City.

Central American Women Speak for Themselves. 1983. Toronto: Latin American Working Group.

Central American Women's Network (CAWN). Newsletter. London: CAWN.

Centro de Información y Servicios de Asesoría (CISAS). 1997. "Adjusting Health Care: The Case of Nicaragua" Pp. 86–90 in *Development for Health*, ed. Deborah Eade. Oxford: Oxfam.

Centro de Investigaciones y Estudios de la Reforma Agraria (CIERA). 1984. *La mujer en la cooperativeas agropecuarios en Nicaragua*. Managua: El Centro de Investigaciones y Estudios de la Reforma Agraria.

Centro Nicaragüense de Derechos Humanos (CENIDH). 1994. *Derechos Humanos in Nicaragua: informe anual abril 1993–abril 1994*. Managua: CENIDH.

Chalmers, Douglas A., et al., eds. *The New Politics of Inequality in Latin America: Rethinking Participation and Representation*. Oxford: Oxford University Press.

Chalmers, Douglas A., Scott B. Martin, and Kerianne Piester. 1997. "Associative Networks: New Structures of Representation for the Popular Sectors?" Pp. 543–82 in *The New Politics of Inequality in Latin America: Rethinking Participation and Representation*, ed. Chalmers et al. Oxford: Oxford University Press.

Chamorro, Amalia. 1989. *La Mujer: Logros y Limites en Diez Años de Revolución*. Managua: Editorial y Escuela de Sociologia a la UCA.

Chavez, Roberto. 1987. "Urban Planning in Nicaragua: The First Five Years." *Latin American Perspectives* 14, no. 2 (spring): 226–36.

Chilcote, Ronald H. 1990. "Post-Marxism: The Retreat from Class in Latin America." *Latin America Perspectives* 17, no. 2 (spring): 3–24.

Chinchilla, Norma Stoltz. 1983. "Women in Revolutionary Movements: The Case of Nicaragua." Working Paper 27. Michigan: University of Michigan.

———. 1990. "Revolutionary Popular Feminism in Nicaragua." *Gender & Society* 4, no. 3 (September): 370–97.

———. 1992. "Marxism, Feminism, and the Struggle for Democracy in Latin America." Pp. 37–51 in *The Making of Social Movements in Latin America: Identity, Strategy and Democracy*, ed. Arturo Escobar and Sonia Alvarez. Boulder: Westview Press.

Chow, Marlene. Ex-AMNLAE leader. Interview by author. February 11, 1994.

Chuchryk, Patricia M. 1989. "Subversive Mothers: The Women's Opposition to the Military Regime in Chile." Pp. 130–51 in *Women, the State, and Development*, ed. Sue Ellen M. Charleton, Jana Everett, and Kathleen Staudt. Albany: State University of New York Press.

———. 1991. "Women in the Revolution." Pp. 143–65 in *Revolution and Counterrevolution in Nicaragua*, ed. Thomas W. Walker. Boulder: Westview Press.

Clemens, Elizabeth S. 1996. "Organizational Form As Frame: Collective Identity and Political Strategy in the American Labor Movement, 1880–1920." Pp. 205–26 in

Comparative Perspectives on Social Movements: Political Opportunities, Mobilizing Structures, and Cultural Framings, ed. Doug McAdam, John D. McCarthy, and Mayer N. Zald. Cambridge: Cambridge University.

Close, David. 1988. Nicaragua: Politics, Economics, and Society. London and New York: Pinter.

————. 1995. "The Newest Nicaragua: Politics, Democracy, and the Search for Stability." Paper presented at the Canadian Political Science Association Annual Conference. Montreal, Canada.

Cohen, Jean. 1982. "Between Crisis Management and Social Movements: The Place of Institutional Reform." Telos 52 (summer): 21–40.

————. 1983. "Rethinking Social Movements." Berkeley Journal of Sociology 28: 97–113.

————. 1985. "Strategy or Identity: New Theoretical Paradigms and Contemporary Social Movements." Social Research 52, no. 4 (winter): 663–716.

Cohen, Jean, and Andrew Arato. 1992. Civil Society and Political Theory. Cambridge: MIT Press.

Colburn, Forrest D. 1986. Post-Revolutionary Nicaragua: State, Class, and the Dilemmas of Agrarian Policy. Berkeley: University of California Press.

Collins, Joseph, with Frances Moore Lappe, Nick Allen, and Paul Rice. 1986. Nicaragua, What Difference Could a Revolution Make? Food and Farming in the New Nicaragua. New York: Grove Press.

Collinson, Helen, et al., eds. 1990. Women and Revolution in Nicargua. London: Zed Books.

Comite Nacional Feminista. 1994. Paper produced for discussion at the Aquelarre Conference. Managua: March 18–19.

Conference on Violence in Nicaragua. 2000. Leeds, England: March.

Corragio, José Luis. 1986. Nicaragua: Revolution and Democracy. Boston: Allen and Unwin.

Criquillon, Ana. 1995. "The Nicaraguan Women's Movement: Feminist Reflections from Within." Pp. 209–38 in The Politics of Survival: Grassroots Movements in Central America, ed. Minor Sinclair. New York: Monthly Review.

Croll, Elizabeth. 1981. "Women in Rural Production and Reproduction in the Soviet Union, China, Cuba, and Tanzania: Socialist Development Experiences." Signs 7, no. 21: 361–74.

Cruz, Arturo J., Jr., with Mark Falcoff. 1990. "Who Won the Election in Nicaragua?" Commentary 89 (May): 31–38.

Cruzes, Fabida. Trainer, Women's Movement House "Nidia White," Puerto Cabezas. Interview by author. July 4, 1994.

Cunningham, Miriam. FSLN Atlantic Coast Representative. Interview by author. February 10, 1994.

Dagnino, Evelina. 1998. "Culture, Citizenship, and Democracy: Changing Discourses and Practices of the Latin American Left." Pp. 33–63 in Cultures of Politics, Politics of Culture, ed. Sonia E. Alvarez, Evelina Dagnino, and Arturo Escobar. Boulder: Westview Press.

Dalton, Russel J., and Manfred Kuechler, eds. 1990. *Challenging the Political Order: New Social Order and Political Movements in Western Democracies*. Oxford: Polity.

Daly Heyck, Denis Lynn. 1990. *Life Stories of the Nicaraguan Revolution*. New York: Routledge.

Daniel, Patricia. 1998. *No Other Reality: The Life and Times of Nora Astorga*. Bangor, Wales: CAM.

Dávila, Esmeralda. Coordinator, training courses, AMNLAE. Interview by author. April 21, 1994; June 16, 1994.

Davis, Charles L., Edwin E. Aguilar, and John G. Speer. 1999. "Associations and Activism: Mobilization of Urban Informal Workers in Costa Rica and Nicaragua." *Journal of Interamerican Studies and World Affairs* 41, no. 3 (fall): 35–66.

Deere, Carmen Diana. 1985. "Rural Women and State Policy: The Latin American Agrarian Reform Experience." *World Development* 13, no. 9 (September): 1037–53.

Deere, Carmen Diana, and Peter Marchetti. 1981. "The Worker-Peasant Alliance in the First Year of the Nicaraguan Agrarian Reform." *Latin American Perspectives* 8, no. 2: 40–73.

Diani, Mario. 1992. "The Concept of Social Movement." *Sociological Review* 40, no.1 (February): 1–25.

Dijkstra, Geske. 1992. *Industrialization in Sandinista Nicaragua: Policy and Practice in a Mixed Economy*. Boulder: Westview Press.

———. 1996. *Technology Questioned: Ideology and Interests in Nicaragua's Economic Policies*. Working Paper Series No. 213 (March). The Hague: Institute for Social Sciences.

Disch, Lisa. 1995. "Please Sit Down But Don't Make Yourself at Home: Arendtian 'Visiting' and the Prefigurative Politics of Consciousness-Raising." Pp. 132–65 in *Hannah Arendt and the Meaning of Politics*, ed. John MacGowan and Craig Calhoun. Minneapolis: University of Minnesota Press.

Draper, Elaine. 1985. "Women's Work and Development in Latin America." *Studies in Comparative International Development* 20, no. 1: 3–30.

Dunayevskaya, Raya. 1982. *Rosa Luxemburg, Women's Liberation, and Marx's Philosophy of Revolution*. New Jersey: Humanities Press.

———. 1985. *Women's Liberation and the Dialetics of Revolution: Reaching for the Future*. New Jersey: Humanities Press.

Dunkerley, James. 1988. *Power in the Isthmus: A Political History of Modern Central America*. London: Verso Books.

The Economist. Weekly news magazine.

Ellsberg, Mary, Jerker Liljestrand, and Anna Winkvist. 1997. "The Nicaraguan Network of Women against Violence." *Reproductive Health Matters* (November 10): 82–92.

Emergency and Reconstruction Civil Committee (CCER). 1999. *Executive Summary*. May.

Envío. Managua: Universidad de Central America.

Escobar, Arturo. 1992. "Culture, Economics, and Politics in Latin America Social

Movements Theory and Practice." Pp. 62–88 in *The Making of Social Movements in Latin America: Identity, Strategy, and Democracy,* ed. Arturo Escobar and Sonia Alvarez. Boulder: Westview Press.

Escobar, Arturo, and Sonia Alvarez, eds. 1992. *The Making of Social Movements in Latin America: Identity, Strategy, and Democracy.* Boulder: Westview Press.

Espinoza, Isolda. Economist, CRIES. Interview by author. February 9, 1994.

Evers, Tilman. 1985. "Identity: The Hidden Side of New Social Movements in Latin America." Pp. 43–71 in *New Social Movements and the State in Latin America,* ed. David Slater. Amsterdam: CEDLA.

Ewig, Christina. 1999. "The Strengths and Limits of the NGO Women's Movement's Mode: Shaping Nicaragua's Democratic Institutions." *Latin American Research Review* 34, no. 3: 75–102.

Fals Borda, Orlando. 1992. "Social Movements and Political Power in Latin America." Pp. 303–16 in *The Making of Social Movements in Latin America: Identity, Strategy, and Democracy,* ed. Arturo Escobar and Sonia Alvarez. Boulder: Westview Press.

Fauné, Mana Angelica. 1994. *Mujeres y Familias Centroamericanas Principales Transformaciones y Problemas: Desde la Perspectiva de las Mujeres.* San José, Costa Rica: May.

Feijoó, María del Carmen. 1989. "The Challenge of Constructing Civilian Peace: Women and Democracy in Argentina." Pp. 72–94 in *The Women's Movement in Latin America: Feminism and the Transition to Democracy,* ed. Jane Jaquette. Boston: Unwin Hyman.

Feijoó, María del Carmen, and Monica Gogna. 1990. "Women in the Transition to Democracy." Pp. 79–114 in *Women and Social Change in Latin America,* ed. Elizabeth Jelin. Translated by J. Ann Zammit and Marilyn Thomson. London: Zed Press.

Feinberg, Richard. 1997. *Summitry of the Americas: A Progress Report.* Washington, D.C.: Institute for International Economics.

Feingold, Cathy. 1998. "Conclusions." Unpublished document.

Fempress. Chile.

Fernández, Anna M. 1995. "Mujeres, Revolución y Cambio Cultural." Paper presented at the Latin American Studies Association Annual Conference. Washington, D.C.: September 28–30.

———. 1996. "The Disruptions of Adjustment: Women in Nicaragua," *Latin American Perspectives* 23, no. 1 (winter): 49–66.

Flora, Cornelia Butler. 1982. "Socialist Feminism in Latin America." Working Paper 14. Women in International Development. Ann Arbor: University of Michigan.

Flynn, Patricia. 1980. "Women Challenge the Myth." *NACLA: Report on the Americas* 14, no. 5 (September/October): 28–32.

Fondo de Población de las Naciones Unidas. 1993. *America Latina y el Caribe: Carpete de Información.*

Fonseca, Hazel. Coordinator, Xochiquetzal. Interview by author. May 25, 1994.

Foley, Monica. CIDA worker, *8 marzo.* Interview by author. June 20, 1994.

Foweraker, Joe. 1995. *Theorizing Social Movements.* London: Pluto.

Franco, Jean. 1998. "Defrocking the Vatican: Feminism's Secular Project." Pp. 278–89 in

Cultures of Politics, Politics of Cultures, ed. Sonia Alvarez, Evelina Dagnino, and Arturo Escobar. Boulder: Westview Press.

Fraser, Antonia. 1989. *Warrior Queens.* New York: Knopf.

Friedman, Debra, and Doug McAdam. 1992. "Collective Identity and Activism: Networks, Choices, and the Life of a Social Movement." Pp. 165–73 in *Frontiers in Social Movement Theory,* ed. Aldon D. Morris and Carol McClurg Mueller. New Haven: Yale University Press.

Gamson, William A. 1992. "The Social Psychology of Collective Action." Pp. 53–76 in *Frontiers in Social Movement Theory,* ed. Aldon D. Morris and Carol McClurg Mueller. New Haven: Yale University Press.

Gamson, William A., and Gadi Wolfsfeld. 1993. "Movements and Media As Interacting Systems." *Annals: AAPSS* 528 (July): 114–25.

Garcia-Guadilla, María Pilar. 1995. "Gender, Environment, and Empowerment in Venezuela." Pp. 213–37 in *EnGENDERing Wealth and Well-Being: Empowerment for Global Change,* ed. Rae Lesser Blumberg, Cathy A. Rakowski, Irene Tinker, and Michael Monteón. Boulder: Westview Press.

Garfield, Richard, Nicola Low, and Julio Caldera. 1993. "Letter from Nicaragua: Desocializing Health Care in Nicaragua." *Journal of the American Medical Association* 270, no. 3 (August): 989–93.

Garreton, Manuel Antonio. 1991. "Political Democratization in Latin America and the Crisis of Paradigms." Pp. 100–118 in *Rethinking Third World Politics,* ed. James Manor. London: Longman.

La Gente. Weekly cultural supplement to *La Barricada* (Spanish). Managua.

Gilbert, Dennis. 1988. *Sandinistas: The Party and the Revolution.* London: Basil Blackwell.

Goetz, Anne Marie. 1991. "Feminism and the Claim to Know: Contradictions in Feminist Approaches to Women in Development." Pp. 133–57 in *Gender and International Relations,* ed. Rebecca Grant and Kathleen Newland. Bloomington and Indianapolis: Indiana University Press.

Gomez, Gladis. Director, CEDIM. Interview by author. Jan 7, 1994; January 25, 1994.

Gonzáles de la Rocha, Mercedes. 1995. "The Urban Family and Poverty in Latin America." *Latin American Perspectives* 22, no. 2 (spring): 12–31.

González Rojas, Nívea. 1993. "La union de hecho estable y la realidad nicaragüense." *Documentos Sobre la Mujer* 18 (July/August): 35–36.

Gorman, Stephen M., and Thomas W. Walker. 1985. "The Armed Forces." Pp. 91–118 in *Nicaragua: The First Five Years,* ed. Thomas W. Walker. New York: Praeger.

Gramsci, Antonio. 1971. *Selections from the Prison Notebooks.* Edited and translated by Quintin Hoare and Geoffrey Nowell Smith. London: Lawrence and Wishart.

Guevara, Ernesto. 1967. *Che Guevara Speaks: Selected Speeches and Writings,* ed. George Lavan. New York: Merit.

Gurr, Ted Robert, ed. 1980. *Handbook of Political Conflict: Theory and Research.* New York: Free Press.

Hahner, June E. 1980. *Women in Latin American History: Their Lives and Views.* Los Angeles: University of California and the Latin American Center Publications.

Hellman, Judith Adler. 1992a. "Making Women Visible: New Works on Latin American and Caribbean Women." *Latin American Research Review* 27, no. 1: 182–91.

———. 1992b. "The Study of New Social Movements in Latin America and the Question of Autonomy." Pp. 52–60 in *The Making of Social Movements in Latin America: Identity, Strategy, and Democracy,* ed. Arturo Escobar and Sonia Alvarez. Boulder: Westview Press.

———. 1994. "Mexican Popular Movements, Clientelism, and the Process of Democratization." *Latin American Perspectives* 21, no. 2 (spring): 124–42.

———. 1995. "The Riddle of New Social Movements: Who They Are and What They Do." Pp. 165–83 in *Capital, Power, and Inequality in Latin America,* ed. Sandor Halebsky and Richard L. Harris. Boulder: Westview Press.

Herrera, Leticia. Representative, FSLN. Interview by author. June 16, 1994.

Hoja Informativa. 1992. Managua: Fundación Agosto César Sandino.

Hofstaeder, Sharon. Witness for Peace. Interview by author. February 22, 1994.

Hoyt, Katherine. 1997. *The Many Faces of Sandinista Democracy.* Athens: University of Ohio Press.

ICPD Watch. 1994.

Ingram, Paula. Mayor of Bluefields. Interview by author. July 8, 1994.

Instituto Nicaragüense de la Mujer (INIM). 1996. *Acciones Realizadas para el Adelanto de las Mujeres Nicaragüenses en el Periodo 1990–1996 y Proyecciones para Su Seguimiento.* Managua: INIM.

Isbester, Katherine. 1996. "Understanding State Disintegration: The Case of Nicaragua." *Journal of Political, Social, and Economic Studies* 21, no. 4 (winter): 455–76.

———. 1998. "The Economic Implications of the Nicaraguan State's Ideology about Women, 1990–1995." *Contemporary Politics* 4, no. 4: 375–89.

Jaquette, Jane. 1989. "Conclusion: Women and the New Democratic Politics." Pp. 185–208 in *The Women's Movement in Latin America: Feminism and the Transition to Democracy,* ed. J. Jaquette. Boston: Unwin Hyman.

———, ed. 1989. *The Women's Movement in Latin America: Feminism and the Transition to Democracy.* Boston: Unwin Hyman.

Jelin, Elizabeth, ed. 1990. *Women and Social Change in Latin America.* Translated by J. Ann Zammit and Marilyn Thomson. London: Zed.

Jenson, Jane. 1994. "Political Economy, Sociology: Political Science?" Lecture series on ReThinking the Political. University of Toronto, Toronto: November 19.

Jonas, Susanne, and Nancy Stein. 1990. "The Construction of Democracy in Nicaragua." *Latin American Perspectives* 17, no. 3 (summer): 10–37.

Jones, Bruce. 1994. "Nicaragua's Economic Situation." Congressional Record, May 4, E845.

Jubb, Nadine. 1996. *Women's Labour Activity in Nicaragua.* Toronto: Latin American Working Group.

———. 1997. "The Development Question in the Nicaraguan Women's Movement." Paper presented at the International Studies Association Annual Conference. Toronto: March 20.

Judson, Fred. 1987. "Sandinista Revolutionary Morale." *Latin American Perspectives* 14, no. 1 (winter): 19–42.

Kampwirth, Karen. 1995a. "Feminism, Anti-Feminism, and Electoral Politics in Post-War Nicaragua and El Salvador." Paper presented at the American Political Science Association Annual Conference. Chicago: August 31– September 3.

———. 1995b. "Social Policy in Nicaragua, 1990–1995." Paper presented at the Latin American Studies Association Annual Conference. Washington, D.C.: September 28–30.

———. 1996. "The Mother of the Nicaraguans: Doña Violeta and the UNO's Gender Agenda." *Latin American Perspectives* 23, no. 1 (winter): 67–86.

———. 1997. "Social Policy." Pp. 115–30 in *Nicaragua without Illusions: Regime Transition and Structural Adjustment in the 1990s*, ed. Thomas W. Walker. Wilmington, N.C.: Scholarly Resources.

Kirkwood, Julieta. 1985. "Feministas y Politicas." *Nueva Sociedad* 78 (July/August): 62–79.

Klandermans, Bert. 1992. "The Social Construction of Protest and Multiorganizational Fields." Pp. 77–103 in *Frontiers in Social Movement Theory*, ed. Aldon D. Morris and Carol McClurg Mueller. New Haven: Yale University Press.

Klein, Hilary. 1995. "Constructing New Alternatives for Women's Liberation: Women's Collectives in Managua, Nicaragua." Senior honors thesis, University of California at Berkeley.

Knight, Alan. 1990. "Historical Continuities in Social Movements." Pp. 78–104 in *Popular Movements and Political Change in Mexico*, ed. Joe Foweraker and Ann L. Craig. Boulder: Lynne Rienner.

Kriesi, Hanspeter. 1996. "The Organizational Structure of New Social Movements in a Political Context." Pp. 152–84 in *Comparative Perspectives on Social Movements: Political Opportunities, Mobilizing Structures, and Cultural Framings*, ed. Doug McAdam, John D. McCarthy, and Mayer N. Zald. Cambridge: Cambridge University Press.

Laclau, Ernesto. 1985. "New Social Movements and the Plurality of the Social." Pp. 27–42 in *New Social Movements and the State in Latin America*, ed. David Slater. Amsterdam: CEDLA.

Lancaster, Roger N. 1992. *Life Is Hard: Machismo, Danger, and the Intimacy of Power in Nicaragua*. Berkeley and Los Angeles: University of California Press.

LaRamée, Pierre, and Erica G. Polakoff. 1997. "The Evolution of Popular Organizations in Nicaragua." Pp. 141–206 in *The Undermining of the Sandinista Revolution*, ed. Gary Prevost and Harry E. Vanden. New York: St. Martin's.

Lernoux, Penny. 1989. *People of God: The Struggle for World Catholicism*. New York: Viking.

Lindo, Matilda. Director, Women's Movement House "Nidia White," Puerto Cabezas. Interview by author. May 21, 1994; July 4, 1994.

Lobao, Linda. 1990. "Women in Revolutionary Movements: Changing Patterns of Latin American Guerrilla Struggle." Pp. 180–204 in *Women and Social Protest*, ed. Guida West and Rhoda Lois Blumberg. New York: Oxford University Press.

Logan, Kathleen. 1990. "Women's Participation in Urban Protest." Pp. 150–59 in *Popular Movements and Political Change in Mexico*, ed. Joe Foweraker and Ann L. Craig. Boulder: Lynne Rienner.

Luciak, Ilja A. 1997. "Women and Electoral Politics of the Left: A Comparison of El Salvador and Nicaragua." Paper presented at the Latin American Studies Association Conference. Guadalajara, Mexico: April 17–19.

MacDonald, Laura. 1995. "A Mixed Blessing: The NGO Boom in Latin America." *NACLA: Report on the Americas* 28, no. 5 (March/April): 30–35.

———. 1997. *Supporting Civil Society: The Political Role of Non-governmental Organizations in Central America*. Basinstoke, England: MacMillan/St. Martin's.

Maier, Elizabeth. 1980. *Nicaragua: la mujer en a revolución*. Mexico, D.F.: Ediciones de Cultura Popular.

Marcus, Bruce, ed. 1982. *Sandinistas Speak*. New York: Pathfinder Press.

Marx Ferree, Myra. 1992. "The Political Context of Rationality: Rational Choice Theory and Resource Mobilization." Pp. 29–52 in *Frontiers in Social Movement Theory*, ed. Aldon D. Morris and Carol McClurg Mueller. New Haven: Yale University Press.

Mason, David. 1992. "Women's Participation in Central American Revolutions: A Theoretical Perspective." *Comparative Political Studies* 25, no. 1 (April): 63–89.

Matus, Auxiliadora. Director, INIM, 1994–1996. Interview and translation by Cathy Feingold. July 14, 1998.

Mayoux, Linda. 1992. "From Idealism to Realism: Women, Feminism and Empowerment in Nicaraguan Tailoring Cooperatives." *Development and Change* 23, no. 2 (April): 91–114.

McAdam, Doug. 1982. *The Political Process and the Development of Black Insurgency*. Chicago: University of Chicago Press.

McAdam, Doug, John D. McCarthy, and Mayer N. Zald. 1988. "Social Movements." Pp. 695–737 in *Handbook of Sociology*, ed. Neil J. Smelser. Newbury Park, Calif.: Sage Publications.

———, eds. 1996. *Comparative Perspectives on Social Movements: Political Opportunities, Mobilizing Structures, and Cultural Framings*. Cambridge: Cambridge University Press.

McAdam, Doug, and Dieter Rucht. 1993. "The Cross-National Diffusion of Movement Ideas." *Annals, American Academy of Political and Social Science* 528 (July): 56–74.

McBriarty, Ana. CIDA worker, *8 marzo*. Interview by author. June 20, 1994.

McCarthy, John D. 1996. "Constraints and Opportunities in Adopting, Adapting, and Inventing." Pp. 141–51 in *Comparative Perspectives on Social Movements: Political Opportunities, Mobilizing Structures, and Cultural Framings*, ed. Doug McAdam, John D. McCarthy, and Mayer N. Zald. Cambridge: Cambridge University Press.

McCarthy, John, and Mayer N. Zald. 1977. "Resource Mobilization and Social Movements: A Partial Theory." *American Journal of Sociology* 82, no. 6: 1212–41.

McCoy, Jennifer L. 1991. "Nicaragua in Transition." *Current History* 90, no. 554 (March): 117–20, 131–32.

McVey, Vicki. 1995. "My Beloved Revolution." Unpublished manuscript.

Melucci, Alberto. 1980. "The New Social Movements: A Theoretical Approach." *Social Science Information* 19, no. 2: 199–226.

———. 1981. "New Movements, Terrorism, and the Political System: Reflections on the Italian Case." *Socialist Review* 11, no. 56: 97–136.

———. 1985. "The Symbolic Challenge of Contemporary Movements." *Social Research* 52, no. 4 (winter): 789–816.

———. 1989. *Nomads of the Present: Social Movements and Individual Needs in Contemporary Society*, ed. John Keane and Paul Mier. Philadelphia: Temple University Press.

———. 1996. *Challenging Codes: Collective Action in the Information Age.* Cambridge: Cambridge University Press.

Mendez, Odelia. Lawyer, CENIDH. Interview by author. February 15, 1994.

Mendoza, Esmeralda. Director, Women's Secretariat, ATC. Interview by author. January 11, 1994.

Metoyer, Cynthia Chavez. 1995. "Efficiency or Burden Shifting? Gendered Outcomes of Stabilization and Adjustment Policies in Nicaragua." Paper presented at Latin American Studies Association International Conference. Washington, D.C.: September 28–30.

Mies, María. 1986. *Patriarchy and Accumulation on a World Scale: Women in the International Division of Labour.* London: Zed.

Mies, María, Veronika Bennholdt-Thomsen, and Claudia von Werlhof. 1988. *Women: The Last Colony.* London: Zed.

Miller, Francesa. 1991. *Latin American Women and the Search for Social Justice.* Hanover, N.H.: University Press of New England.

Millet, Richard. 1977. *Guardians of the Dynasty.* Maryknoll, N.Y.: Orbis Books.

Ministry of Social Action (MAS). 1997. *Política Nacional de Población.* Managua: MAS.

Molyneux, Maxine. 1986. "Mobilization without Emancipation? Women's Interests, The State, and Revolution." Pp. 280–302 in *Transition and Development: Problems of Third World Socialism*, ed. Richard Fagan, Carmen Diana Deere, and José Luis Coraggio. Berkeley: Monthly Review Press and Center for Study of the Americas.

———. 1981. "Women in Socialist Countries: Problems of Theory and Practice." Pp. 167–202 in *Of Marriage and the Market: Women's Subordination Internationally and Its Lessons*, ed. Kate Young, Carol Wolkowitz, and Roslyn McCullagh. London: Routledge and Kegan Paul.

Moore, Barrington. 1978. *Injustice: The Social Bases of Obedience and Revolt.* New York: M. E. Sharpe.

Morgan, Martha I. 1990. "Founding Mothers: Women's Voices and Stories in the 1987 Nicaraguan Constitution." *Boston University* 70, no. 1 (January): 1–107.

Morgan, Sarah. 1995. "Toward a New Revolution in Health: The Emergence of Alternative Health Care Networks in Nicaragua since the 1990 Elections." Undergraduate thesis, Hampshire College.

Morris, Aldon D., and Carol McClurg Mueller, eds. 1992. *Frontiers in Social Movement Theory.* New Haven: Yale University Press.

Moses, Caroline, and Linda Peake, eds. 1987. *Women, Human Settlements, and Housing.* London: Tavistock.

Mueller, Edward N. 1980. "The Psychology of Political Protest and Violence." Pp. 69–99 in *Handbook of Political Conflict*, ed. Ted Robert Gurr. New York: Free Press.

Las Mujeres Autoconvocadas. 1994. *La Sociedad Democratica Vista y Aspirada por Las Mujeres*. Managua: June.

Munck, Geraldo. 1990. "Identity and Ambiguity in Democractic Struggles." Pp. 23–42 in *Popular Movements and Political Change in Mexico*, ed. Joe Foweraker and Ann L. Craig. Boulder: Lynne Rienner.

Munguia, Marta. Director, ¡Acción Ya!. Interview by author. March 28, 1994.

Murguialday, Clara. 1988. "Ser mujer en Nicaragua: Diez años de lucha de AMNLAE." *Nueva Sociedad* 94 (March/April): 54–64.

———. 1990. *Nicaragua, revolución y feminismo (1977–89)*. Madrid: Esitorial Revolución S.A.L.

Nash, June, and Helen Safa, eds. 1985. *Women and Change in Latin America*. South Hadley, Mass.: Bergin and Garvey.

———. 1980. *Sex and Class in Latin America: Women's Perspectives on Politics, Economics, and Family in Third World*. South Hadley, Mass.: Bergin and Garvey.

National Coalition of Women. 1996. *Agenda Mínima*. Managua: March.

Navarro, Amílcar. National Director, UNAG. Interview by author. February 9, 1994.

Navarro, Marysa. 1989. "The Personal Is the Political: Las Madres de Plaza de mayo." Pp. 241–58 in *Power and Popular Protest: Latin American Social Movements*, ed. Susan Eckstein. Berkeley and Los Angeles: University of California Press.

Navarro-Génie, Marco. 1993. "The Children of Sandino: Tomás Borge and the Millenarian Inheritance." Paper presented at the Canadian Political Science Association Annual Conference. Ottawa: June 6–8.

New York Times. Daily newspaper. New York City.

Newland, Kathleen. 1991. "From Transnational Relationships to International Relations: Women in Development and the International Decade for Women." Pp. 122–32 in *Gender and International Relations*, ed. Rebecca Grant and Kathleen Newland. Bloomington and Indianapolis: Indiana University Press.

Nicaraguan Solidarity Campaign (NSC). *2000 Special Report*. London: NSC.

NICCA Bulletin. New York City.

Nielson, Kai. 1995. "Reconceptualizing Civil Society for Now: Some Somewhat Gramscian Turnings." Pp. 41–67 in *Toward a Global Civil Society*, ed. Michael Walzer. Providence: Berghahn Books.

Nolan, David. 1984. *The Ideology of the Sandinistas and the Nicaraguan Revolution*. Coral Gables, Fla.: Institute of Interamerican Studies.

El Nuevo Diario (Spanish). Daily newspaper. Managua.

Nuñez Soto, Orlando. 1988. *La Insurrección de la Consciencia*. Managua: Imprenta UCA.

Oberschall, Anthony. 1993. *Social Movements: Ideologies, Interests, and Identities*. London: Transaction.

———. 1996. "Opportunities and Framing in the Eastern European Revolts of 1989." Pp. 93–121 in *Comparative Perspectives on Social Movements: Political Opportunities, Mobilizing Structures, and Cultural Framings*, ed. Doug McAdam, John D. McCarthy, and Mayer N. Zald. Cambridge: Cambridge University.

Ocampo, José Antonio. 1991. "Collapse and (Incomplete) Stabilization of the Nicaraguan Economy." Pp. 331–68 in *The Macroeconomics of Populism in Latin America*, ed. Rodiger Dornbusch and Sebastian Edwards. Chicago: University of Chicago Press.

Ocón, María Dolores N. 1992. "Los Servicios Alternativos de la Salud de la Mujer en Nicaragua." Document prepared for Pan-American Health Organization, Women Health and Development Program. Managua: September.

———. 1993. "Servicios Alternativos de Salud de la Mujer en Nicaragua." Document prepared for the Pan-American Health Organization, Women and Health Program, Managua: September. (Author is assumed to be Lola Ocón.)

O'Donnell, Penny. 1991. *Death, Dreams, and Dancing in Nicaragua*. Crows Nest, New South Wales: Australian Broadcasting Corporation.

Okin, Susan Moller. 1989. *Justice, Gender, and the Family*. New York: Basic Books.

Olivera, Mercedes, Malena de Montis, and Mark A. Meassick. 1992. *Nicaragua: El Poder de las Mujeres*. Managua: Cenzontle.

Olson, Mancur, Jr. 1965. *The Logic of Collective Action*. Cambridge: Harvard University Press.

Oxfam-Quebec. 1994. *La Sociedad Civil en Nicaragua y la Conferencia de Poblacion y Desarrollo*. Managua: December.

Padilla, Martha Luz, Clara Murguialday, and Ana Criquillon. 1987. "Impact of the Sandinista Agrarian Reform on Rural Women's Subordination." Pp. 125–41 in *Rural Women and State Policy: Feminist Perspectives on Latin American Agricultural Development*, ed. Carmen Diana Deere and Magdalena Leon. Boulder: Westview Press.

Palacios, Dhina. Social worker, Commission on Women and Children's Police Stations. Interview by author. May 24, 1994.

Pallais, María Lourdes. 1992. "Violeta Barrios de Chamorro: La reina-madre de la nación." *Nueva Sociedad* 118 (March/April): 89–98.

Patterson, Henry. 1997. "Pacts and Poverty: The Democratization Process in Nicaragua 1990–1996." *Contemporary Politics* 3, no. 3 (September): 209–24.

Pasos, Mayra. 1995. "The Women's Movement Today." Speech at York University. Toronto: March 6.

Pasos, Mayra. Interview and translation by Cathy Feingold. July 21, 1998.

Perez, Paola, and Ivonne Siú. 1986. "La Mujer en al economia nicaragüense: cambios y desafíos." Paper presented at the Fifth Congress of ANICs. Managua: OGM.

Picado, Francisco, and Sebastian O'Grady. 1995. "Nicaragua: Stability Still Eludes Capitalists." *Militant* 59, no. 29 (August 14). Reprinted through Peacenet.

Pizarro, Ana María. 1993. "Encuentro Nacional de Mujeres Sobre Politicas de Población y Desarrollo: Por un Futuro Digno y Seguro para Todas y Todos." Managua: Fondo de Población de las Naciones Unidas.

La Prensa (Spanish). Daily newspaper. Managua.

Puntos de Encuentro. "What Is Puntos de Encuentro?" Author, translator, and date unknown.

Quandt, Midge. 1997. "Interview with Arelys Bellorini." Pp. 84–98 in *Voices of Sandin-*

ismo in Post-Election Nicaragua. Translated by Mark Lester. Nicaragua Network Education Fund.

Radcliffe, Sarah A., and Sallie Westwood, eds. 1993. *Viva: Women and Popular Protest in Latin America.* London: Routledge.

Rakowski, Cathy A. 1995. "Engendering Wealth and Well-Being—Lessons Learned." Pp. 285–94 in *EnGENDERing Wealth and Well-Being: Empowerment for Global Change,* ed. Rae Lesser Blumberg, Cathy A. Rakowski, Irene Tinker, and Michael Monteón. Boulder: Westview Press.

Ramirez-Horton, Susan E. 1982. "The Role of Women in the Nicaraguan Revolution." Pp. 147–59 in *Nicaragua in Revolution,* ed. Thomas W. Walker. New York: Praeger.

Ramos, Josefina. Codirector, Center for Constitutional Rights. Interview by author. May 11, 1994.

Randall, Margaret. 1981. *Sandino's Daughters: Testimonies of Nicaraguan Women in Struggle.* Vancouver: New Star Books.

———. 1992. *Gathering Rage: The Failure of Twentieth-Century Revolutions to Develop a Feminist Agenda.* New York: Monthly Review Press.

———. 1994. *Sandino's Daughters Revisited: Feminism in Nicaragua.* New Brunswick, N.J.: Rutgers University Press.

Randall, Vicky. 1987. *Women and Politics.* 2nd edition. London: Macmillan.

Ríos, Patricia. Nurse, Sí Mujer. Interview by author. April 25, 1994.

Robinson, William I. 1996. *Promoting Polyarchy: Globalization, U.S. Intervention, and Hegemony.* Cambridge: Cambridge University.

Ruchwarger, Gary. 1987. *People in Power: Forging a Grassroots Democracy in Nicaragua.* South Hadley, Mass.: Bergin and Garvin.

———. 1989. *Struggling for Survival: Workers, Women, and Class on a Nicaraguan State Farm.* Boulder: Westview Press.

Rusmore, Kaki. 1994. "Building Women's Democratic Leadership: The Experience of the ATC's Women's Secretariat." Paper presented at the Latin American Studies Association Annual Conference. Atlanta: March.

Saettem, Guri. Coordinator, Norwegian Committee in Solidarity with Nicaragua. Interview by author. January 19, 1994; April 1994.

Safa, Helen Icken. 1990. "Women's Social Movements in Latin America." *Gender and Society* 4 (September): 354–69.

———. 1995. "Economic Restructuring and Gender Subordination." *Latin American Perspectives* 22, no. 2 (spring): 32–50.

Saint-Germain, Michelle A. 1993a. "Paths to Power of Women Legislators in Costa Rica and Nicaragua." *Women's Studies International Forum* 16, no. 2: 119–38.

———. 1993b. "Women in Power in Nicaragua: Myth and Reality." Pp. 70–102 in *Women As National Leaders,* ed. Michael A. Genovese. Newbury Park, Calif.: Sage Publications.

Sanchez, Alejandro. Subdirector, Commission for Human Rights. Interview by author. May 12, 1994.

Santa Cruz, Adriana. 1985. "Los Movimientos de Mujeres: Una Perspectiva Latinoamerica." *Nueva Sociedad* 86 (September/October): 141–46.

Sargent, Lydia, ed. 1981. *Women and Revolution: A Discussion of the Unhappy Marriage of Marxism and Feminism.* Boston: South End Press.

Schild, Verónica. 1990. "The Hidden Politics of Neighbourhood Organizations: Women and Local Level Participation in the Poblaciones of Chile." *Canadian Journal of Latin American and Caribbean Studies* 15, no. 30: 137–58.

———. 1994. "Recasting 'Popular Movements': Gender and Political Learning in Neighbourhood Organizations in Chile." *Latin American Perspectives* 21, no. 2 (spring): 59–80.

Schneider, Cathy. 1992. "Radical Opposition Parties and Squatters Movements in Pinochet's Chile." Pp. 260–75 in *The Making of Social Movements in Latin America: Identity, Strategy, and Democracy,* ed. Arturo Escobar and Sonia Alvarez. Boulder: Westview Press.

Schultz, Victoria. 1980a. "¡Organizar!" *NACLA: Report on the Americas* 14, no. 2 (March/April): 36–39.

———. 1980b. *Women in Arms.* Video. Hudson River Productions.

Scott, Alan. 1990. *Ideology and New Social Movements.* London: Unwin Hyman.

Seitz, Barbara J. 1992. "From Home to Street: Women and Revolution in Nicaragua." Pp. 161–74 in *Women Transforming Politics: Worldwide Strategies for Empowerment,* ed. Jill M. Bystydzienski. Bloomington and Indianapolis: Indiana University Press.

Sí Mujer. 1991. Pamphlet. Managua.

Seranno, Alicia. Director of Projects, AMNLAE. Interview by author. April 21, 1994.

Sevilla, Rogalia. Director, *8 marzo.* Interview by author. June 20, 1994; June 27, 1994.

Síu Bermúdez, Ivonne. 1993. *Perfil del Movimiento de Mujeres Nicaragüenses.* Managua: Centro de Documentación e Información de la Mujer.

Siú, Ivonne. Director, CEDIM. Interview by author. July 1, 1994.

Slater, David, ed. 1985. *New Social Movements and the State in Latin America.* Amsterdam: CEDLA.

Snow, David A., E. Burke Rochford Jr., Steven K. Worden, and Robert D. Benford. 1986. "Frame Alignment Processes, Micromobilization, and Movement Participation." *American Sociological Review* 51, no. 4 (August): 464–81.

Solá, Roser, and María Pau Trayner. 1988. *Ser Madre en Nicaragua: Testimonies de una historia no escrita.* Barcelona: Icaria Editorial.

Solocerno, José. Director, UNAG, Matagalpa. Interview by author. January 18, 1994.

Spalding, Rose. 1994. *Capitalists and Revolution in Nicaragua: Opposition and Accomodation 1979–1993.* Chapel Hill: University of North Carolina Press.

Stahler-Sholk, Richard. 1990. "Stabilization, Destabilization, and the Popular Classes in Nicaragua, 1979–1988." *Latin American Research Review* 25, no. 3: 55–88.

———. 1995. "Breaking the Mold: Economic Orthodoxy and the Politics of Resistance in Nicaragua." Paper presented at the Latin American Studies Association Annual Conference Washington, D.C.: September 28–30.

———. 1997. Structural Adjustment and Resistance: The Political Economy of Nicaragua under Chamorro." Pp. 74–113 in *The Undermining of the Sandinista Revolution,* ed. Gary Prevost and Harry E. Vanden. New York: St. Martin's.

Stewart, Barbara. Coordinator, Documentation Center, CRIES. Interview by author. April 26, 1994.

Tarrow, Sidney. 1990. "The Phantom at the Opera: Political Parties and Social Movements of the 1960s and 1970s in Italy." Pp. 251–73 in *Challenging the Political Order: New Social and Political Movements in Western Democracies,* ed. Russell J. Dalton and Manfred Keuchler. Cambridge and Oxford: Polity Press and Basil Blackwell.

——. 1991. *Struggle, Politics, and Reform: Collective Action, Social Movements, and Cycles of Protest.* Western Societies Program Occasional Paper 21. Ithaca: Cornell University and the Center of International Studies.

——. 1994. *Power in the Movement: Social Movements, Collective Action, and Politics.* Cambridge: Cambridge University Press.

——. 1996. "States and Opportunities: The Political Structuring of Social Movements." Pp. 41–61 in *Comparative Perspectives on Social Movements: Political Opportunities, Mobilizing Structures, and Cultural Framings,* ed. Doug McAdam, John D. McCarthy, and Mayer N. Zald. Cambridge: Cambridge University Press.

Thayer, Millie. 1994. "After the Fall: The Nicaraguan Women's Movement in the 1990s." Paper presented at the Latin American Studies Association Annual Conference, Atlanta: March.

Tilly, Charles. 1978. *From Mobilization to Revolution.* New York: Random House.

——. 1984. "Social Movements and National Politics." Pp. 297–317 in *Statemaking and Social Movements: Essays in History and Theory,* ed. Charles Bright and Susan Harding. Ann Arbor: University of Michigan Press.

Tinoco, Jilma. Director of Gender Program, University of Central America. Interview by author. May 10, 1994.

Trottoir, Paulette. Oxfam-Quebec. Interview by author. January 10, 1995; April 20, 1994.

Vance, Irene. 1987. "More Than Bricks and Mortar: Women's Participation in Self-Help Housing in Managua, Nicaragua." Pp. 139–65 in *Women, Human Settlements, and Housing,* ed. Caroline Moser and Linda Peake. London: Tavistock.

Vanden, Harry E., and Gary Prevost. 1992. *Democracy and Socialism in Sandinista Nicaragua.* Boulder: Lynne Reinner.

Vargas, Milú. 1989a. "Mujer y Derechos Politicos." November.

——. 1989b. "Las Plataformas Electorales de los Partidos Políticos y la Mujer." In *Mujer y Partidos Políticos,* ed. Patricia Vargas Fernandez, Milú Vargas, and Josefina Ramos. Managua: November.

——. 1993. "The Women's Movement in Nicaragua." Speech at the Harborfront. Toronto: March 18.

——. 1994. "Por la Unidad en la Diversidad." Paper presented at Seminario: Aspectos de Género y Cooperación en América Latina. Managua: March 14–16.

——. Legal advisor for MINSA, alternative representative for FSLN, Co-Director of Center for Constitutional Rights. Interview by author. April 27, 1994.

Vargas, Virginia. n.d. "The Women's Movement in Peru: Rebellion into Action." Publishing information unavailable.

Vega, Adela. *Campesina*, Aranjúez. Interview by author. December 28, 1993.

Vega Vargas, Gustavo Adolfo. 1993. *Procedimiento Penal: Particularidades de la Ley no. 150*. Managua: Centro de Derechos Constitucionales, May.

Walker, Thomas. 1981. *Nicaragua: Land of Sandino*. 3rd edition. Boulder: Westview Press.

———, ed. 1982. *Nicaragua in Revolution*. New York: Praeger.

———, ed. 1985. *Nicaragua: The First Five Years*. New York: Praeger.

Weber, Henri. 1981. *Nicaragua: The Sandinist Revolution*. Trans. Patrick Camiller. London: Verso Books.

Weeks, John. 1985. "The Industrial Sector." Pp. 281–95 in *Nicaragua: The First Five Years*, ed. Thomas W. Walker. New York: Praeger.

Wessel, Lois. 1991. "Reproductive Rights in Nicaragua: From the Sandinistas to the Government of Violeta Chamorro." *Feminist Studies* 17, no. 3 (fall 1991): 537–49.

Wiarda, Howard J., and Harvey F. Kline, eds. 1996. *Latin American Politics and Development*. 4th edition. Boulder: Westview Press.

Wiegersma, Nan. 1994. "State Policy and the Restructuring of the Women's Industries in Nicaragua." Pp. 192–205 in *Women in the Age of Economic Transformation: Gender Impact of Reforms in Post-Socialist and Developing Countries*, ed. Nahid Aslanbeigui, Steven Pressman, and Gale Summerfield. London: Routledge.

Williams, Harvey. 1986. *Women and Revolution: Women's Changing Role in Nicaragua*. East Lansing: Michigan State University Press.

Women's International Resource Exchange (WIRE). 1985. *Nicaraguan Women: Unlearning the Alphabet of Submission*. New York: Women's International Resource Exchange.

Wood, Ellen Meiksins. 1995. *Democracy against Capitalism: Renewing Historical Materialism*. Cambridge: Cambridge University Press.

The World's Women 1970–1990: Trends and Statistics. 1991. New York: United Nations.

Woroniuk, Beth. 1987. "Women's Oppression and Revolution: The Nicaraguan Debate." Unpublished paper written for Canadian University Students Overseas.

Young, Iris. 1981. "Beyond the Unhappy Marriage: The Critique of the Dual Systems Theory." Pp. 43–69 in *Women and Revolution: A Discussion of the Unhappy Marriage of Marxism and Feminism*, ed. Lydia Sargent. Boston: South End Press.

Zeledón, Dora. 1993. "Mujer, Genero, Poder: Esperiencias Sectoriales en Defensa de un Proyecto Popular." Paper presented at IPADE: June.

———. Coordinator, AMNLAE. Interview by author. February 3, 1994; April 13, 1994.

Zuniga, Paola. Worker, Puntos de Encuentro. Interview by author. March 21, 1994.

Index

52 Percent Majority Conference, 133–34, 139, 144, 153

abortion: AMNLAE demands for, 84, 94; available in Managua, 224*n2*; banned under Chamorro, 112–15, 117, 121, 181, 197, 225*n4*; CONAPRO H-M demands for, 87, 94, 103; constitutional negotiations, 81; and foreign aid, 148; topic avoided by Baez, 133

Agrarian Reform Decree, 68–69, 103, 223*n5*

agriculture: effect of contra war, 67–68; effect of Hurricane Mitch, 200, 204; predominance, 27, 67; reforms, 68–70, 73, 76, 222–23*n1*, 229*n1*; under Alemán, 200, 202, 207, 210; women's roles, 25, 27, 69–74, 223*n6*

Alemán, Arnoldo: 1996 election, 175–76; 2000 election, 211; background, 175–76; constitutional negotiations, 208–11, 214; foreign aid, 201–3, 205; and government corruption, 199–201, 205; against women's rights, 122, 186, 211–14; and Hurricane Mitch, 204–5

Allende, Salvador, 31, 219*n4*

American Convention on Human Rights, 79

American Declaration of the Rights and Duties of Man, 79

AMNLAE. *See* Association of Nicaraguan Women "Luisa Amanda Espinoza" (AMNLAE)

AMPRONAC. *See* Association of Nicaraguan Women Confronting the National Problem (AMPRONAC)

Aquelarre Conference, 164–65

Arce, Bayardo, 49

Argentina, 31

Association of Nicaraguan Women Confronting the National Problem (AMPRONAC): communication, 42, 179; formation, 5, 18, 29–34; growth, 34–35, 41, 43; link with FSLN, 47–48, 190; link with MPU, 40–41, 47; objectives, 34, 36–37, 43–44; overthrow of Somoza, 42; structure, 32–33, 41, 43–44, 47, 59; successes, 18, 34–36, 43, 77, 95, 97, 184, 190, 220*n13*

Association of Nicaraguan Women "Luisa Amanda Espinoza" (AMNLAE): 1990 election, 224*n3*; 1996 election, 170–72, 228*n11*; alliances with other women's groups, 91, 95–96, 145, 170; conflict with other women's groups, 134–39, 141–42, 152; and constitutional negotiations, 76–82, 102; and contra war, 54, 55–57, 59, 62; decline, 8–9, 62, 64–65, 83–85, 128, 191; failures, 18–19, 78–79, 100–101, 184, 191; foreign aid, 57, 227*n10*; formation, 48–49; goals, 48, 50, 59, 62, 65, 83–84, 170; health campaigns, 51–52, 57, 146, 149–50, 178, 183; legal reform campaigns, 52–54, 57, 79, 94; link with FSLN, 16, 18–19, 25*n9*, 49–50, 54, 56–57, 59, 62, 77, 83–85, 87–91, 95, 100, 127–28, 130–31, 170; Literacy Crusade, 50–51, 57; role, 7, 89; structure, 57–59, 62–63, 89–90, 128–34, 139, 144, 221*nn6*, *9*; successes, 8, 18, 77, 95, 97, 101, 191; and women in agriculture, 71, 222*n1*

Association of Rural Workers (ATC): de-

249

Nuñez, Carlos, 5, 90, 94
Nuñez, Vilma, 206, 209

Oberschall, Anthony, 31
Ocón, María Dolores, 170
Ocotal, 8, 10
Ortega, Daniel: 1990 election, 96; 1994 leadership campaign, 109, 172; 1996 election, 170; on abortion, 49; accused of sexual abuse, 199, 206–7, 211, 214; constitutional negotiations, 209–10; grip on FSLN, 172, 211; role after Insurrection, 46
Ortega, Humberto, 29
Oxfam-Quebec, 227n10

Paris Club, 205
Party of the Erotic Left (PIE), 85
Pastora, Edén, 5
PIE. *See* Party of the Erotic Left (PIE)
Popular Credit Bank, 210
Popular Unity Movement. *See* United People's Movement (MPU)
Prensa, La, 35, 116, 135, 180, 220n11
Professional Women for Development Network, 178
Professional Women's Network, 170
Protestant Church, 160
public spaces: and constitutional negotiations, 77, 80–81; limits under Chamorro, 116; and semiautonomous groups, 66, 74, 83; used by AMPRONAC, 34, 53–54; used by women's movement since 1990 election, 54, 138, 141, 175, 185–86; value, 15–16, 20, 169, 188–89

Quintana, Marta Magali, 87

Ramírez, Sergio, 29, 170, 226n1
Ramos, Josefina, 143
Ramos, Sandra, 109
Reagan, Ronald, 7, 9, 54–55, 60, 221–22n11
resource mobilization: by AMPRONAC, 31–32, 39; by CONAPRO H-M, 87, 90, 92, 104; and constitutional negotiations, 80; importance of communication, 42; lost without identity, 85; theory, 12–13, 15, 17, 187, 189; by women's movement after 1990 election, 125, 137, 141, 146, 178, 185; by women's secretariats, 75, 104
Río San Juan, 204

Rubio, Amparo: background 1–3; during Chamorro government, 9–11; during contra war, 7–8; during Insurrectionary War, 3–6; with Ministry of Interior, 7–8; shocked by outcome of 1990 election, 126; trains for FSLN, 3–4

Saint-Germain, Michelle, 36
Sánchez, Domingo, 208
Sandinismo: abandoned by women, 77; defined, 29; embraced by AMNLAE, 63; reigning ideology post Somoza, 48, 82; restructured for women's rights, 88
Sandinista Defense Committee (CDS), 59
Sandinista Extra-Ordinary Conference, 108–9
Sandinista Front of National Liberation (FSLN): 1984 election, 8, 59–61, 221–22n11; 1990 election, 9, 19, 66, 83, 96–100, 128, 151, 224n3, 225n7; 1996 election, 170–77; agricultural policies, 67–69, 72, 74–76, 103, 222n1, 229n11; attempts to democratize, 168–74, 184, 226n4; communication, 87, 135, 179; connection with Christian communities, 3, 38; constitutional negotiations, 77–82, 214; contra war, 47, 55–56, 163; economic policies, 65, 68–69, 101, 223n4; first elected leader, 109; government structure, 45–46, 72, 127–28; health care issues, 51, 183; Insurrectionary War, 4, 5–6, 27–29, 39, 40, 42, 45; lack of support for women's issues, 64, 82, 84–85, 103, 109, 127, 224n2; late 1990s, 199, 204, 205–11, 213–14; legal reforms for women, 52–53; link with AMNLAE, 16, 18–19, 25n9, 49–50, 54, 56–57, 59, 62, 77, 83–85, 87–91, 95, 100, 127, 128, 130–31, 170; link with AMPRONAC, 30–33, 36, 44, 190; link with CONAPRO H-M, 86, 87, 90, 92, 94; link with FAO, 40, 220n12; link with MPU, 40–41; link with UNO, 108; negotiates with Chamorro government, 11, 207; objectives, 36–37, 229n6; and semiautonomous women's groups, 65, 101, 103–4; supported by *Tercerismo,* 29; supports women's rights, 8–9, 31, 37–38, 43, 45–46, 53, 88–90, 192, 193, 195; view of homosexuality, 226n5; women in, 1, 4–6, 27, 38–39, 60–61, 168–77, 221n9, 225n9; women's movement breaks from, 124–25, 128, 131–32,